A Hand-Book of Louisiana

GIVING

General and Agricultural Features, Together With Crops That Can be Grown

AND

Description of Each Parish, Climate, Health, Education, Industries, Railroads, Water-Courses, Forestry, Etc.

ISSUED BY THE
Louisiana State Board of Agriculture and Immigration

HARRY D. WILSON,
Commissioner, Baton Rouge, La.

Marula

An imprint of Arcadia Publishing

Louisiana's Invitation
Louisiana State Board of Agriculture and Immigration
Harry D. Wilson, Commissioner, Baton Rouge

A Marula Historical Reprint
Originally published in 1917

Published by Arcadia Publishing
Charleston SC

ISBN 978-0-7385-9468-2

Printed in the United States of America

For all general information contact Arcadia Publishing at:
Telephone 843-853-2070
Fax 843-853-0044
E-mail sales@arcadiapublishing.com
For customer service and orders:
Toll-Free 1-888-313-2665

Visit us on the Internet at www.arcadiapublishing.com

PREFACE

IN THE PREPARATION and compilation of data for the publication of such a book as will give with accuracy and clearness the varied and immense resources of a State which is only yet in the infancy of its development it is necessary to cull from every available source possible.

In this book we have taken from our previous hand-books, we have given copious extracts from Hon. Jos. E. Ransdell's "On to Dixie" speech in the House of Representatives in the Sixty-first Congress, almost his entire speech, "The Lure of the Southland," recently delivered in the United States Senate; we have copied from the National Magazine the article of Garnault Agassiz on "The Untold Treasures of Louisiana," and are under obligations to Professors W. R. Dodson, W. H. Dalrymple, E. S. Richardson, E. Pegram Flower and many others for courtesies extended, and to the United States Agricultural and Census Bureaus for valuable data.

HARRY D. WILSON, Commissioner.

INDEX TO ILLUSTRATIONS.

INDEX.

INDEX—Continued

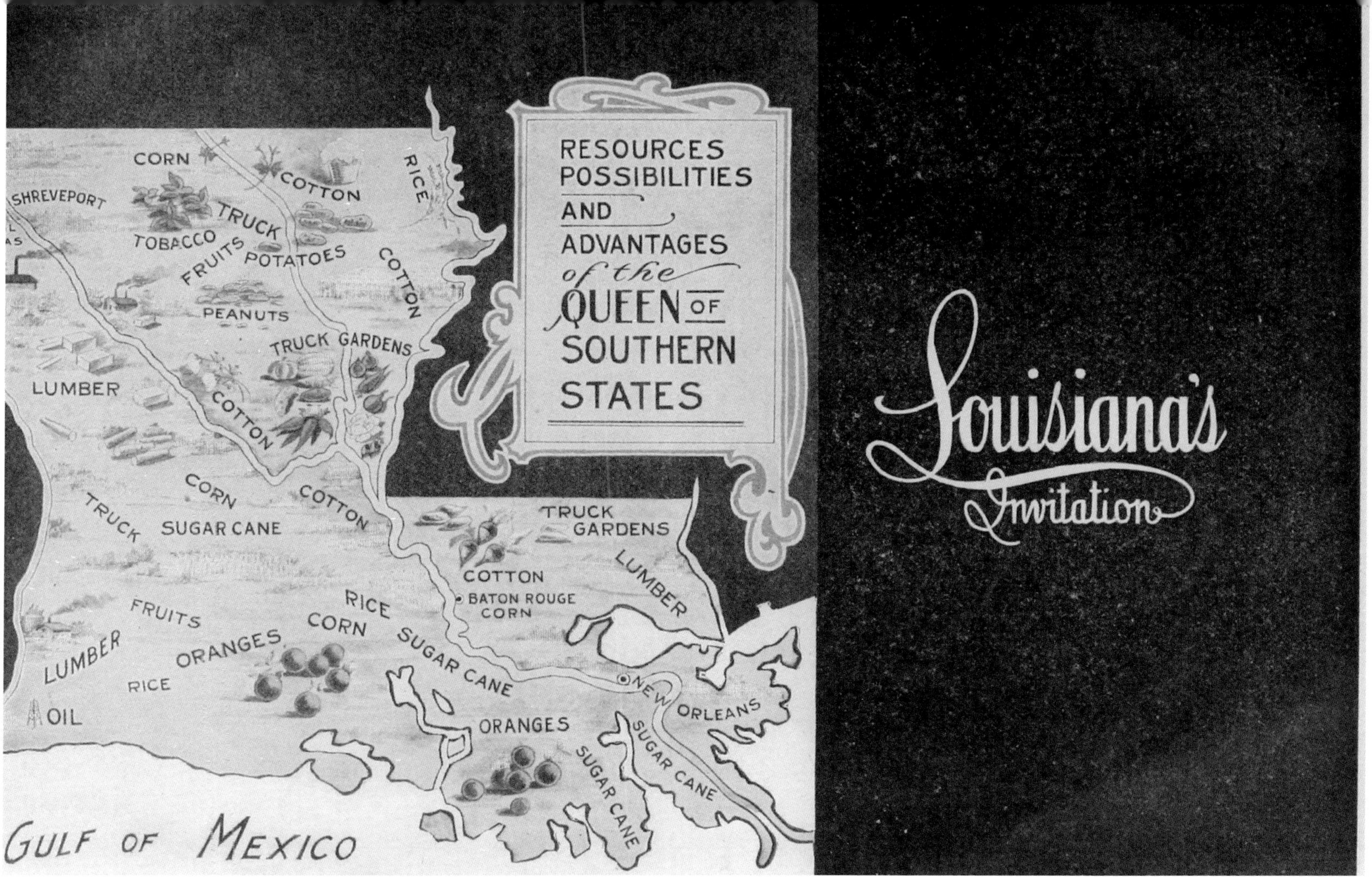
RESOURCES
POSSIBILITIES
AND
ADVANTAGES
of the
QUEEN OF
SOUTHERN
STATES
Louisiana's
Invitation
SHREVEPORT
CORN
COTTON
RICE
TRUCK
TOBACCO
FRUITS
POTATOES
COTTON
PEANUTS
TRUCK GARDENS
LUMBER
COTTON
CORN
COTTON
TRUCK
SUGAR CANE
TRUCK
GARDENS
LUMBER
COTTON
BATON ROUGE
CORN
FRUITS
RICE
CORN
SUGAR CANE
LUMBER
ORANGES
RICE
OIL
NEW ORLEANS
ORANGES
SUGAR CANE
SUGAR CANE
GULF OF MEXICO

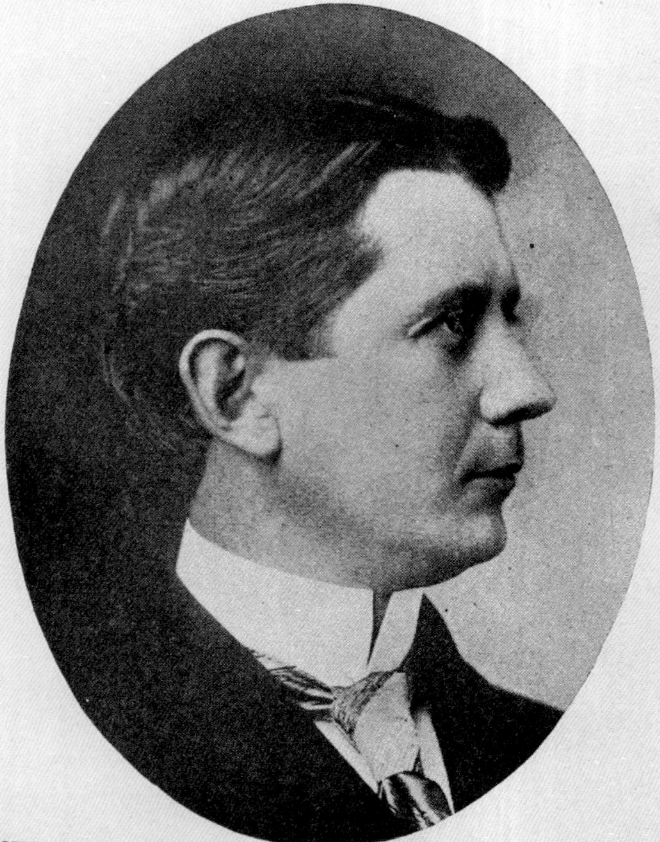

HIS EXCELLENCY RUFFIN G. PLEASANT, GOVERNOR OF LOUISIANA.

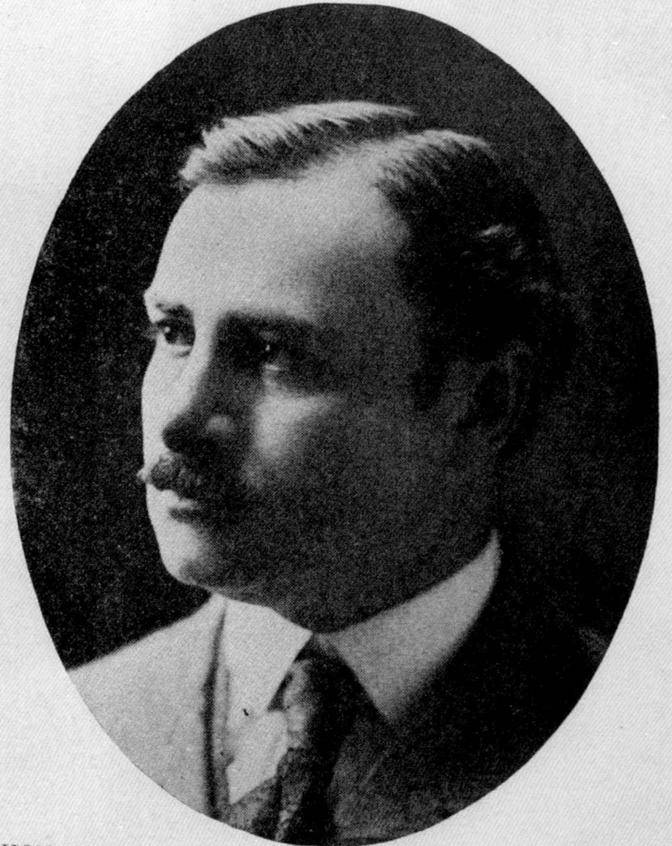

HON. FERNAND MOUTON, LIEUTENANT GOVERNOR.

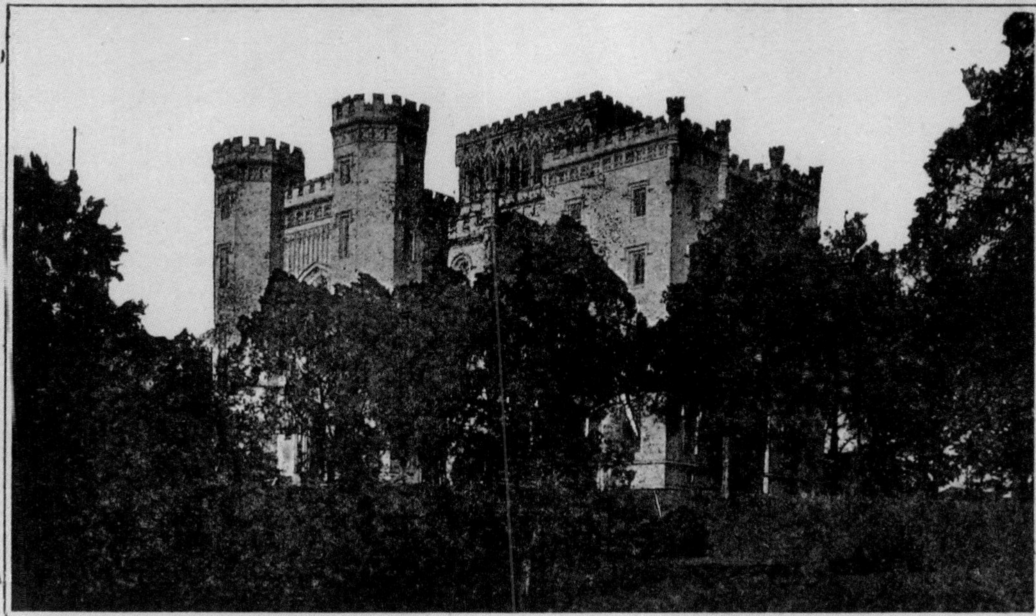

STATE CAPITOL OF LOUISIANA.

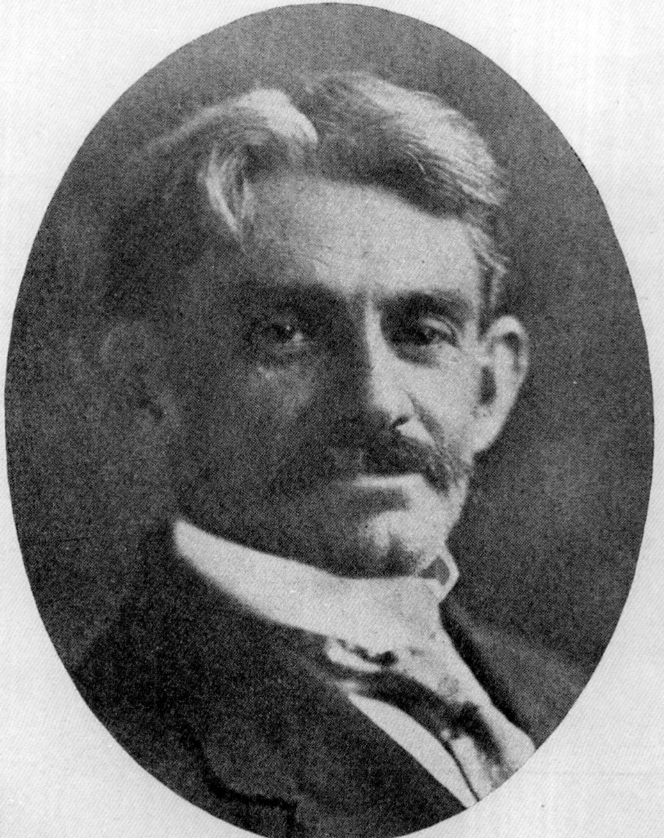

HARRY D. WILSON, COMMISSIONER OF AGRICULTURE AND IMMIGRATION.

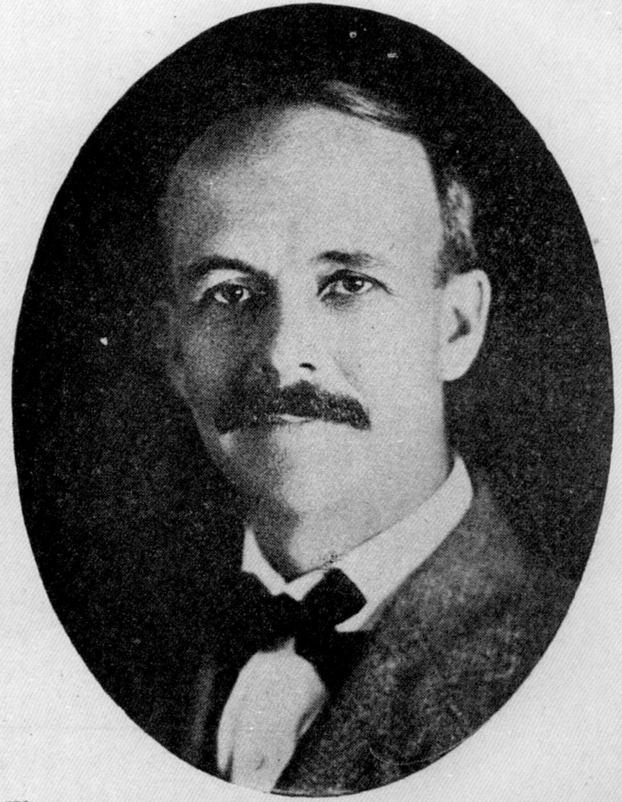

W. R. DODSON, DIRECTOR OF THE EXPERIMENT STATIONS AND STATE CHEMIST.
An untiring worker for agricultural interests.

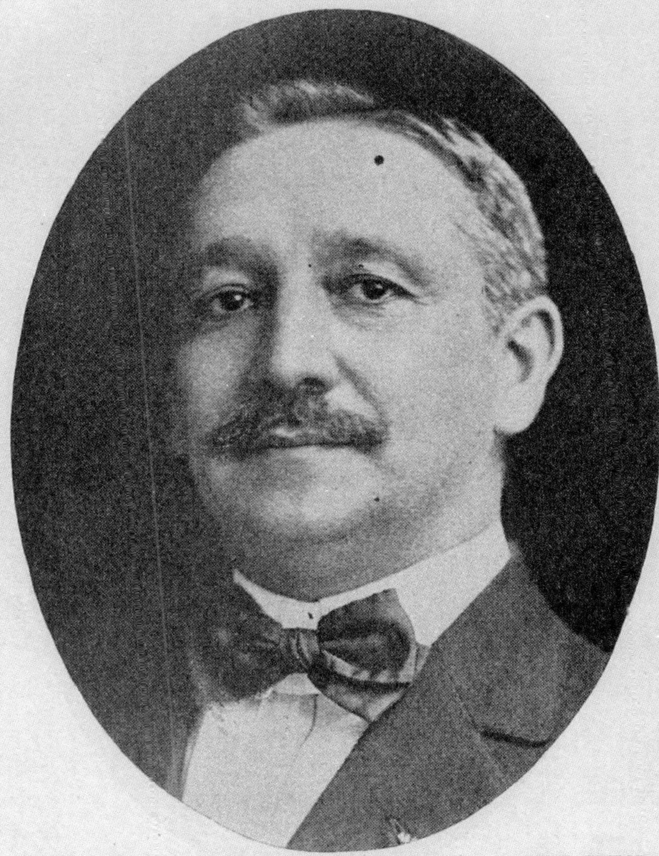

JUSTIN F. DENECHAUD, SECRETARY OF THE IMMIGRATION DIVISION.

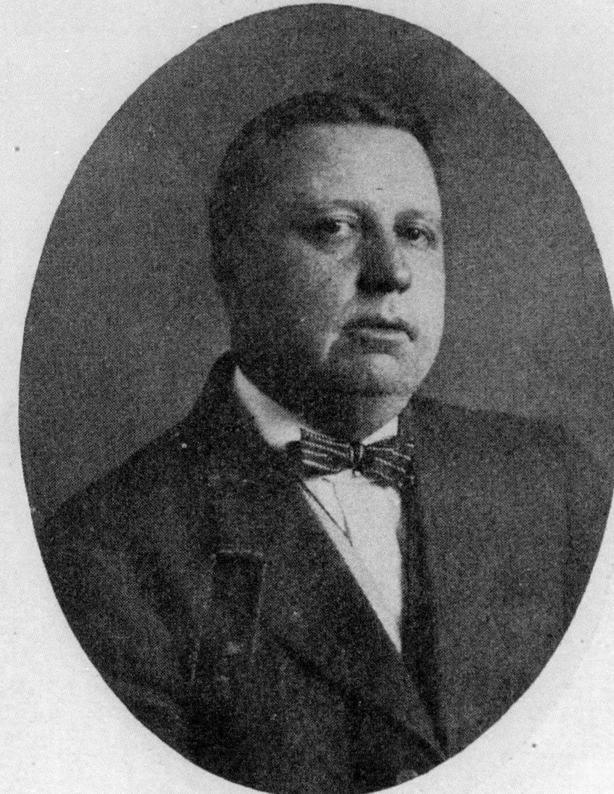

EUGENE JASTREMSKI, SECRETARY OF THE STATE BOARD OF AGRICULTURE AND IMMIGRATION.

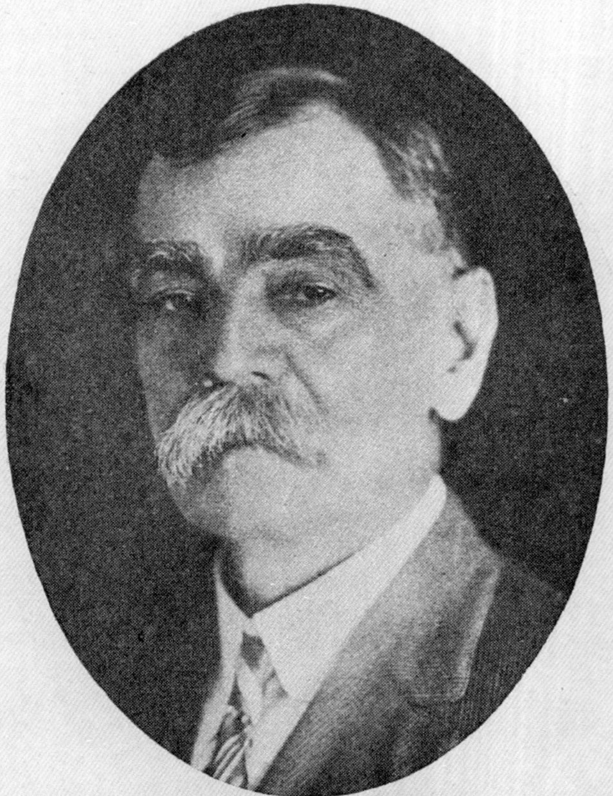

HOWELL CARTER, STATISTICIAN AND MANAGER COMMERCIAL FEED STUFF DIVISION.

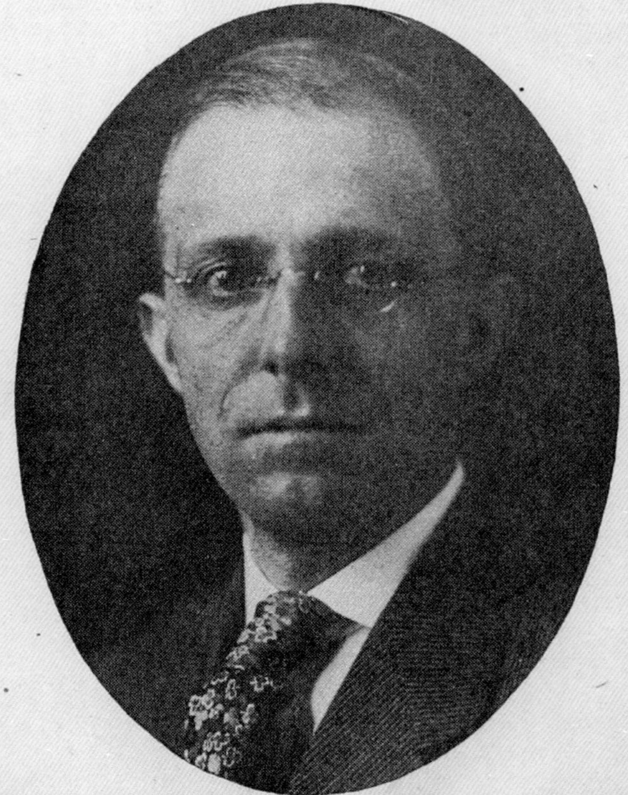

MILLARD S. PERKINS, MANAGER OF COMMERCIAL FERTILIZER DIVISION.

Should the Patron Saints of Agriculture and Husbandry seek in the State of Louisiana fit representatives for their "Hall of Fame", they could point to these two and say they possess the requisites necessary.

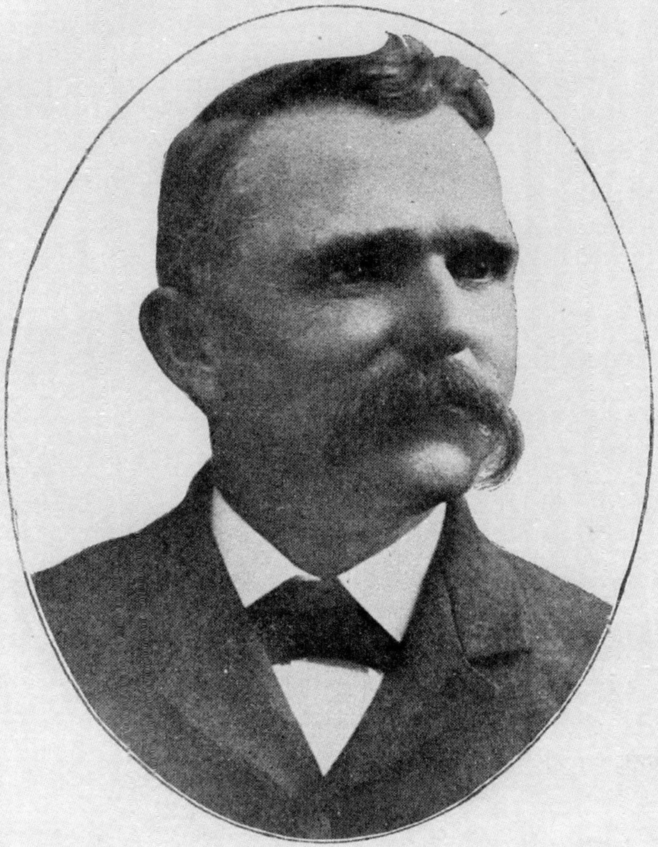

DR. WILLIAM C. STUBBS, the well-known Agricultural Chemist and ex-Director of the Louisiana Experiment Stations, though now voluntarily retired, is not "defunct" as he jokingly says of himself, for his agricultural works are always before us and his wonderful advancement of the sugar interests ever assures him a "sweet" place in Louisiana hearts.

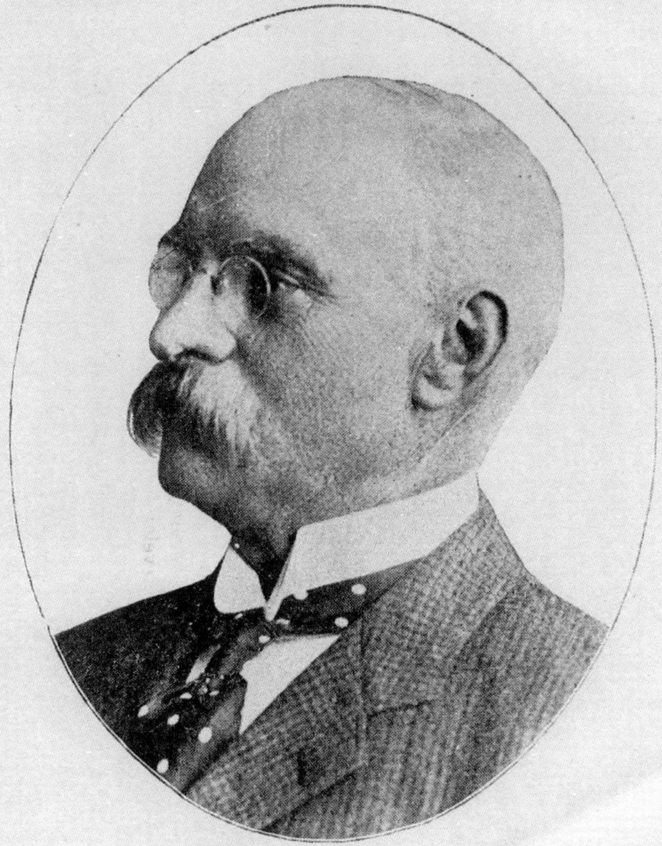

DR. W. H. DALRYMPLE, the Louisiana State University's well-known Veterinarian of nation-wide reputation, whose long-continued and persistent labor in teaching his balanced-ration idea and his indefatigable work in the cause of tick eradication which will ultimately prove to be the key to unlock the door to untold treasures accruing from Louisiana's animal husbandry.

LOUISIANA'S INVITATION

THE HOSPITALITY of Louisiana is proverbial, and she now stands with open arms at her borders to welcome the stranger. Nature is exceedingly bountiful within her gates; agriculturist, manufacturer or artisan will find here what all men should seek, "a festival of well requited labor," with a genial climate, an honest, sunny-tempered people, and all the advantages of Twentieth Century civilization. Those who have come to her in recent years stand ready to testify in her behalf. Her marvelous development of the past ten years is but the forerunner of a more marvelous development in the future. She invites you to come and be a part of this development. The last United States Census Report shows that capital invested in farms yielded, in Louisiana, an income of 27.3% annually on the investment, and this, gentle stranger, is 70% higher than the general average for the whole United States. Corn, cotton, sugar-cane, rice, fruits and berries, truck, forage crops, and almost everything grown under the sun, can be raised on her rich and responsive soil. Her advance as a manufacturing State has been marvelous. In 1890 she was the sixth ranking manufacturing State in the South, and in 1900 she had jumped to second place. Large and valuable deposits of coal in the northwestern, and an unlimited supply of fuel oil and gas in the various parts of the State, are the additions to her mineral wealth, discovered during recent years. Situated in the heart of the raw material district, with the richest soil on earth, with cheap fuel, oil, coal and gas, with nearly four thousand miles of navigable streams and three thousand miles of railways, with the Panama Canal now completed, can you have one lingering doubt of her future greatness and imperial splendor? If this material side appeals not to you, examine her aesthetic beauty. She has her throne builded beneath the sunniest sky that lights the globe, and her shores are laved by the waters of the great Gulf. She lives perfumed by the choicest flowers, when bleak winter's chill has enclasped her more northern sisters. Boreas, when most furious, stops in his maddened career, to pet and woo her. She is rich in all and holds out a generous and charitable hand to the children of her poorer sisters.

BANKS.

Louisiana has hundreds of banks, national and State. They are sound financial institutions, with ample funds to take care of the growing and gathering of her crops, the operating of her manufacturing industries and her commercial industries. For the promotion of new enterprises, outside capital is largely depended upon, but if a Federal Farm Loan Bank can be established every want in that line will be filled.

ASSESSMENT.

In 1915 the total assessment of the State was $590,568,506.00.

THE PEOPLE.

"Of the typical population of Louisiana, also, a special mystery seems to be made, but Louisianians have much reason to be proud of their historical descent. They have a history as authentic and as valuable as the annals of the Puritans of Massachusetts, or that of Catholic Maryland. The rearing of the State's colonial structure by one nation, and its blending into colonial dependence upon another, contains no special mystery. They are a hospitable, brave and generous people, whether tracing their history back to French Bienville or Laussat; to Spanish O'Reilly or Salcedo, or to American Claiborne.

"That is the native State autonomy, which, blended with English, Irish and Scotch immigration, and the descendants of the Cavalier and Huguenot settlers from Virginia, Kentucky, Georgia, Alabama, and the Carolinas, make up the population of Louisiana. A people exhibiting all those finer traits which betoken the cultivation of noble traditions and refined associations, evidenced in the generous hospitality, the chivalric spirit, the punctilious courtesy, the knightly hand, the Christian knee, the clean firesides, and the holy altars cherished in the hearts and homes of as proud and pure an aristocracy as the world has ever known."

AREA, PRODUCTION, CLIMATE AND POPULATION.

Louisiana has nearly 45,000 square miles of territory, containing some 28,000,000 million acres. Of this amount about 13,000,000 acres are of alluvial origin, and the rest good upland. With proper drainage and levee protection there is very little of the alluvial region that cannot be cultivated. Thousands of acres of so-called marsh and swamp are being reclaimed and put into cultivation every year. Capital and brain have converted barren wastes into rich, productive fields. The uplands are almost all susceptible of cultivation. Of her 28,000,000 acres, only about 5,000,000 are in cultivation.

CLIMATE.

Its proximity to the Gulf of Mexico secures a prevalence of southern winds, cool and moisture-ladened, which mitigates the extremes of weather experienced by the States of the North. Though our summers are prolonged, the heat is never oppressive, the thermometer rarely reaching 95 degrees. In carefully kept records of the three Experiment Stations for eight years, 98 degrees has been the highest recorded temperature at New Orleans, 99 degrees at Baton Rouge, and 100 degrees at

Calhoun. These maxima amounts have been rarely reached, not oftener than one or two days in a summer.

The winters are usually mild, with an average temperature of about 53 degrees in the southern, and about 45 degrees in the northern part of the State.

Above all other requirements for a good climate, the differences between summer heat and winter cold should not be too great. Louisiana stands, in this respect, almost at the head of the States. She is blessed with a uniform temperature.

Ice appears here but seldom, and the climate of the entire State, from October to May, is an ideal one, attractive alike to the invalid and tourist, and thousands of visitors from the North are yearly seeking this State in quest of health or enjoyment. The hotels furnish attractive homes for the opulent and fashionable, while men of moderate means can find cheap and excellent homes in the smaller hostelries and private boarding houses of the city, in the towns and villages scattered over this State.

The comparative temperature of New Orleans, and of Jacksonville, and San Francisco, is seen below, for the winter months of November, December, January and February, as compiled from the Weather Bureau records, at New Orleans, La.:

New Orleans, La.	Mean.	Average highest	Average lowest	Highest on record	Lowest on record
November	61	68	54	85	30
December.............	56	64	49	81	20
January...	54	62	47	82	15
February............	58	65	51	82	16
	—	—	—	—	—
Season............	57	65	50	85	15
Jacksonville, Fla.					
November	63	72	52	86	26
December.........	57	68	47	81	19
January	55	64	44	81	15
February....	60	70	50	84	14
	—	—	—	—	—
Season............	59	68	48	86	14
San Francisco, Cal.					
November	56	64	50	78	41
December.........	52	57	47	72	34
January	50	56	44	69	29
February....	52	58	45	76	35
	—	—	—	—	—
Season............	52	59	46	78	29

Regarding the heat of summer in Louisiana, there prevails in many parts a totally erroneous opinion. It is believed that it must be warmer here than in other States because Louisiana is located farther South. Such reasoning is utterly false; living in close proximity to the Mexican

Gulf, and having during the months of March, April, May, June, July and August, almost constantly south winds, we always have a cooling sea breeze.

Another widespread error is the impression that a white man cannot work in this climate during the summer, and that only the negro can stand the heat. As far as the heat is concerned, the truth has been stated above; in regard to labor, it should be said that there are certain people who can never work, because they do not want to—during the summer it is too hot, and during the winter too cold for them, and they are willing to believe that only the negro can stand the heat.

Our German gardeners and farmers, as well as thousands of other nationalities, have performed labor in garden and field for many years. They need no negroes, and feel so comfortable that they prefer the summer to the winter. On extremely hot days they work in the field only during the morning and afternoon hours, "laying off" during the midday heat, as they do in other sections under similar conditions.

Cases of sunstroke are reported from Northern and Western cities; they occur here but seldom.

RAINFALL.

The average yearly rainfall at New Orleans is about 70 inches, decreasing in quantity as one goes northward, with 45 inches as an average in the extreme northern portion. The heaviest showers fall in summer during the growing season. Winter comes next in its quantity of rainfall, while our springs and autumns are our dry seasons, with only occasional showers. Such seasons are conducive to the welfare of our staple crops—corn, cotton, sugar-cane and rice; dry springs permitting a successful planting and cultivation of these crops, and dry autumns, so essential to the rapid and economical harvesting of them. Our regular rains are from the southwest, yet in summer they sometimes come from the northwest, and when they do they are usually accompanied by thunder and lightning.

RIVERS AND WATER COURSES

NO STATE IN THE UNION has so much alluvial lands or so many miles of navigable waters. The widest part of the flood plain, as well as the delta of the Mississippi River lies within its border. The alluvial and marsh lands derivable from this river are over 13,000 square miles. The bottoms of the Red, and its tributaries before it enters this valley, about 1,700, the marsh lands west of the delta, about 4,000; other alluvial and swamp lands, about 600 square miles, making in the aggregate a little over 19,000 square miles of alluvial land, or nearly one-half of the State.

The Mississippi and the Red are the chief drainage channels of the State, and almost all of the larger streams of these basins diverge from them, and hence, are called bayous. Before the days of the levees they

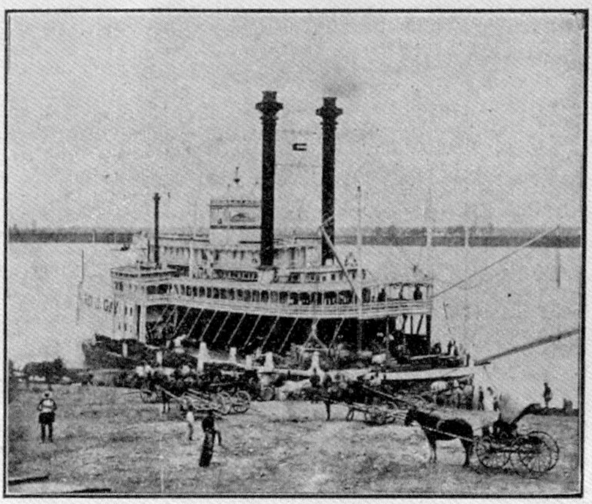

A Steamboat Landing on the Mississippi River.

formed so many channels, or outlets for the escape of water in floods. Such a network of connection has thus been formed that it is now difficult sometimes to trace the course of an individual stream. As a rule, some large bayou flows along the edge of the bottom plain. Bayou Macon is on the west of the Mississippi flood plain, Ouachita River on the extreme west of the central plain, Bayous Boeuf, Cocodrie and Teche on the west of the flood plain of the Red River. In North Louisiana the rivers follow the trend of the subterranean rocks. In the east they flow southeasterly in the Ouachita, and southward into the Red. In the extreme south those west of the Mississippi flow southward into the Gulf; those east, southeast, into the lakes.

NAVIGABLE WATERS IN LOUISIANA.

(In all of which boats operate during some season of the year.)

Streams—	Miles of Navigation	Head of Navigation
Amite River	61	Port Vincent.
Atchafalaya River	218	Red River.
Barataria Bayou	78	Harvey's Canal.
*Bartholomew Bayou	145	State Line, Arkansas.
Bayou Louis	25	Florence.
Big Creek	20	Ferry Landing.
Bisteneau Lake	30	Minden.
Black River	70	Mouth of Ouachita.
Bodcau Lake	10	Bellevue.
Boeuf River	300	Lake Lafourche.
Boeuf Bayou	11	
Bunches Bend	12	
Calcasieu River	132	
Cane River	60	Grand Ecore.
Choctaw Bayou	25	Pinhook.
Corney Creek	50	Spearsville.
Courtableu Bayou	36	Washington.
D'Arbonne Bayou	75	Farmerville.
DeGlaise Bayou	75	Evergreen.
Delarge Bayou	20	
Dorchite Bayou	6	Minden.
Forks of Calcasieu	32	
Grand Caillou Bayou	13	
Lafourche Bayou	318	Donaldsonville.
Lacombe Bayou	15	Bayou Lacombe.
Little River (including Catahoula Lake)	150	St. L., I. M. & S. R. R. Bridge.
Louis Bayou	15	Bayou Castor.
Macon Bayou	200	Floyd.
Manchac Bayou	18	Hope Villa.
Mermentau Bayou	81	Lake Arthur.
*Mississippi River	560	St. Paul, Minn.
Natalbany River	12	Springfield.
*Ouachita River	217	State Line.
Palmyra Lake	25	Palmyra.
*Pearl River	103	Carthage, Miss.
Petite Anse Bayou	8	Salt Mine.
*Red River	510	Fulton, I. T.
Rouge Bayou	15	Shoals, Texas.
Sabine Bayou	75	Catahoula Lake.
Sabine River	387	
Teche Bayou	91	St. Martinsville.
Tensas River	150	V., S. & P. Bridge.
Tickfaw River	16	V., S. & P. Bridge.
Terrebonne Bayou	27	
Tangipahoa River	15	
Tchefuncta Bayou	20	Covington.
Vermilion Bayou	49	Pin Hook Bridge.
Other streams	155	
Total	4,794	

*Portion of navigable streams lying in other States.

Miles of Navigation in Each State of the Mississippi Valley.

State	Miles	State	Miles
Louisiana	4,794	Minnestota	720
Arkansas	2,100	Wisconsin	660
Mississippi	1,380	Ohio	560
Montana	1,310	Texas	550
Dakota	1,280	Nebraska	440
Illinois	1,270	West Virginia	500
Tennessee	1,260	Pennsylvania	380
Kentucky	1,027	Kansas	240
Indiana	1,230	Alabama	200
Iowa	840	New York	70
Indian Territory	830		

Comparative Table Showing Total Mileage, Single Track, Main Line, Branches and Spurs, Operated in Louisiana on June 30, for Seventeen Years.

Years Ending June 30	Total Miles Operated Single Track	Increase in Miles	Per Cent Increase
1899	2,264.32	.....	...
1900	2,425.40	161.08	.066
1901	2,662.00	236.60	.097
1902	2,912.73	250.73	.094
1903	2,969.67	56.94	.019
1904	3,413.70	444.03	.150
1905	3,505.33	191.63	.056
1906	3,886.74	261.41	.073
1907	4,290.25	433.51	.110
1908	4,765.78	475.53	.095
1909	4,950.65	184.87	.037
1910	5,021.18	70.53	.014
1911	5,175.47	154.29	.030
1912	5,257.05	81.58	.015
1913	5,232.83	†24.22	†.004
1914	5,160.33	†72.50	†.014
1915	5,240.15	79.82	.015

† Decrease.

LIST OF RAILROADS IN LOUISIANA AND THEIR TRACK MILEAGE ON JUNE 30, 1915.

Name of Road	Total Miles Main Lines, Branches and Spurs
Alexandria & Western Railway Comapny	14.70
Arkansas, Louisiana & Gulf Railway Company, The	39.20
*Arkansas Southeastern Railway Company	31.00
Brimstone Railroad & Canal Company	7.73
Chicago, Rock Island & Pacific Railroad Company, The	147.73
†Chicago, St. Louis & New Orleans Railroad Company	.....
*Dorcheat Valley Railroad Company	.....
Franklin & Abbeville Railway Co., The	44.16
Glenmora & Western Railway Co.	12.00
Gulf, Colorado & Santa Fe Railway Company	63.96
Gulf & Sabine River Railroad Co.	28.23
Houston & Shreveport Railroad Company	39.78
‡Iberia, St. Mary & Eastern Railroad Company	39.46
Iberia & Vermilion Railroad Company	16.09

Name of Road	Total Miles Main Lines, Branches and Spurs
Illinois Central Railroad Company	188.12
†Jasper & Eastern Railway Company	.....
Kansas City, Shreveport & Gulf Terminal Company, The	.....
Kansas City Southern Railway Company, The	249.08
Kentwood & Eastern Railway Company	48.03
Kentwood, Greensburg & Southwestern Railroad Company	14.20
Kinder & Northwestern Railroad Company	12.00
Lake Charles & Northern Railroad Company	44.35
Lake Charles Railway & Navigation Company	9.00
Lake Providence, Texarkana & Wn. Railroad Company	8.00
Leesville East & West Railroad, The	2.00
Louisiana & Arkansas Railway Company	222.60
Louisiana & Northwest Railroad Company, The	96.69
Louisiana & Pacific Railway Company	24.60
Louisiana Railway & Navigation Company	342.48
Louisiana Southern Railway Company	65.31
Louisiana Western Railroad Company	207.74
Louisville & Nashville Railroad Company (N. O. & M. Div.)	44.64
Mansfield Railway & Transportation Company	15.85
*Milliken & Southwestern Railroad Company	.....
Missouri, Kansas & Texas Railway Co. of Texas, The	19.29
Monroe & Southwestern Railway Company	10.66
Morgan's Louisiana & Texas Railroad & Steamship Company	416.34
Neame, Carson & Southern Railroad Company	32.58
Natchez, Urania & Ruston Railway Company	14.00
New Iberia & Northern Railroad Company	49.35
New Orleans & Northeastern Railroad Company	61.86
New Orleans Great Northern Railroad Company	136.70
New Orleans, Natalbany & Natchez Railway Company	29.01
New Orleans Southern & Grand Isle Railway Company	59.71
New Orleans Terminal Company	26.08
New Orleans, Texas & Mexico Railroad Company	172.72
North Louisiana & Gulf Railroad Co	25.70
Oberlin, Hampton & Eastern Railroad Co	11.00
Opelousas, Gulf & Northeastern Ry. Co., The	57.03
Ouachita & Northwestern Railroad Co	65.41
Pontchartrain R. R. (Branch L. & N. R. R. Co.)	4.96
Red River & Gulf Railroad Co	14.20
St. Louis, Iron Mountain & Southern Ry. Co	573.68
St. Louis Southwestern Railway Co	37.50
St. Tammany & New Orleans Rys. & Ferry Co	13.60
Sibley, Lake Bisteneau & Southern Ry. Co	28.00
Texas & Pacific Railway Co., The	720.85
Tioga & Southeastern Railway Co	18.00
Tremont & Gulf Railway Co	66.74
Vicksburg, Shreveport & Pacific Railway Co	183.20
Victoria, Fisher & Western Railroad Co	31.00
Woodworth & Louisiana Central Railroad Co	23.00
Yazoo & Mississippi Valley Railroad Co., The	236.15
Zwolle & Eastern Railway Co	23.00
Totals	5,240.15

*Ceased operation. †Not an operating road.

WHAT LOUISIANA'S LAND WILL GROW

THE GENERAL IMPRESSION prevails that the South can only grow cotton, sugar-cane, tobacco and rice; that other crops cannot be grown successfully, and that hay-making and stock-raising are impossibilities in this sunny land.

This erroneous impression has been produced by the persistency of our planters and farmers in growing the above crops, a persistency largely inherited and acquired, with our large plantations filled with ignorant, unskilled laborers, who have been disciplined since youth in planting methods. But the climax has been reached. Planting

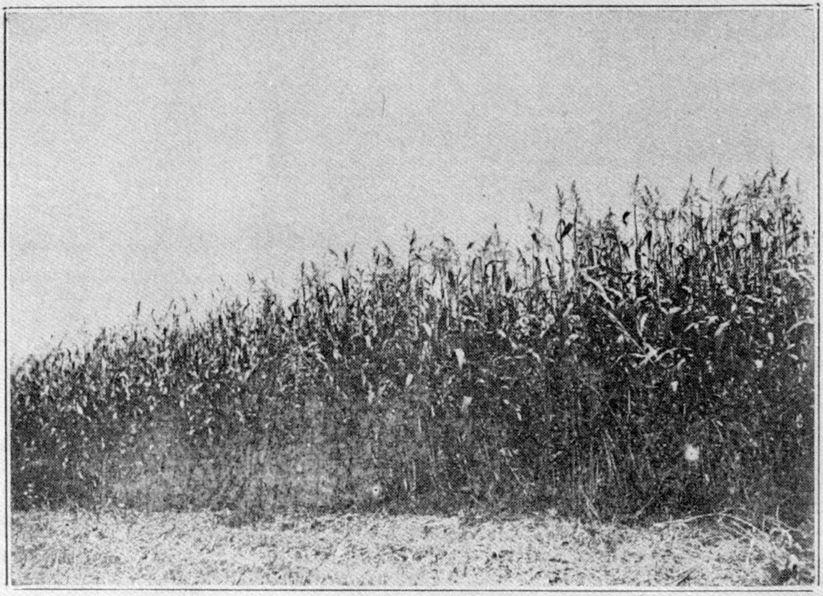

FIELD OF SORGHUM FOR SILAGE.

on a large scale is no longer popular. Unreliable labor, low prices, soil exhaustion and high money rates have shorn this business of all its pleasures and most of its profits. Disintegration and division is now the order for the day, and the large plantation of yesterday will be tomorrow the abode of many happy and prosperous farmers.

The question may be asked, What else can be grown in Louisinaa? The reply is a sweeping one; nearly everything capable of growth in a temperate or sub-tropical country. Wheat has been, and is now, grown in the northern part of the State. Oats sown in the early fall, and using the rust-proof varieties for seed, will make as finely here as anywhere on earth. Over 100 bushels per acre have been grown on the alluvial and bluff lands of the State, while the hill lands of north Louisinaa have frequently given over sixty bushels per acre. Spring oats are sometimes successful, but are not generally to be recommended. Rye and barley, if home-grown seed be used, will thrive all over the State, and are frequently sown for winter pastures. The stock are turned on during the winter, and at the beginning of spring they are removed and the grain permitted to mature, frequently with large results.

Corn can be grown easily all over the State, and if the same attention and methods of cultivation were given it here as in the corn-growing States of the West, the average yield per acre would be but little under that produced there. But corn has been a side issue with the cotton and cane planter, and cultivated as little as possible. Under this "touch-and-go" method, the yield of the State during the past years was but little below 25,000,000 bushels. By proper rotation, fertilization and cultivation, this yield could easily be doubled, and it is claimed by the United States Government report to have already reached that point. Upon the alluvial lands of south Louisiana the sugar experiment station has made 100 bushels per acre. Sixty to ninety bushels have been obtained at the State experiment station at Baton Rouge upon the bluff lands, and thirty to sixty bushels are the yields upon the rotation fields of the north Louisiana experiment station, situated at Calhoun, upon the yellow sandy loams of the oak and short-leaf pine hills. It is reported that 28 boys of the Louisiana Corn Clubs of 1910 grew each more than 100 bushels per acre and the average yield of 256 boys was 61 bushels and the experiments all along that line indicate that Louisiana is developing into a great corn-growing State.

One caution is needed in planting grains of all kinds here—that is, for a general crop use home-grown, acclimated seed; e. g., corn grown here is planted in early March, and harvested in August and September, while seed from the extreme North planted at the same time will prob-

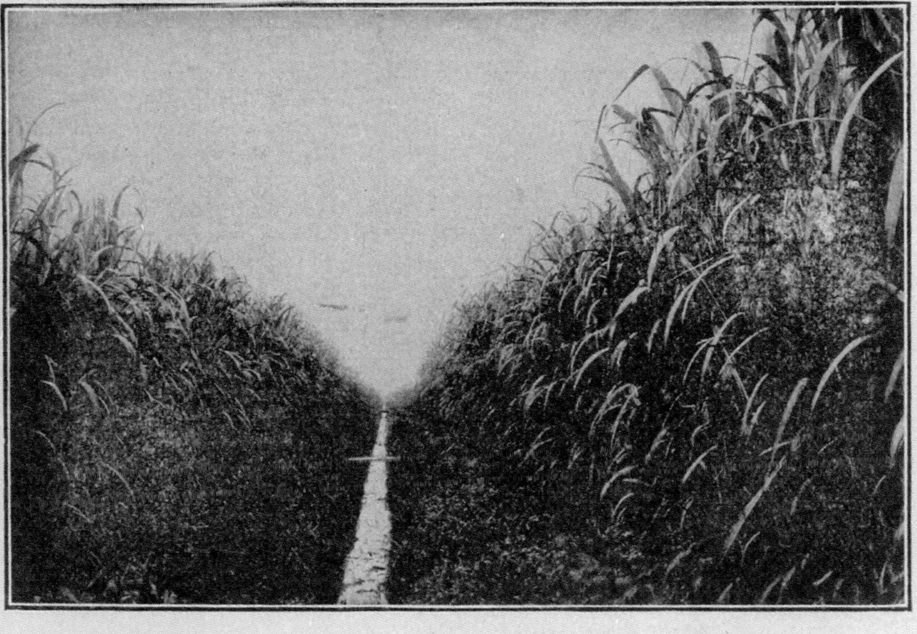

A FIELD OF SUGAR CANE.

ably mature in May, and that, too, with only a partial crop. Wheat and oats, per contra, planted in the fall from seed raised in the extreme North, will not ripen before June or July, if at all (the rust frequently destroying it before ripening), while home-raised seed, sown at the same time, will be ready for harvest in May. If, therefore, we desire an early crop of corn, we obtain seed from the North, and if an early crop of oats, wheat, barley or rye we send South for the seed. The reasons are obvious when we remember that each comes to us inheriting the habits of the country from which it came. In the North the summers are short, and the time of the growth of the corn is, therefore, limited. In the South, the winters are short, and, therefore, the period of repose is materially shortened, and early maturity follows. This involves the whole question of acclimation. In Louisiana, under good culture, the corn crop will be from 20 to 100 bushels per acre. The latter, of course, being the fancy figures and as yet only made in exceptional cases.

German and cat-tail millets, the sorghums, both saccharine and non-saccharine, clovers, grasses and root crops, soy beans, cow peas, teosite and other forage crops can be grown over the entire State in larger quantities per acre than elsewhere, since the tendency of our climate and the extreme fertility of our soils are to make "weed."

Vegetables of all kinds can be, and are, grown in large quantities. Besides those grown in the North and West are many others, peculiar to the South, such as okra, globe artichoke, lima beans, etc., beets, cabbage, lettuce, radishes, turnips. Mustard, cauliflower, English peas, etc., are grown through the winter in open ground. In fact, every home, however humble, has its garden, in which most of the vegetables are grown. Besides these home gardens there are thousands of acres devoted to truck-growing and market-gardening. From the latter our own cities and towns are supplied, while the former utilize many thousands of cars in transporting their products to the Western markets.

Of fruits a variety of superior excellence can be grown here. The apple is grown in the northern part of the State. The pear, particularly the Chinese type, all over the State. The peach will grow everywhere, but it fruits best in the hill lands . The native and Japanese varieties of plums do well everywhere.

Grapes can be grown in every parish, but succeed best in the uplands. Blackberries, dewberries and mulberries grow wild in every parish; so do the wild plums in the hill lands. Strawberries are perfectly at home everywhere, and in some sections are largely grown for the markets. As early as February 18 they were on sale in the markets this year. Raspberries, currants and gooseberries do not thrive so far South.

Pecans grow and bear abundantly all over the State. Some of the larger varieties, especially the paper shell, command fancy prices on the market. English walnuts are grown in some of the southern parishes.

Oranges, kumquats and pomelos are grown throughout south Louisiana, while lemons, guavas, bananas and pineapples are grown on the extreme Gulf Coast. The kumquat and pomegranate are found in nearly every yard of South Louisiana. Figs are cultivated in every parish, while in south Louisiana they are largely grown for the canneries.

No mention is made in this article of our staple crops—cotton, sugar-cane and rice—since they are inseparably connected in every man's mind with Louisiana and New Orleans.

This bare recital will show the wonderful capabilities of our soil and climate from an agricultural standpoint. Turning to the forests, we find a wealth of Nature's products ready for the harvest, to be turned by man's skill and ingenuity into the various forms and shapes suitable for man's varied wants. Timber and lumber trees, stave timber, box timber, hub timber, spoke timber, tray timber, hoop timber, ship timber, bucket timber, etc., crown our hills, decorate our valleys and fill our swamps. Shade trees of the densest foliage and of most beautiful shape everywhere abound. The evergreens and deciduous trees grow side by side in every forest. The magnolia and the live oak intertwine their boughs with the beech and the ash, while the holly and the dogwood bask in their shadows. Willows abound in our swamps, ready for conversion into charcoal or to be made into baskets and boxes.

Louisiana does not appeal alone to the utilitarian. Her æsthetic products are perhaps more wonderful than her useful ones. Flowers of brilliant tints and attractive forms fill her fields, her woods and her swamps. Her climate favors the growth of native flowers as well as the delicate and highly-prized exotics. Roses bloom in great profusion throughout the winter in open air, while japonicas, hibiscus and poinsettas of beautiful shades and brilliant tints are found in many yards. Tea roses, olives and magnolias (fuscata) and cape jasmines perfume the air with their delicious fragrance, while chrysanthemums and geraniums give brilliancy to every garden.

Palms of endless varieties furnish the centerpieces of many private yards, and ornament our parks and public squares.

COTTON AND COTTON FACTORIES

THE COTTON INDUSTRY in Louisiana is one of tremendous import and significance. The powerful influence it exerts on trade, its absorption of capital, both as product and manufacture, places it high in the scale of commercial economics. There is no section of the world more fortunately situated for the production of cotton than Louisiana. In the past it has been of such potent significance that it has been called "King." Its future depends on the establishment of factories in the South. Cotton-producing offers an inviting field for speculative investors, because the lands which grow it can be purchased cheaply; it can be produced at a nominal cost. The first thing to be done is for the raisers of cotton to send less cotton to the East, and manufacture more of it at home.

Of all the industries which Louisiana has which offer inducements, that of cotton manufacturing offers supreme attractions. The advantages of location of a cotton factory anywhere in the State, on the scene of the production of raw material, is now a trite topic. Fifteen or twenty years ago New England contended that it was preposterous for the South to think of manufacturing any grade of goods from cotton. In a few years the South has practically driven the East out of all lines of coarser manufacture, and now is demonstrating that this promise was not over-estimated. This subject is receiving a great deal of attention in Louisiana. It has been successfully tried in the Carolinas. The inducements in this field are tremendous. There are many things which place Louisiana at the head of cotton-producing States, as a field for the erection of factories. First, the cheapness of fuel, oil and coal and natural gas; second, the cost and quality of labor; third, the abundance of raw material; fourth, the facilities for transportation, both rail and water, and the opportunities for export trade furnished by the great port of New Orleans.

Free sites can be obtained in many of the smaller towns for the erection of factories; cheap brick and lumber are always plentiful for the erection of the factory; cheap labor is abundant, and is always obtainable in Louisiana. Shreveport, Monroe and Clinton have tried cotton factories and other cities and towns are moving actively. New Orleans has had a number of successful mills, all turning out a good grade of goods, which have never failed to find a quick and ready market and pay good dividends.

The cotton seed oil business has grown to be one of the most important industries of the State. Nearly every town has one or more mills, and there are now fifty-one of these mills located in the State.

STOCK RAISING AND DAIRYING

NO PORTION OF THE GLOBE is better adapted to stock riasing than the State of Louisiana. Our soils unaided will supply native grasses sufficient to maintain cattle and horses through at least nine months in the year. The great variety of grasses, clovers and forage crops which can be grown so successfully upon all of our soils; our short winters, requiring shelter and extra feed for only a few months in the year; our numerous water courses, with their infinite number of tributaries, furnishing an abundant supply of water at all seasons, all conspire to make Louisiana a most desirable location for stock raising. The question may be asked, if these natural advantages exist, why is it that more have not engaged in this industry? The ready reply is found in the fact that heretofore our entire agricultural world has been absorbed in the growing of our leading staples: sugar-cane, rice and cotton. Another potent reason may be found in the absence of packing factories, where a ready market for cattle, sheep and hogs might be found the year round. Both of these reasons are now gradually melting away. Sugar-cane and cotton no longer afford the handsome profits of the past to the planter, and the latter particularly is now diversifying his crops and paying more attention to the raising of stock. A large majority of the horses of the State have been raised at home. Mules have been raised in sufficient quantities to demonstrate that, with proper care and attention, the finest and largest can be grown here, but only in a few instances has mule raising been pursued as a profession or special occupation. But many farmers are now raising both mules and horses for home demand, and some to sell. This home raised stock shows greater superiority for work than those raised elsewhere. The same natural conditions and advantages apply as to cattle.

In addition to ample pasturage and luxurious forage for cattle raising, fattening cattle for market has superior advantages in Louisiana, as is shown in many articles further on.

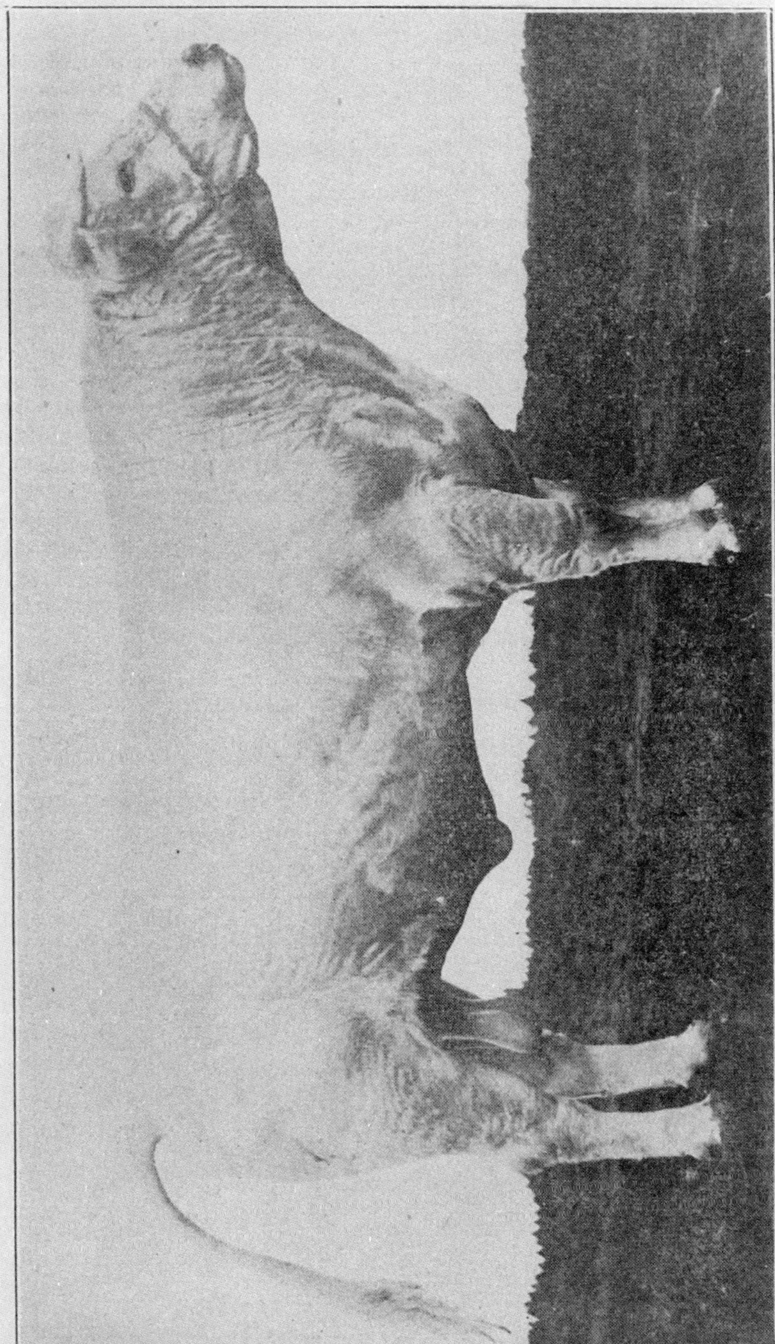

A LOUISIANA WHITE SHORT HORN.

Cotton seed meal and hulls from the many cotton seed oil mills, the rice bran, polish and shorts from our rice mills, and cheap molasses from our sugar factories provide superior economic feeding rations for cattle feeders. Annually thousands of head of cattle from this and other States are fattened at our mills and shipped to the Northern and Western markets. Improved breeds of the dairy type, Jersey and Guernsey, and the beef type, Herefords, Durhams, Polled Angus and Devons, are being rapidly adopted, and the State is making great strides now in this direction.

Hogs, likewise, are easily raised, and great interest is now being manifested in that line of farming. The "razor back" is fast disappearing and in his place comes the Poland China, the Berkshire, Red Jersey and Essex. There are now several breeders in the State with herds as good as any.

Hog raising, by the adoption of proper rotation of crops, making the hog gather each crop, can be made exceptionally profitable, provided one can find a ready home market when they are fit for the shambles. With packing houses convenient, hog raising will soon become a leading industry of this State and a most profitable one. By planting an acre or two in February or early March of a variety of early ripening sugar corn, in rows three feet apart and six to twelve inches in drill, it will be ready for the hogs in May. Succeed this with a similar patch of early sorghum, which will be ripe in June. Follow with Spanish peanuts, ripe in July, or early cow peas, ripe at same time. Add to these Chufas and artichokes a late corn field with cow peas, and a good lot of sweet potatoes, and you have the material to grow and fatten mnay hogs. These lots should be arranged so that the hogs could gather them all and simultaneously have access to a field of grass or clover, with an abundance of fresh, pure water. This is possible on nearly every farm. By adopting such a plan as the above, some of our best farmers have raised hogs for half a cent a pound.

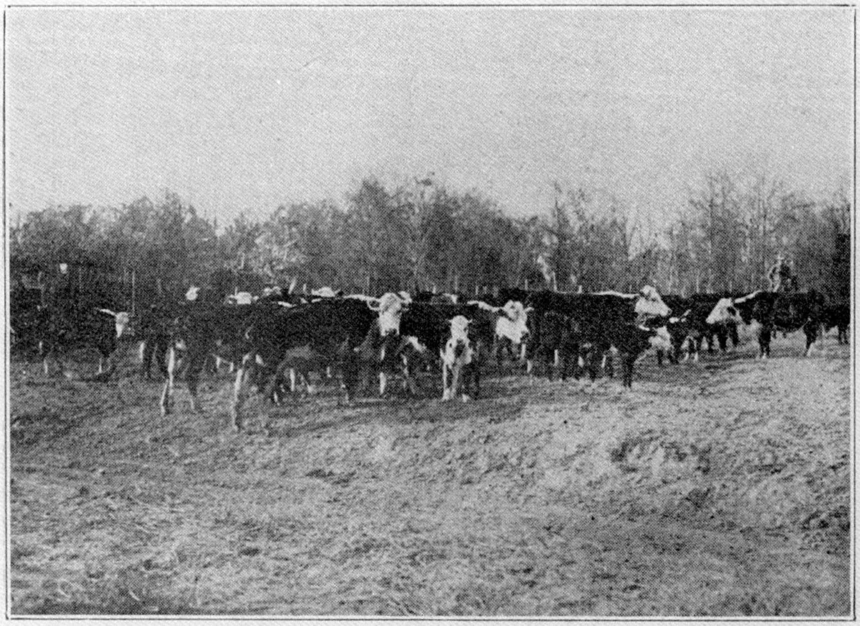

LIVE STOCK

CAN LIVE STOCK be successfully raised in Louisiana? The most forceful reply to this question would seem to be that farm animals of the most popular breeds are being successfully raised in the State, and this is doubtless due to the excellence of the climate and to the superabundance of food crops which Louisiana is capable of producing.

CATTLE.

Of the breeds and varieties at present in the State, the following may be mentioned:

Beef Breeds.—Shorthorn, Polled Durham, Aberdeen-Angus, among the larger breeds, and the Red Poll and Devon, representing the smaller.

Within the last few years the prices paid for males of the beef breeds have ranged up into the thousands of dollars, and animals of the choicest families are constantly being introduced.

Dairy Breeds.—Jersey, Guernsey and Holstein-Friesian chiefly. Some of the most famous families of these breeds are represented in the State.

The main impediment to the cattle industry in Louisiana, like other Southern States, has been the presence of the cattle tick. However, the work of eradication is being vigorously prosecuted by the Federal and State authorities, and a compulsory tick eradication law is now on the statute books, which means that the entire State is to be tick-free within the next very few years.

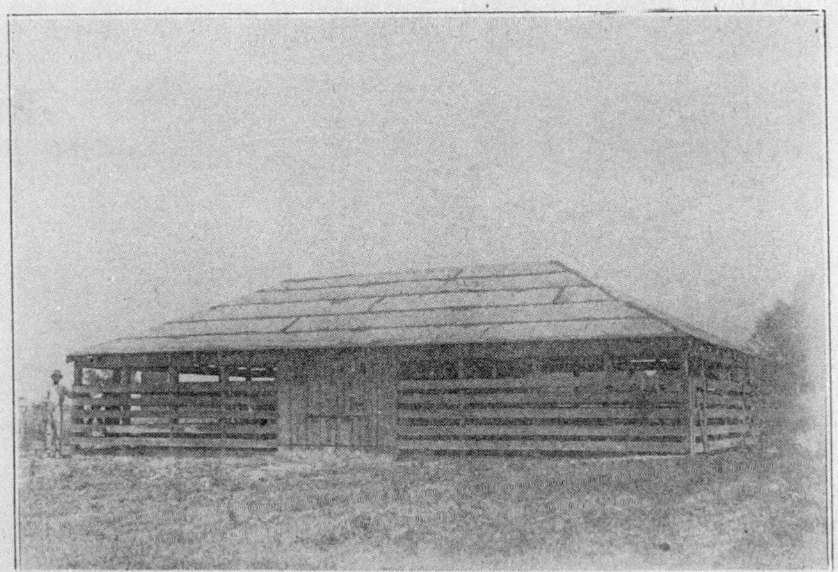

AN INEXPENSIVE HOG HOUSE.

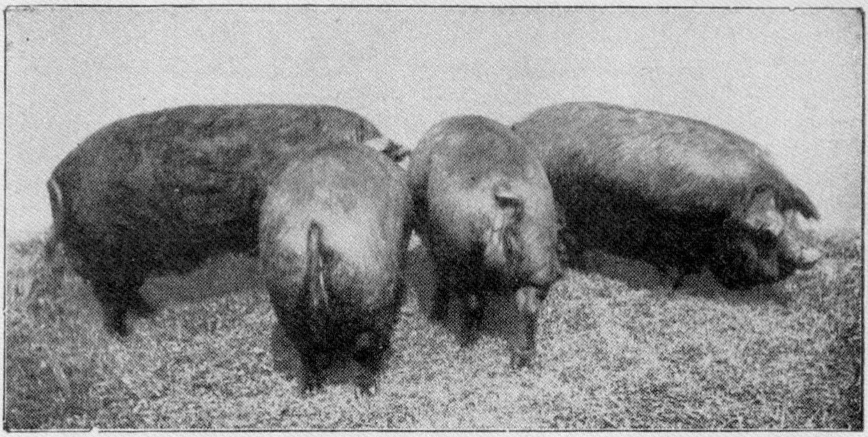

SAMPLE OF LOUISIANA HOGS.

HOGS.

Breeds.—Duroc-Jersey, Berkshire, Poland-China, Hampshire, Tamworth, Essex, Yorkshire, and other white breeds.

The raising of hogs is fast becoming a very extensive industry in Louisiana and promises to become one of our chief branches of animal husbandry in almost every section.

It may be said of the hogs, as of the animals previously mentioned, that in Louisiana there are represented some of the best strains in the country.

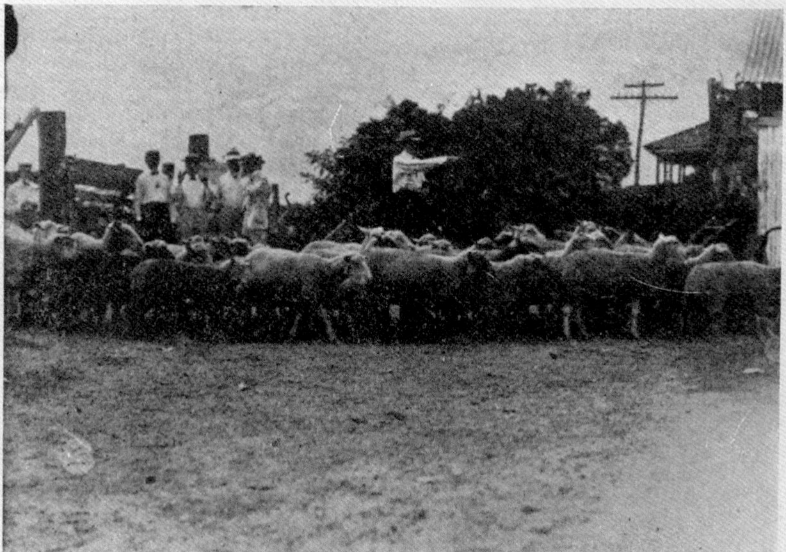

A FLOCK OF SHEEP IN POINTE COUPEE PARISH.

SHEEP.

Breeds.—Shropshire, Southdown, Hampshire, Dorset, and perhaps a few other breeds, including some of the Merinos.

The climate of Louisiana seems better suited to the middle-wool, or mutton, breeds than to the heavy, long-wooled sheep, such as the Lincoln, Cotswold, etc., and there are great possibilities in the raising of mutton sheep and lambs, especially in the hands of those who are familiar with this line of husbandry. Under intelligent management, sheep do well in the State, and there is a profitable and large consuming market for mutton in the city of New Orleans.

HORSES AND MULES.

The heavy draft breeds of horses have not, as yet, gained a very extensive foothold, on account of the mule having been for so long the chief draft animal; but many farmers are gradually adopting horses of the heavier breeds, and they seem to be giving entire satisfaction.

Of the lighter breeds of horses there are to be found the German Coach, French Coach, English Hackney, "Kentucky" saddle horse, and the standard-bred, or light harness horse, besides ponies.

Mules are quite a profitable "crop," and with the proper foundation stock are being raised in Louisiana as well as anywhere.

LIVE STOCK ORGANIZATIONS.

In connection with live stock it may be said that almost every variety has its own special organization or association to look after and stimulate its development in the State. Among these may be mentioned the Louisiana Beef Breeders' Association, the Louisiana Jersey Breeders' Association, the Louisiana Swine Breeders' Association, etc., and, in addition, Louisiana has a State Live Stock Sanitary Board, or "Health of Animals Department," to control the various infectious and contagious diseases to which live stock may be susceptible. And this State Board also operates a serum plant at Baton Rouge for the benefit of the hog-raisers, where they may secure potent anti hog cholera serum at a minimum of cost.

THE LOUISIANA STATE LIVE STOCK SANITARY BOARD.

The Louisiana State Live Stock Sanitary Board is to the live stock population of the State what the Louisiana State Board of Health is to the people. It was created for the purpose of preventing, controlling and eradicating the infectious and contagious diseases of animals and thus protect the farmer's property.

The State Live Stock Sanitary Board prepares and distributes the serum to protect the farmer's hogs against hog cholera and has already saved thousands of dollars' worth of hogs in the State.

The State Live Stock Sanitary Board prevents the introduction of diseased animals from other States and thus protects the State from outbreaks of contagious diseases among our live stock.

The State Live Stock Sanitary Board requires that all cattle for breeding or dairy purposes, over six months old, coming into the State of Louisiana, must be accompanied by a certificate from a qualified veterinarian approved by officials of the State from which the shipment is made, showing their absolute freedom from tuberculosis, and in this way prevent the introduction and spread of that insidious disease among the herds of cattle in the State.

The State Live Stock Sanitary Board is at the head of the tick eradication work in the State, and it is through the co-operation of this Board with the Federal Bureau of Animal Industry, at Washington, that this work is being systematically carried on for the benefit of our cattle owners.

The State Live Stock Sanitary Board operates under one of the best live stock sanitary laws in the United States and was created solely in the interest of the farmers and stock owners of the State.

The State Live Stock Sanitary Board earnestly requests the co-operation of every farmer and stock owner in the State in order to make its work as effective as possible in preventing the introduction of the contagious diseases of animals from the outside and in controlling and eradicating them within the State.

The State Live Stock Sanitary Board is the friend of the stock owners of the State; it was created solely for their protection and it earnestly requests their hearty support and assistance in carrying out its provisions and regulations.

The State Live Stock Sanitary Board invites correspondence from the stock owners of the State regarding infectious and contagious diseases of their animals, and it urgently requests that all suspicious cases or outbreaks of these diseases be promptly reported to the Secretary and Executive Officer.

The prevention, control and extermination of our animal plagues can be accomplished only by intelligent sanitation.

The office of the Louisiana State Live Stock Sanitary Board is located in the State Capitol, Baton Rouge, Louisiana. Dr. E. P. Flower is Executive Officer.

DAIRYING IN LOUISIANA

THE PRODUCTION OF MILK and its products is still in its infancy in Louisiana, although this State offers the dairyman many advantages over other States. Nature affords a splendid climate, native pastures and an abundance of pure water and plenty of cool shade. Besides these, the Southern dairyman has the advantage over his Northern competitor in that our short winters require shelter and extra feed for only a few months in the year. Moreover, the feed for the winter—such as hay, turnips, etc.—can be raised in winter months. Oats and vetch sowed in September and October furnish satisfactory feed for January and February. Cotton seed meal and hulls from the many cotton seed oil mills, the rice bran from our rice mills and the molasses from the sugar factories provide superior economic feed for the cattle.

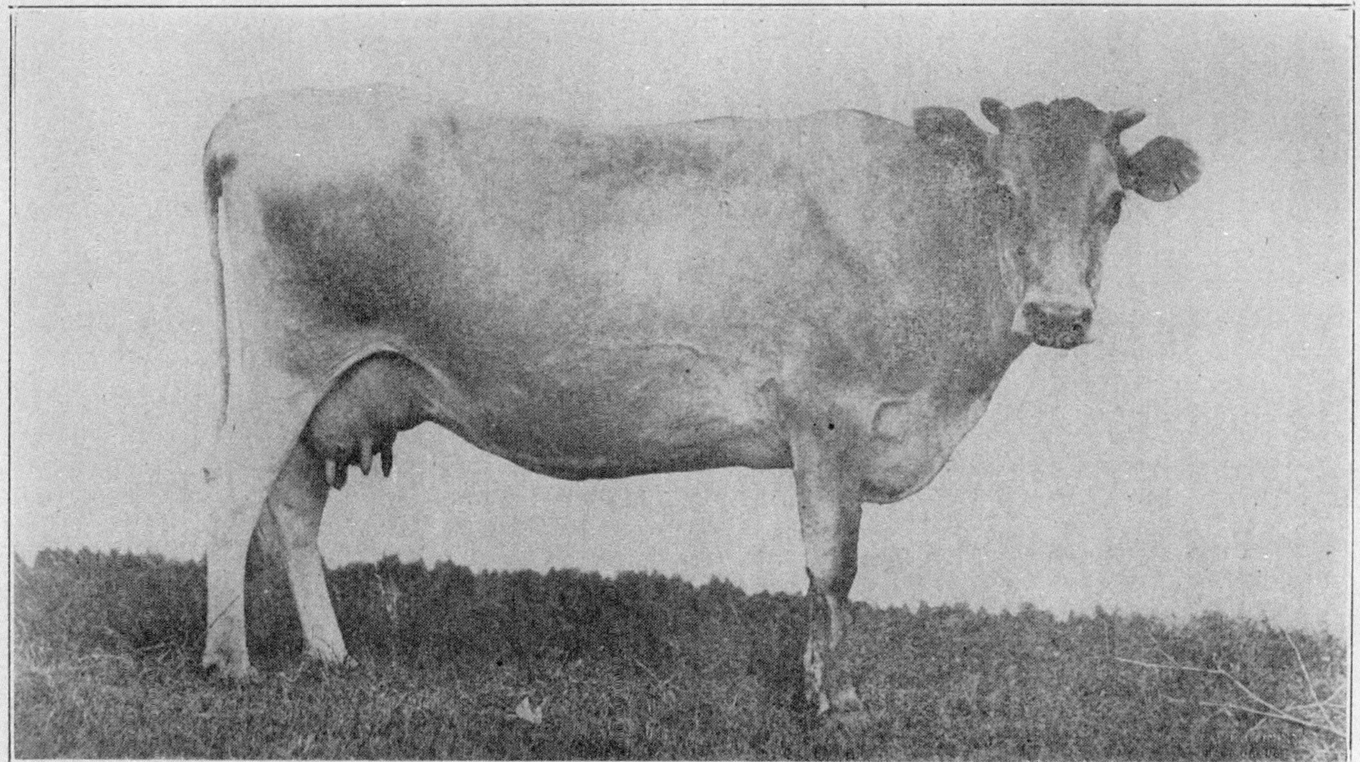

ONE OF LOUISIANA'S MONEY MAKERS.

Only within the last few years has the attention of the people of New Orleans been pointedly drawn to the matter of its milk supply. Heretofore nearly all the milk used in that city was produced in dairies within the city limits. It is now recognized by all authorities and scientists that milk should not be produced in thickly populated centers, but in the open country, and the dairies within the city limits were closed by law and compelled to move outside of certain prescribed and safe lines. As a result the supply of milk was still further reduced, though the quality and cleanliness, thanks to the strict supervision of the Board of Health, has been improved. Large dairies have also been established at some distance from the city, in localities that can be reached in one or two hours by rail. Hammond, which is fifty-two miles from New Orleans, furnished a large part of the milk consumed in that city, and a number of farmers at Roseland also ship fresh milk daily to New Orleans, and all along on the Illinois Central and Yazoo & Mississippi Valley railroads hundreds of gallons are being shipped daily. In New Orleans a company with a perfect and sanitary plant and proper facilities for pasteurizing milk is buying and disposing of all the milk it can secure, and will help much to develop the dairy industry of the country adjacent to New Orleans. The net price paid to the producer has been 20 cents a gallon in summer and 22 cents in winter, or 4½ cents per degree of butter fat. This company and other responsible parties will make a contract for all the high-grade milk the farmers can produce, and every farmer who delivers his milk at the railway station can collect his payments weekly.

It will thus be seen that New Orleans is in need of thousands of gallons of milk and its need will increase with each year. In the production of butter, cheese and other milk products, too, a rational man-

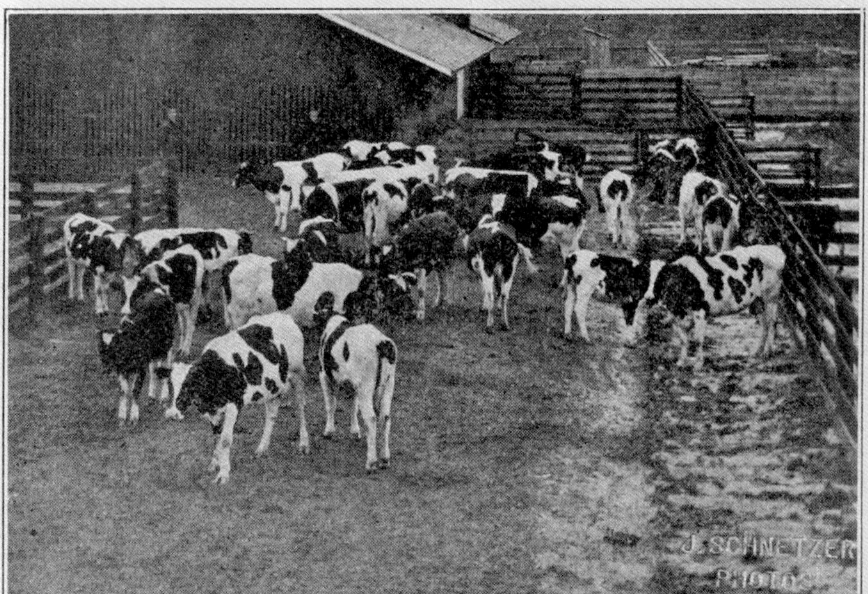

A HERD OF TANGIPAHOA DAIRY CATTLE.

agement can introduce many improvements and no better opportunity can offer itself to those seeking to establish the dairy industry in this vicinity. The selection of the proper dairy cow, improved dairy machinery and appliances and the necessary knowledge to operate the dairy become the only considerations. Otherwise the conditions for success in dairying in this vicinity are the most favorable. Cheap land suitable for this purpose in great abundance and conveniently located near the city, on either side of the fourteen railroads entering the city, and which deliver the milk here in one or two hours; a strong demand which assures to the producer a firm price and ready sale of all the milk he has to offer; and, lastly, climate and agricultural conditions which furnish the dairyman advantages such as he will not find in regions further North. Under these circumstances the dairy business in Louisiana properly handled offers rare opportunities to any one with the necessary experience and small capital required, and there is not the least doubt that the time will come when it will be one of the most important industries of the State.

SOY BEANS

IN THIS AGE OF PROGRESS, where opportunities are constantly flashed upon us, we must be on the alert to seize always the best in sight.

In 1798 indigo was the chief crop of this section of the country, selling at 75 cents per pound, but cotton made its appearance among the farmers and at four dollars per hundred (no gins at that time being thought of) was considered more remunerative, and it slowly increased until the gin was invented, and then it became the great crop of the South, overshadowing all others to such an extent that the one-crop system became baneful, and it is now a recognized fact that diversity is the farmers' slogan that should be sounded all over our Southern land; it is the "shibboleth" that will open the doors to prosperity, but selections for diversified crops should be seriously considered. The soil and climate are factors that should not be overlooked; the adaptability to Southern cultivation would be another consideration, and now, after eight years' actual observation, after a careful examination into its merits, we unhesitatingly recommend soy beans as one crop that should occupy a prominent place on every farm in the State of Louisiana.

It is practically a companion to cotton; its similarity in culture is its first recommendation, and we trust that it will not be long before it is known as one of Louisiana's great staple crops.

The introduction of anything new is sometimes attended by slow growth. Sugar cane, for instance, was first introduced by the Jesuit Fathers into Louisiana in 1751, and no real development took place until fifty years after, and today it is grand among our agricultural interests.

Rice, too, slowly traveled along as a small adjunct to our other products until Southwest Louisiana forced it into our first lines.

Thus we see that it took the invention of the gin to place cotton upon its proper pedestal; the crushing rollers of the mill was the first key to unlock the doors of the world's great storage of sweetness; and irrigation placed rice as one of the great products of Louisiana's soil. but all

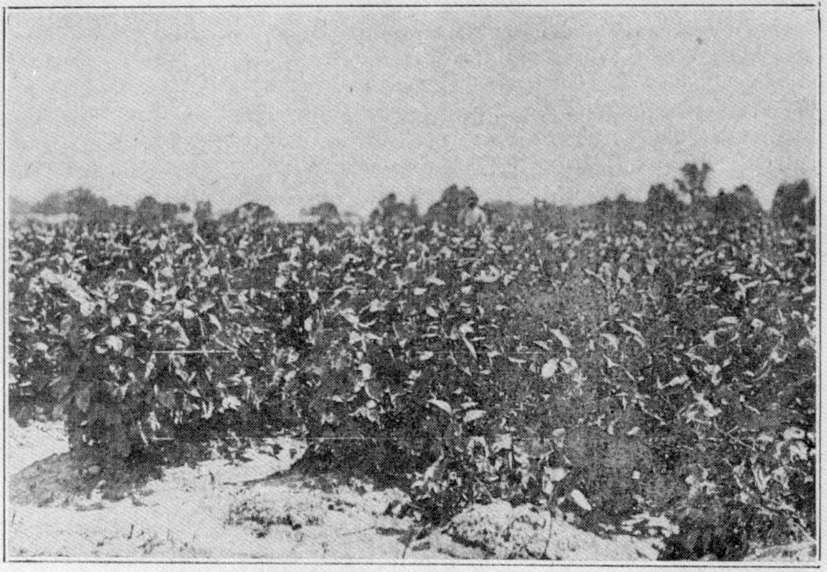

A FIELD OF SOY BEANS.

these developments took time and study, but in recommending soy beans no such delays are necessary, for, besides the great feeding qualities of this product, the cotton seed oil mills, with only a few small changes, are ready to convert into oil and meal.

The oil mills of North Carolina have already begun to crush the soy beans, having this season crushed over a hundred thousand bushels, making 2,400 tons of meal and 94,500 gallons of oil.

The average extraction from a ton of cotton seed is about 800 pounds of meal, 800 pounds of hulls, 35 to 40 gallons of oil and 90 pounds of linters. From soy beans 1,600 to 1,700 pounds of meal are procured, and 35 to 40 gallons of oil made. The average yield of cotton seed per acre is from one-eighth to one-quarter ton, whereas, the beans yield from 25 to 50 bushels per acre. The cotton stalk is valueless as a feed and expensive to get rid of, while the soy bean vine yields about one ton per acre of feed that is equal to wheat bran or alfalfa. Cotton takes from the soil, while beans add to its fertility.

If we stop a moment and think of cotton seed, the despised product which the ingenuity of man was strenuously used to get rid of, when we think of the envied looks of many owners of gins when they found a neighbor had located upon a running stream and had the double satisfaction of possessing cheap motive power and at the same time gotten rid of a great nuisance by dumping the seed into the stream below, today one of the South's great assets is that once obnoxious product that has developed into a commercial importance that ranks high indeed.

Strawberries, too, that have been only one of our garden luxuries in the past, today bring into Louisiana several millions of dollars, and the accomplishment of this great development was produced only by co-operation among the farmers and railroads, and now by co-operation between farmers and cotton seed oil men we feel absolutely sure that this new agricultural "Richmond" will win out in the great field of diversification which we have planned to fight out and which will place Louisiana in the front ranks of agricultural States.

And why should soy beans not win its place among these diversified crops? It can be planted from early spring until the middle of July. It can follow Irish potatoes, oats or any other spring crop.

The soy bean is one of the most important agricultural plants of Northern China and Japan. It is said that the production is so great in Manchuria that already that country is annually exporting hundreds of thousands of tons to Europe, and the western coast of America is gradually becoming a market for this product. Henry says: "No other plant in the United States grown so little at this time as the soy bean is so full of promise to agriculture, especially to animal husbandry."

Soy bean meal is a valuable dairy and poultry feed because of the high content of protein. On the Pacific coast, where soy bean meal has been manufactured for several years as a dairy feed, the material has become very popular at $37.50 per ton. An idea of its importance commercially is suggested by the fact that the United States has been annually importing 5,000,000 pounds of soy bean cake, 19,000,000 pounds of soy bean oil and 4,000,000 pounds of soy bean seed.

In conclusion, special attention is called to the following tables from Henry's "Feeds and Feeding":

DIGESTIBLE NUTRIENTS IN 1000 POUNDS.

	Crude Protein. Pounds.	Carbohydrates. Pounds.	Fat. Pounds.
Wheat bran	12.50	41.6	3.0
Alfalfa hay	10.60	39.0	0.9
Soy bean (grain)	30.70	22.8	14.4
Soy bean (hay)	11.70	39.2	1.2
Red clover	7.60	39.3	1.8
Timothy hay	3.00	42.8	1.2
Corn stover	2.10	42.4	0.7
Linseed meal	30.20	32.6	6.7

The above is conclusive evidence of the great value of soy beans as a feeding stuff, and the following from the same authority shows how they stand as a fertilizer:

FERTILIZER CONSTITUENTS IN 1,000 POUNDS.

	Nitrogen. Pounds.	Phosphoric Acid. Pounds.	Potash. Pounds.
Wheat bran	25.6	29.5	16.2
Alfalfa hay	23.8	5.4	22.3
Soy bean (grain)	58.4	13.7	24.7
Soy bean (hay)	25.6	6.8	23.3
Red clover	20.5	3.9	16.3
Timothy hay	9.9	3.1	13.6
Corn stover	9.1	3.0	11.5
Linseed meal	54.2	17.0	12.7

With these corroborative evidences of the great value of soy beans and feeling sure that it must soon be developed into one of Louisiana's great staple crops, it is with an urgent appeal that the farmers all over the State are asked to try this crop, even if it be but on a small scale. Our cotton seed mills will be glad to take care of your surplus crop.

Plant in rows 30 to 33 inches apart. Use your corn planter (the nine-hole plate), which will drop them two to three inches in the drill; be sure and not plant too deep, as they will not come up.

The mammoth yellow bean is the one to plant.

POULTRY RAISING

WHILE IT IS USUALLY regarded as a side issue on the farms, poultry raising is an important industry. Thousands of dollars' worth of eggs and chickens, in the aggregate, find their way to all the local markets, and furnish many thrifty housewives with pocket money. There are many poultry breeders in the State, and thoroughbred or high-bred poultry are found on nearly every farm. The most popular farm breeds are the Leghorns, Plymouth Rocks, Langshan, Rhode Island Reds, Indian Game and Wyandotte, the Bronze Turkey, and the Pekin Duck. No better opportunity is anywhere offered than in Louisiana for poultry raising.

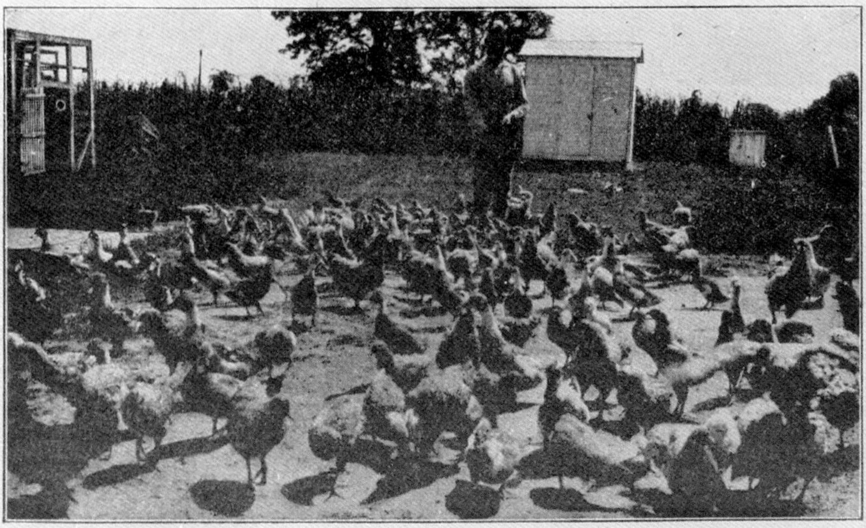

A POULTRY FARM.

BUREAU OF MARKETING

ONE OF THE MOST IMPORTANT additions to the work of the Agricultural Department is the Bureau of Marketing. Every day communications are received from various parts of the State announcing what products they have for sale or exchange. At the same time, letters are received from others asking where certain animals or products can be procured. The department at once places these parties in communication and thus sales or exchanges are made and nothing seems to be giving the farmers such general satisfaction as the Bureau of Marketing. The daily press publishes every week a list of the offerings and wants and every Monday the department sends out a bulletin embodying the week's work.

RESOURCES AND POSSIBILITIES

THE HON. JOSEPH E. RANSDELL, while a member of Congress from the Fifth District, in a speech to that body, gave so much valuable information concerning Louisiana that we quote with pleasure the following extracts:

"The eyes of the world are today being turned toward Dixie, and in the next twenty-five years we are to witness a most marvelous development in that section. Long retarded and checked in growth by the civil war and its disastrous industrial results, the South has arisen from her ashes a fairer and a mightier land. She has laid aside her sable garments and, bedecked in a gown of bright colors, is looking confidently to the glorious future that awaits her, for she knows that a benign Providence has favored her above other lands, and that by virtue of her natural advantages she will become the most prosperous section of our great common country.

We have marvelous resources of every kind and sort which are just beginning to be developed and in no portion of the world are there as good opportunities for success as in the land of Dixie. If Horace Greeley were alive today his advice to young men would be, "Go South!" When he said to them, "Go West!" a great field opened there, and many fortunes were made by following his sage counsels. The scene has shifted. The great opportunities of the West have been seized, but there are innumerable openings in the South awaiting fertile brains and vigorous hands.

If the new settler is accustomed to grain and cereals, with cattle and hogs, he need not change his crops or methods in the South, unless it be to substitute rice for wheat, should he settle in the lower half of the Gulf States, although wheat does well in northern portions. He need not become a cotton grower unless he wishes to, for corn and the cereals, with forage crops of many kinds, coupled with some branch or branches of animal industry—especially hogs—will furnish the most attractive and profitable employment. If he be a dairyman, that line is open to him with marked advantages in many respects. If he be a gardener or fruit grower, the Gulf and lower Atlantic coast sections, with immunity from cold and delightful climate, can not be excelled. Indeed, he can choose his own branch of agriculture and find ideal conditions in the South.

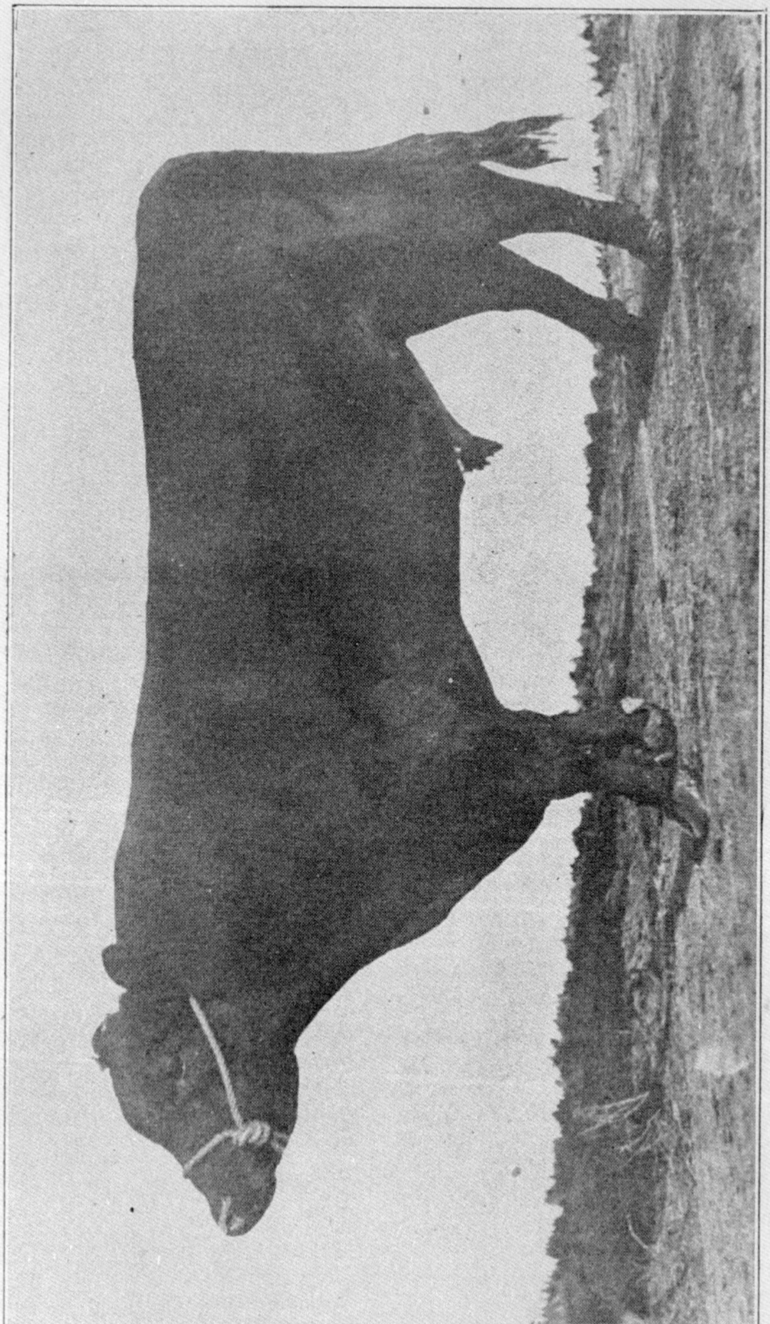

ABERDEEN ANGUS BULL.

And we would welcome them gladly. We need a great many of them. Why, sir, the last federal census showed the density of the population in the State of Texas as something like 11.6 per square mile, in Louisiana 30.4, in Georgia 37.6, and in Arkansas 24.7 per square mile, while of New York it was 152.6, in New Jersey 250.3, in Ohio 102, in Pennsylvania 140.1, and in Massachusetts 348.9 per square mile. The South has not been peopled yet; it is a new land. The best opportunities of the North and West have been seized and developed; but such is not true of the South, which still offers exceptional inducements in any line of business that a good, industrial man wishes to pursue.

ANIMAL INDUSTRY.

With forage crops naturally goes animal industry. There are no enemies to hogs, sheep, horses and mules in the Southern States which do not exist everywhere, and all of these animals succeed well. Our winters are so mild that with a proper variety of crops grazing can be secured every day in the year, and animals require much less dry food and close attention than in the North. Conditions with us are especially favorable to hogs, and I doubt if any State in the Republic has as many advantages for the lowly porker as my own Louisiana. Food crops of every kind grow in great profusion throughout the year, so that no housing is necessary, and the health of the pigs is fine whenever properly cared for. The same is true of horses, mules and sheep. Kentucky and Tennessee are justly famous for the best horses and mules on the continent, but I have seen as good animals raised in Louisiana as ever trod the ground.

I am sometimes asked if we can make good butter in Louisiana. Yes; most emphatically. And why not? We have the most succulent grasses and clovers, and every variety of food necessary for good milk thrives with us. Dairying can be made a very profitable industry in many parts of the South, including Louisiana.

CLIMATE.

In point of climate the South compares favorably with any other section. Her summers are longer, but the extremes of heat are no greater than in more Northern regions, and the change from cold to heat is so gradual that the system becomes accustomed to it. Sunstrokes of man or beast are very uncommon in the South. I was born and reared in Louisiana, where my life has been spent, and I remember only one slight case of sunstroke in human beings. The nights are usually pleasant and sleep refreshing in the hottest weather of July and August.

While our summers are long, our winters are very short and mild, and the seasons of spring and fall are delightful. Great extremes of cold are never experienced, and when we get a cold snap it lasts only a few days, followed by a greater period of warm sunshine. Farming operations, such as the preparation, seeding and cultivation of the soil are interrupted by freezes only for very brief periods in the lower tier of States, and are practically continuous throughout the year. Interruption of general business by cold is almost unknown.

HEALTH.

There are many false impressions about the health of the South, and misrepresentations on this subject are prevalent. Owing to the fact that our system of securing vital statistics is imperfect in rural districts, just as it is in most of the States, I can not make accurate comparisons between different sections, but will produce enough to show any fair-minded man that the whites of the South are as healthy as any in the Union. We have in round numbers in the Southern States about 19,000,000 whites and 9,500,000 negroes. The latter race is not healthy for reasons which the scope of this speech prevents me from discussing. Statistics show a much heavier mortality among negroes than whites, hence I shall refer only to Caucasians in making my comparisons.

The mortality statistics of the United States census for 1908 show that in Boston, which I take as a typical Northern city, the death rate from all causes was as follows:

In the year 1906, 18.9 per 1,000 souls; 1907, 19.2 per 1,000 souls; 1908, 19.1 per thousand souls.

While in New Orleans it was:

In 1906, whites, 18.1 per 1,000 souls; 1907, whites, 20.1 per 1,000 souls; 1908, whites, 19 per 1,000 souls.

So it appears that by comparing the whites of New Orleans with the entire population of Boston, where practically all are Caucasians, we find exactly the same average death rate in the two cities. And I wish to add that since the completion of a splendid system of sewers and waterworks, the health of New Orleans has improved materially, and in 1909 the death rate was only 15.52 per 1,000, according to the city officials.

These same census tables show:

At Detroit, Mich., in 1906, 17 per 1,000; 1907, 16.5 per 1,000; 1908, 15.6 per 1,000.

At Savannah, Ga., in 1906, whites, 17.2 per 1,000; 1907, whites, 17.9 per 1,000; 1908, whites, 15.1 per 1,000, or a very slight advantage for Detroit, which is considered one of the health resorts of the Great Lakes.

And again they show:

New Haven, Conn., in 1906, 19.1 per 1,000; 1907, 18.6 per 1,000; 1908, 16.9 per 1,000.

Memphis, Tenn., in 1906, whites, 16 per 1,000; 1907, whites, 15.8 per 1,000; 1908, whites, 15.6 per 1,000.

Which is a decided advantage for the Southern City.

And finally:

Cincinnati, Ohio, in 1906, 20.8 per 1,000; 1907, 18.5 per 1,000; 1908, 18.5 per 1,000.

Mobile, Ala., in 1906, whites, 21 per 1,000; 1907, whites, 19 per 1,000; 1908, whites, 17.3 per 1,000.

Or an advantage for the city on the Gulf.

A very interesting table giving a comparison of general death rates in American cities from 1871 to 1904, inclusive, was compiled by Mr. Frederick Hoffman and published by the American Statistical Association, March, 1906, pages 5-7. It shows that for the twenty years 1885 to 1904, inclusive, the average mortality per 1,000 of population in

Northern and Western cities was 19.75 per annum, and of whites in the Southern cities it was 19.34, or a lower death rate in the cities of the South.

And in considering the death rate of the South for the past twenty years it must be remembered that two of the most fatal diseases of that section—yellow fever and malaria—were not understood until recently. The last yellow fever outbreak that was in scourge could readily be controlled and there is no longer any reason for alarm about it. Scientists have shown our people how to prevent malaria by screening their houses against mosquitoes, and also that common disease-bearer, the house fly. No intelligent immigrant from Europe or the North need have any greater fear of sickness in the South that he is subject to at home.

A thoroughly reliable, disinterested and competent witness on this subject is Dr. Walter Wyman, Surgeon-General of Public Health and Marine Hospital Service of our Government, who delivered an admirable address on "Southern Health Conditions" before the Southern Commercial Congress in this city December 7, 1908. He said:

"Impressions have prevailed concerning health conditions in the South which, though perhaps justified twenty-five years ago, are now entirely unwarranted. A principal cause for false impression is undoubtedly due to yellow fever, which formerly so frequently afflicted our Southern States, but which, it may fairly be claimed, is no longer a factor to be considered in the determination of health conditions.

"Such diseases as malaria nad typhoid fever are subject to the same causative agencies as prevail elsewhere; and as to tuberculosis, the climate is favorable in that it freely permits and encourages life in the open air. With regard to this and other diseases, the conditions seem more favorable than in colder localities where people are prone to shut themselves up with the disease.

"I would not be understood to claim that sanitary or health conditions throughout the South are all that could be desired, nor could I say the same concerning the North or any foreign country, but I do mean to say that, with its salubrious climate, one may settle in any of our Southern States and by observing for himself and his family the sanitary laws and principles now so well understood he will be under as favorable conditions for health and length of life as he could be anywhere."

A witness from my home town, Lake Providence, in northeast Louisiana, on the banks of the Mississippi, in the very center of the big bottom lands, is Hon. E. J. Hamley, one of the best men in the State. He states, in a recent letter to me:

"I will say that I left the northeastern part of Missouri for Lake Providence, La., in October, 1879, and I have lived here continuously since that time. All of my children have been born and reared in this town.

"I know of no healthier part of the United States than I have found right here. My health and the health of my family has always been good, and I believe that I can honestly say that I have not spent $100 for doctor bills for myself in the whole time I have been living here.

"I know of no better and healthier country for a young man to make a start in than right here, provided he is willing to take off his coat and go to work."

One of the many splendid citizens contributed by Iowa to Louisiana is Mr. S. L. Cary, of Jennings, who never ceases to thank his stars for finding a home in the Pelican State. He writes me:

"Next to Vermont, Louisiana has most old people to population, and the Gulf Coast line the lowest death rate in the States. In 1880 the southwest Louisiana census gave the average family nine persons. For home-making, the easiest, best conditoin I have ever seen, and next to this, money-making is easy.

"I was here at 56; now at 83; and the last twenty-seven years the healthiest and happiest of all my life.

"As school children we were taught that Louisiana was a low, swampy, unhealthy country, the home of the alligator. The truth says, 'Thank God for the lowlands of Louisiana; 80 bushels of rice, 40 tons of sugar cane and $300 in oranges are entirely possible on a single acre of land."

Another good man who went from Minnesota to Livingston Parish, La., is Mr. M. M. Garig, of Denham Springs, who writes:

"The number of very old people will attest to the healthfulness of the country. Myself and boys work in the fields in the sun. In thirty-five years I have not seen a case of sunstroke. It is not nearly as hot as in Minnesota. Allow me to say the man that wishes to escape the rigors of Northern winters will make no mistake by visiting this part of the sunny south—Livingston Parish, La."

And I conclude this branch of my subject with an extract from a letter from Dr. B. A. Ledbetter, of New Orleans, president New Orleans Medical Society, and a member of the Louisiana State Board of Health, as follows:

"Your inquiry as to general health conditions of Louisiana has been received, and it gives me pleasure to say to you that I believe Louisiana, from a health standpoint, is second to no State in the Union. It is useless for me to state that Louisiana, like Texas, has a variety of climate such as few other States enjoy. In the northern portion of our State you find a high, dry climate, particularly free from malaria and one of the best in the world for tubercular and similar diseases. In the central and southern portions of Louisiana the altitude is not so great. In south Louisiana, which includes the city of New Orleans, we have the delightful Gulf breezes, which make New Orleans one of the coolest and most delightful summer as well as winter resorts in the world."

These two States—Louisiana and Texas—are typical of the entire South, and I say with the utmost candor that health, prosperity, a warm welcome and happiness await every immigrant to Dixie who comes to bear an honest man's part in his new home, and does his duty.

THE LANDS OF THE STATE.

Speaking of the Mississippi Valley, Mr. Joseph E. Wing, of Mechanicsburg, Ohio, who is familiar with lands throughout the Union and a scientific as well as a practical Ohio farmer and leading business man, recently wrote me as follows:

"There are millions of acres in the South that have soils richer than those of central Illinois, that garden spot of the corn belt. These lands are unoccupied or thinly inhabited. They are now dreary, desolate, mosquito-inhabited, moss-hung lands along various southern streams,

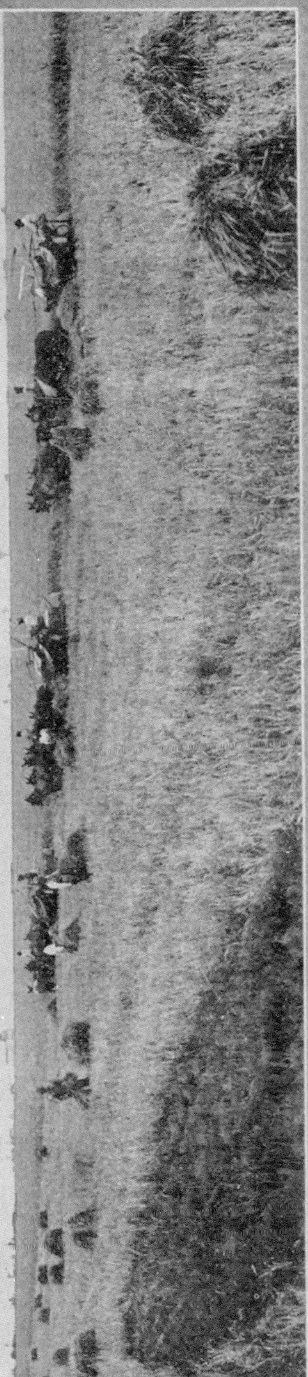

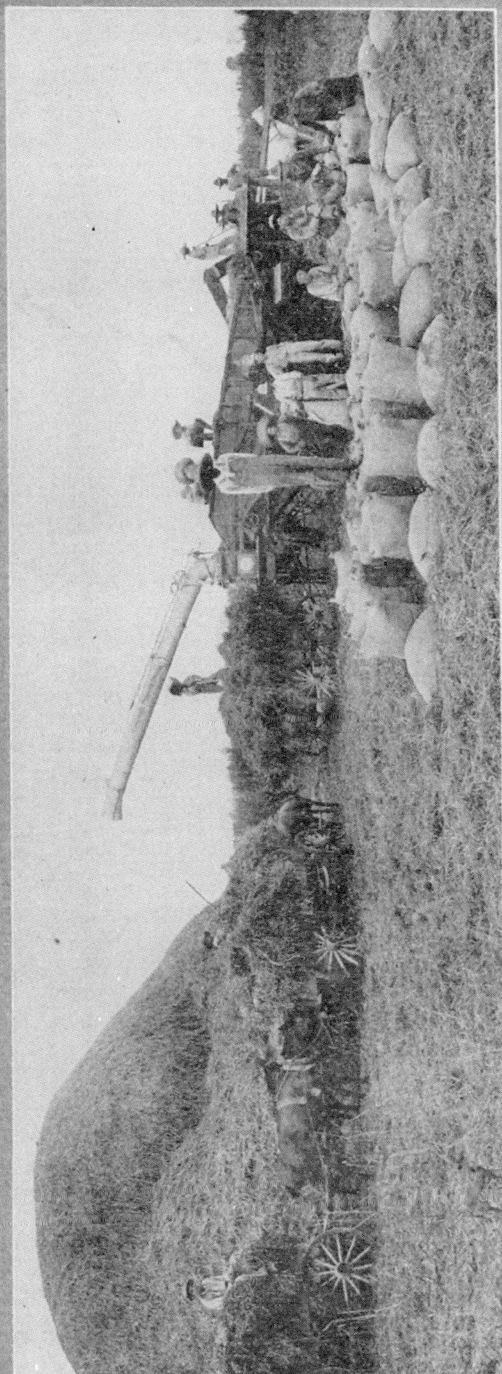

the swamp lands. The lands bordering the Mississippi River are made from the very cream of northern soils. These soils to an immense depth are the deposits of silt brought down by floods from washings of Ohio, Indiana, Illinois, Iowa, and other rich-soiled northern States. Technically, these soils are immensely rich in potash and phosphorus, the essential elements of fertility. The black "buckshot" soils bordering the Mississippi River are also very rich in carbonate of lime. Carbonate of lime is the thing in soils that has always stood for enduring fertility. Carbonate of lime makes land ready for alfalfa and other soil-enriching clovers.

"A man can take that land along the Mississippi River in Louisiana or one of the adjoining States and grow on it more alfalfa per acre than he can in Illinois or Iowa. On the alfalfa sod he can grow as much corn per acre as he can grow in Illinois, and perhaps he can grow more corn. He can live in a mild climate, delightful nearly every day from middle September till middle June. I firmly believe that, living right, the health of the white man in Louisiana will be better than the health of the man in Illinois, and the same is true of his family. He can grow there cheap bacon, beef, mules. He can grow rice, cotton if he desires, corn, alfalfa, wheat. Why, then, does he not do it?

"The reason is not far to seek. The land is undrained. Only here and there are dry fringes along the margins of bayous. Nearly the whole of it is unbroken forest, submerged during part of the year. The descent of the stream is too slight for drainage, the surface of the land too flat. A few years ago the levees along the Mississippi River were too weak to afford protection. Now they are made strong, but the trouble from deficient outlet for the heavy rainfall remains. The sluggish rivers need straightening. The Tensas has a channel four times as long as it would be if a few short canals were dug across bends; maybe it is ten times as long as it need be, because of its tortuous course. Other streams and bayous are similarly tortuous.

"Individual effort, unfortunately, can not accomplish much in solution of this problem. Some of the streams that block drainage are navigable streams. A comprehensive system of drains must be inaugurated. There must be main canals; these must lead to large streams; these must be widened in places, deepened in places, straightened. It is not a difficult problem. It is not even an expensive or costly thing to accomplish. A dollar spent in drainage here will do more than four spent in difficult irrigation enterprises in the West. These irrigation works are good; we rejoice to see them done; the whole people will be the richer for them, yet the Government ought not to forget its other needy territory.

"I know well the lands of America from one end to the other. I have studied soils and farms and farmers from Boston to San Francisco and from Washington to Florida. Thus I speak with knowledge when I say that we have no more priceless treasure than this Delta region of the Mississippi. It can be made to hold thousands of farms, small farms, each with its home, its children, and schools. I have lived in the Delta in July and been there during nearly every month. White men can there keep strong and well if they can escape mosquito infection and sleep out of doors behind screens on porches during the warm weather. Malaria

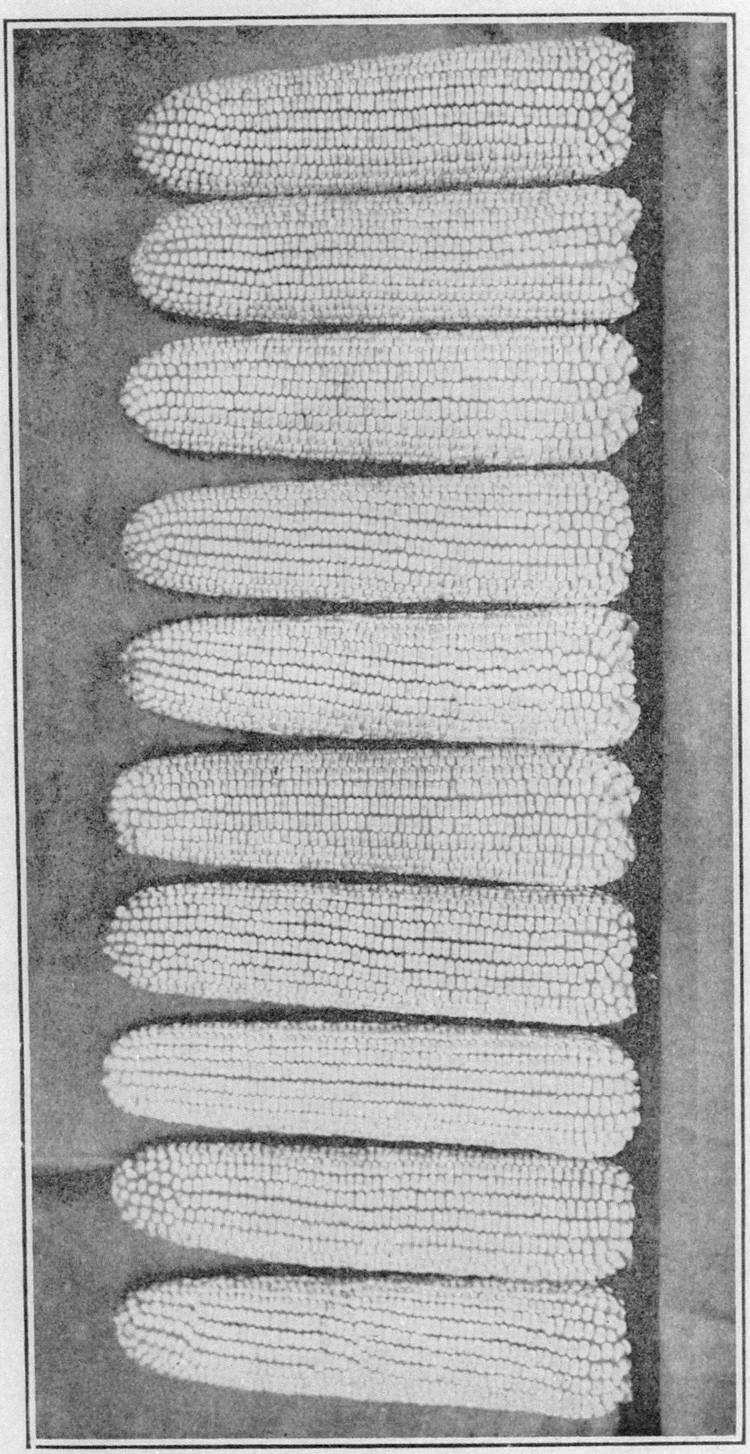

A SAMPLE OF LOUISIANA CORN.

is easily escaped. When drainage comes, mosquitoes can be nearly eradicated, and then there will be no more malaria there than there is in Illinois.

I thank Mr. Wing for these frank, truthful words.

LOUISIANA QUEEN OF THE SOUTH.

I must now emphasize some of the strong points of my native State, Louisiana—the queen of the South.

Louisiana is unique in several particulars. A large portion of her surface is of recent formation, caused by the rich sediment of the Mississippi settling and making land as its rushing floods commingle with the quiet waters of the Gulf. This makes her, geologically speaking, the youngest of our States, and, like Benjamin, she occupies a tender spot in her father's heart.

Louisiana has four great crops—sugar, rice, cotton, and corn. She easily leads the Union in the production of sugar and rice and is a heavy producer of cotton and corn. Practically every soil product and fruit of the Temperate Zone does well. Her grasses and climate are admirably adapted to animal industry; cattle for beef and dairying, horses, mules, and sheep thrive; and she is the natural home of the hog, which does exceptionally well. Indeed, it is said by competent judges that Louisiana is the best State in the Union for raising hogs.

Col. F. L. Maxwell, a Union soldier from Illinois, who cast his lot at Mound, Madison Parish, La., forty-five years ago, and has accumulated a large fortune by farming, says:

"As requested, I give you my opinion on the advantages of Louisiana to the investor and home-seeker. Louisiana has some 14,000,000 acres of alluvial lands, only one-fifth of which are in cultivation. All of this land is capable of being cultivated and can be easily and cheaply drained."

"The opportunities in Louisiana for profitable investment to both the home-seeker and the investor are greater than in any other section; the climate is mild and healthful, without the extremes of heat and cold; and plenty of sunshine and rainfall (an average of about 52 inches per annum). We have no sunstrokes or cold blizzards; we have excellent churches and schools; quick and easy transportation facilities.

"As a corn country this is not excelled by the famous Wabash and White River bottoms of Indiana or the corn belt of central Illinois, Iowa, Nebraska, or Kansas, and excels all other States in ribbon cane, cotton, rice, clover, alfalfa, Bermuda, peas, soy beans and all kinds of vegetables.

"Louisiana produces the finest oranges that grow; she produces apples, peaches, figs, and all kinds of fruits, and is the home of the large pecan. The wonderful crops of succulent grasses grown nearly all the year make this a great stock and dairy country, and the best mules I have ever owned are those I raised on my own property. Hogs, cattle, mules and horses can be produced cheaper than in any other section I know of."

COME TO DIXIE.

In conclusion, let me again invite to Dixie the sturdy citizens of the North and West who have gone to Canada, or contemplate a change of domicile, and all good immigrants. The South wishes them and will welcome them with open arms. My own Louisiana will gladly receive a

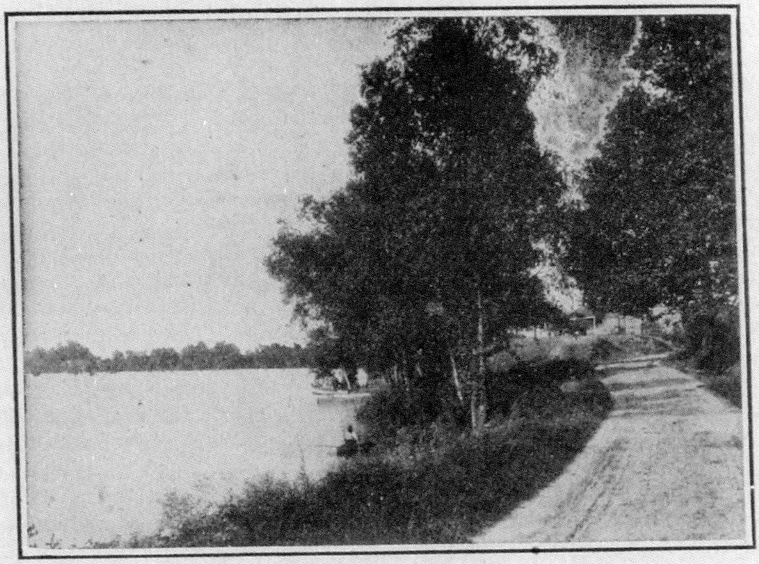

A GOOD ROAD ALONG THE RIVER BANK.

million such people as are exiling themselves from the best country on earth and the dearest flag that ever floated over freemen. The South has fields for corn and wheat and the cereals peculiarly classed as northern. She has fields for rice, cane and cotton. She has lumber and minerals for the Nation. She has waters for power and upon which to float the richest argosies. She has a climate far superior to Canada, and is as healthy a land as any in the Union.

"Come, then, to the Southland, and make it your home; come to Louisiana."

APPENDIX F.

United States Department of Agriculture,
Bureau of Plant Industry,
Office of Farmers' Cooperative Demonstration Work.

Washington, D. C., February 25, 1910.

Hon. Jos. E. Ransdell, M. C.,
Washington, D. C.

My Dear Congressman: You have asked me to give an opinion on the agricultural possibilities of the South. The subject is so large that it will be necessary for me to classify and consider it under about four heads, as follows:

1. Corn, hay, pasture, and forage crops.
2. Stock raising.
3. Fiber plants.
4. Truck farming.

It has been thought till recently that the South would not raise large crops of Indian corn, but a little demonstration has proven that the soils and climate are specially adapted for that purpose and that larger crops can be raised than in the so-called corn States. Climatic conditions are much more favorable for the corn plant, and as a large portion of the plant is of atmospheric origin, climate is of primary consideration. All that is necessary is to prepare the soil in the best way and use good farm methods, and the South will develop into one of the best corn regions of the United States. We have produced the past year under test from 80 to 150 bushels of corn per acre. For pasture and hay the South is also superior to most of the Northern States, first because of the greater rainfall and secondly because of more favorable climatic conditions. The reason the South has not developed in this line is because the farmers have been so engrossed in other crops that they have paid but little attention to hay and pasture lands and have failed to use the best methods. Under trial the past year we have been able to produce from four to six tons of hay per acre where the soil was thoroughly prepared and the proper seed used. Then, there is a great variety of forage plants, such as the velvet beans, the cowpea, soy beans, Japan ribbon cane, etc., that grow with amazing vigor in the Southern States and are exceedingly nutritious, so that there can be an abundant supply for stock all seasons of the year.

In three respects a large portion of the South is superlatively adapted to stock raising; first, because of the abundant forage that can be provided, as stated above, and, secondly, because of the temperature, which is so mild that it does not tax the vitality of the animal, an d it reduces the amount of food necessary to sustain life and vigor; thirdly; as compared with the extreme North, there is a great reduction in the expense of providing shelter in the winter, all of which means an addition to the vigor of the animal and its immunity from disease, such as tuberculosis, etc. Then, the longer period of pasture makes it more economical. The comparatively low price of lumber for building purposes is another important item.

These facts are especially emphasized in case of pork production. Hogs can be pastured the year round on a variety of pasture forage that will nearly mature them for market without the addition of corn. Under the final adjustment of agriculture in the United States I believe that a large portion of the South will be found preeminently adapted to dairying; to the production of horses, mules, and swine; poultry; and in the mountain districts to sheep; that it will be found that they can be raised more economically there than in most any other portion of the world.

It is simply necessary to call attention to the great value of southern conditions for the production of the semi-tropical plants, sugar cane, rice and cotton, three of the best cash crops in the world. The United States already produces 70 per cent of the fiber that practically clothes the world. The rich alluvial lands along the Gulf are well adapted to the sugar cane. The river bottoms and the coastal prairies take kindly to rice and produce it in great quantities. The past year an experiment made by our department showed 93 bushels per acre of rice. Nearly all the Southern States produce cotton. As an example of what can be realized in cotton, some very sandy lands the past year produced as high as two bales, netting the owner more than $100 per acre.

Along the Atlantic and Gulf coasts, and even in the interior, are large tracts of sandy loam land perfectly adapted to truck-growing. They have not as yet been more than partially developed, but ultimately they are going to constitute the permanent garden lands of the United States. Single acres have yielded in celery, lettuce, and such crops more than $1,000 per acre.

It is unnecessary to dilate upon these facts. The South has not been understood; neither its soil nor its climate has been appreciated. Lands are far below their value at the present time, and there is no better place on the continent for young, thrifty, and vigorous men to start in agriculture than in many of these Southern States.

Respectfully submitted,

S. A. KNAPP, Special Agent in Charge.

APPENDIX L.

"A Belgian's Opportunities in Louisiana."

(Speech of August Van Asselburg before the Louisiana Farm Lands Congress at Alexandria, La., April 22, 1910.)

Louisiana is the home of a Belgian farmer. As I say this, I am talking about that farmer what got to rent his farm. The poor farmer in Belgium never will be the owner of a farm. Plenty of it never will be the owner of a horse. Some of it can go as far as that they got a little old Shetland pony, but the most of it do the plow work with his milk cow and the wagon work with the wheelbarrow, and then he make only one crop in the year, and pays $10 to $15 per acre for rent and about $1 per acre for license (contribution).

I was working a farm in Belgium of 30 acres. It cost me every year $240 rent, license included, and I was as good a farmer and as good a worker as any Belgian man, and at the age of 36 years, working day and night to save expenses of hired hands, I got nothing. Was not paid for my work. I could show no money, only we was making a living; what are called at the present day a poor living; and I was thinking on giving up farming, for it was too hard to keep it up any longer. But it happened that an old Belgian farmer came to the old country on a visit from Alexandria, Rapides Parish, in May, 1902. The people told me that he was good looking and that he got plenty of money and that he got a farm of 100 acres of his own. It was a wonder to me how that could be, for I know that he left the old country without a nickel. But one time I meet the old man, and he told me the story in Belgium. He told me of the happy farm life in Louisiana. It was hard to believe it, but today it is proven to me that the old man was right, and it was more happy than he told me.

I came to Alexandria in September, 1903, beginning to farm in 1904, and right now I can say that a good and saving Belgian farmer in Alexandria can furnish his table with that stuff to eat the year round as the rich man do in Belgium, and generally that it left always a little money on top each year. This is proven by every Belgian farmer of Alexandria: about all of them got his own farm and nobody came here with money. Some of it count his property by hundreds of acres and all that came from the farm, and no wonder to me. We make here two and three crop per year, and each one is more valuable than the one crop in Belgium, and we pay here not half the rent, and the expenses are not as big as in Belgium.

To close, I can say, and it is proven by me, that I make during five years working as a truck farmer several thousand dollars clear money, and it happened last year, 1909, that I make between $4,000 and $5,000 clear money on not quite 50 acres of ground; and then another thing, if it was that you not make that money that I am talking about, what is possible to do for a Belgian farmer, it will pay him all right to come here and go to farming and see the happiness of his family.

OPENINGS IN THE SOUTH

A REMARKABLE REVIEW of the present status of the South was given in the Senate Friday by Senator Ransdell, of Louisiana. His presentation of the conditions, resources and needs of the South was masterly for its grasp of general questions and its wealth of detail. The wonderful riches of that splendid region, in soil, minerals, timbers, waters and climate, together with the opportunities that await enterprising settlers, were never set forth more impressively. Senator Ransdell's speech is a compendium of information which every American should read and every homeseeker take to heart.

It is gratifying that the new spirit of the South is for immigration and expansion. Its people no longer look indifferently upon the rich and vitalizing flood of immigration that swept to the West and built up empires, while passing by the greater opportunities in the South. The departure of tens of thousands of Americans for Canada, taking millions of dollars with them, has aroused the South and caused it to make an appeal to these citizens to turn southward instead of northward when they seek to better their condition.

Unquestionably the region under the American flag that will make greatest strides in the next decade is the South, from Virginia to southern California. Already the movement is in full swing, as is shown by increasing land values, bigger and more diversified crops, extension of mining, manufactures and commerce, road building, rising cities and great prosperity. The climate facilitates agricultural development in all directions, and the water resources excel those of any other part of the Union.

The senator from Louisiana has performed an act of patriotism in directing the attention of his countrymen to the undeveloped riches of the South and the opportunities that await desirable immigrants from the North. Doubtless many a man will date the turn in the tide of his fortunes from the hour when he received and acted upon the hints in Senator Ransdell's speech.—Reprinted from The Washington Post.

The Lure of the Southland

MR. RANSDELL:

Mr. President, while the Agricultural bill is under consideration, I desire to address the Senate in regard to several matters which concern very closely the farmers of the United States and, indeed, the country at large. I allude to the large exodus of our best citizens into the British possessions north of the United States, and to the rapid congestion of our cities caused by the growing unpopularity of life on the farm, and by the large influx of foreign immigrants, the majority of whom settle in cities. I shall explain these questions briefly, for there is little dispute concerning them, and shall offer at some length what seems to me the best solution of these problems, which is that these people should go south and reap the benefit of its golden opportunities.

THE SOUTH THE NATION'S HOPE.

The eyes of the world are turned to the southern portion of our Republic, and we are witnessing a marvelous development in that section. Long retarded and checked in growth by the War between the States and its disastrous consequences, the South has arisen from her ashes a fairer and mightier land. The ravages of the war were fearful. In 1860 the value of taxable property in the South was six and one-third billion dollars, while in 1870 it had fallen to three and one-half billions, a decrease of nearly 50 per cent because of the war. In addition to this economic loss, hundreds of thousands of her sons had sacrificed their lives in her cause.

But the South was rich in the indomitable spirit of her citizens. With the same resistless energy and do-or-die perseverance that had charcterized their actions during the war, the men and women of the South turned their attention to the pursuits of peace. Literally they converted "their swords into plowshares and their spears into pruning hooks."

I am not here, however, to recite the disasters that befell my section in the sixties. These facts are matters of history. It is my purpose, however, to show how the South, in spite of all obstacles, has not only kept pace with but has actually outstripped the rest of the Nation.

She has laid aside her sable garments and, bedecked in a gown of bright colors, is enjoying her marvelous present prosperity and looking forward confidently to a still more glorious future, for she knows that a benign Providence has favored her above other lands, and that by virtue of her natural advantages and the enterprise and genius of her people she is becoming the most prosperous section of our great common country. Southward the star of empire takes its course.

I shall call your attention to the limitless resources of this great region; to its agricultural products, which include the best of nearly every known crop; to its live stock, which graze on land as rich as any in the world; to its inexhaustible treasuries of timber and mineral wealth; to its vast manufacturing industries; to its colossal mercantile and banking interests; to its admirable transportation system by road, rail, and river; to its golden opportunities for willing hands and honest hearts; to its crying need for men and money; and, above all, to its potential possibilities which make the South the Nation's greatest asset.

It has been the habit for certain gentlemen from other sections to smile tolerantly when some one from the South painted in bright colors the glories of Dixie. Some people have a sort of hazy idea that the South is a land of poetry and indolence; of romance and pretty women; of lazy negroes, who bask in the semitropical sun; and that our products are limited principally to cotton, tobacco, and lumber. I shall attempt to correct these misapprehensions.

It is not my purpose to make any boast for the South. I shall call the attention of the Senate to some plain facts which must be recognized, and the sooner the better, not only for the South but also for the North, East, and West, for in the cooperative development of all parts of our Nation alone is true prosperity to be found.

The South, consisting of the sixteen States of Alabama, Arkansas, Florida, Georgia, Kentucky, Louisiana, Maryland, Mississippi, Missouri, North Carolina, Oklahoma, South Carolina, Tennessee, Texas, Virginia, and West Virginia, comprises an area of 945,000 square miles, approximately one-third the total area of the country. Its population in 1915 was about 35,000,000, or an average of about 37 people to the square mile. These figures show that the South comprises as much territory as France, Germany, Austria, Belgium, Great Britain, Italy, and Spain combined, but these nations have an average density of population of 338 to the square mile. Think of it, Mr. President! Thirty-seven people to the square mile in the South and in the European countries I have mentioned 338 to the square mile. The mere statement of these facts indicates the room for expansion.

Our doors are open wide to all desirable immigrants, especially those from other States. The South will gladly furnish homes to every one of our splendid citizens who has gone to Canada or contemplates such a move, and would welcome all the boys and girls who have left, or expect to leave, the hardships of northern and eastern farms to seek unfamiliar work in congested cities. We can supply farms to a great many of the foreigners who seek our shores, and we are really anxious to receive all good people from whatever land they come. We have great resources of every kind and sort which are just beginning to be developed, and in no portion of the world are there as good opportunities for success as in the land of Dixie. If Horace Greely were alive today, his advice to young men would be, "Go South." When he said to them, "Go West," a great field opened there, and many fortunes were made by following his safe counsels. The scene has shifted. The great opportunities of the West have been seized, but there are innumerable openings in the South awaiting fertile brains and willing hands.

THE SOUTH NEEDS MEN AND MONEY.

With all her marvelous resources begging for further development, the most crying need of the South is men and money. I can not impress too strongly upon you that the South needs labor and capital; and I assert that returns from investments there will astound even the most sanguine.

We have many advantages over Canada, where the winters are so long and severe as to make life very uncomfortable for man and beast, and to restrict agriculture to wheat, and the hardiest cereals, vegetables, and fruits.

In the South there is every variety of crop and every form of animal life thrives. Our winters are so mild that light clothing and a small amount of fuel suffices, and one can work out of doors practically every day in the year. Our summer heats are not as great as those of Canada, and our white farmers work in the fields throughout the hottest weather with impunity.

Between 1900 and 1910 farm values in the entire Union increased 108 per cent, while in the South they advanced 136 per cent. I hope Senators are paying attention to some of these comparisons. Figures are a little dull, but those who listen to me will ascertain from cold facts that the South is going forward with much greater rapidity in every line than any other section of this Nation.

THE SOUTH'S VARIED FARM PRODUCTS.

Every variety of soil can be procured in the South—from the rich sugar and rice lands of Louisiana to the fertile corn, melon, and peach fields of Georgia and South Carolina; from the blue grass and limestone of Kentucky, Tennessee, and Missouri, with their wonderful horses, mules, and hogs, to the fertile plains of Texas, with its vast herds of cattle and sheep; from the tobacco and peanuts of North Carolina and Virginia to the wheat and oats of Maryland and Oklahoma; from the orange, the grapefruit, and the figs of Florida and Louisiana to the delicious apples of West Virginia and Arkansas; and from the succulent Johnson and Bermuda grasses of Alabama to the alfalfa, lespedeza, and other clovers of Mississippi, where hogs and cattle luxuriate. Cotton flourishes in 11 of them and wheat does well in many sections. If the new settler is accustomed to grain and cereals, with cattle and hogs, he need not change his crops or methods in the South, unless it be to substitute rice for wheat, should he settle in the lower half of the Gulf States, although wheat does well in northern portions. He need not become a cotton grower unless he wishes to, for corn and the cereals, with forage crops of many kinds, coupled with some branch or branches of animal industry, especially hogs, will furnish the most attractive and profitable employment. If he be a dairyman, that line is open to him with marked advantages in many respects. If he be a gardener or fruit grower, the Gulf and lower Atlantic coast sections, with immunity from cold, and delightful climate, can not be excelled. Indeed, he can choose his own branch of agriculture and find ideal conditions in the South.

OTHER INDUSTRIES OF THE SOUTH.

But suppose he be a manufacturer? We are now manufacturing fully one-half of the cotton made in the United States. We are manufacturing an immense quantity of iron and steel. We are manufacturing about one-half of all the lumber in the United States, and our timber supply is immense.

Every kind and sort of manufacturing is going forward by leaps and bounds. We have innumerable manufacturing establishments converting our vast wealth of raw material from field, forest, and mine into finished products. If he be a school-teacher, a banker, a railroad or steamboat man, we can furnish him splendid schools, banks, railroads, and navigable rivers. If he be a merchant, we have a population of 35,000,000, with many fine cities and towns and every line of mercantile business. If he be a miner, we can show him mines of everything in the mineral calendar. Our supplies of coal, iron, phosphate, marble, limestone, bauxite, salt, sulphur, oil, gas, and so forth, are inexhaustible and just beginning to be developed. He can select his own calling and find opportunities in the South, under a mild, delightful climate, and, as I shall show later, under as good health conditions as anywhere in the United States.

When a man is about to change his residence, the first question that suggests itself to him is, What are the climatic and health conditions in my prospective home? He wishes to assure himself that he and his family can live in health and comfort in the new home. Since health and climate are considerations of such primary importance to those who contemplate a change of residence, I shall go somewhat into detail on both subjects.

THE SOUTHERN CLIMATE—THE NATION'S BEST.

The climate of the South is one of its most valuable assets. While all countries may not grow cotton, corn, or wheat, they all have certain characteristic weather conditions which, in the aggregate, go to make up climate, and oftentimes the climate of a country is its blessing or its curse, fixed and unchangeable. If a blessing, it remains as a permanent asset that can never be taken away or appreciably changed by the agency of man; and if a curse, no hope for better things can ever be entertained.

Happily our southland is blessed with a climate which compares favorably with that of any other section of North America and has great advantages over many of them, especially the British Northwest, or even that of the more northern sections of our own country. This is true both from the standpoint of successful agricultural, manufacturing, and commercial enterprises and that of personal health and comfort.

In farming, as in any other occupation, the yearly profits are largely proportional to the total time during which work may be prosecuted, and herein lies the South's most important asset as an agricultural region. The farmer's profits are produced in nature's workshop, and, other things being equal, the section in which she holds open shop longest and does the largest number of hours' work during the year is the locality in which the largest profits should result. The growing season is the period each year in which the farmer's profits must be made. During the remainder of the year not only are dividend-producing farm operations practically at a standstill but many expenses must be incurred and much of the products of the growing season are necessarily consumed.

In the British possessions immediately north of the United States and also in the adjoining States of the Union the length of the crop-growing season, on the average, is from 115 to 140 days, while over the Southern States it is more than 250 days. Thus the profit-producing period is only about 35 per cent of the year in these northern districts, while it is about 75 per cent in the South, and the consuming and profitless portion of the year ranges from 25 per cent in the South to something like 65 per cent in the North.

With the diversified farming operations that are rapidly being adopted in the South and the generous response of its soil to improved methods of cultivation, the factor of nearly continuous production throughout the year becomes one of great importance, and should be given weighty consideration in any comparison of the relative value of different communities for the pursuit of agricultural enterprises.

There are many other important features, from an agricultural standpoint, in which the South has great advantages, among which may be mentioned the period in which it is possible to plant crops. In the case of corn, for instance, the crop in many of our so-called great corn States, in order to mature before the usual early autumn frost, must be planted within a definite short period of time, and if unfavorable weather prevails during that period or immediately preceding it, delaying the seeding or preparation of soil, great damage is almost certain to result if the usual early frost is not delayed, especially if rapid growth be retarded by cool weather during the season. Just such conditions as these prevailed only last year in many portions of the northern corn belt, and vast damage resulted to the crop. In the South the long period in which planting may be done and the ample length of the growing season obviates such disasters and insures a crop free of frost injury.

The long growing season also makes possible such a diversity of crops that no serious and widespread disasters, due to drought or otherwise, as befall less favored one or two crop communities, are possible. In case of prospective failure of one crop, it is frequently possible to replant and grow another of the same or different character during the same season.

Next to temperature, which determines the length of the growing season as above outlined, the most important climatic element from an agricultural standpoint is rainfall, and here again the South is amply supplied and has the advantage, when compared with our neighboring Canadian Provinces and Northern States. In the latter sections the average annual rainfall is much less than in the South and consequently damaging droughts are of more frequent occurrence. Its abundant precipitation and infrequent disastrous droughts insure the South a remarkably uniform crop production, as is evidenced by comparing the average per-acre yield of cotton year by year. A failure is unknown and the production year after year is comparatively constant.

From the facts brought out in the foregoing remarks, it appears unquestionable that from a purely business standpoint there are afforded in the South unparalleled opportunities for wide-awake, progressive farmers or business men. However, there are other considerations to be taken into account when one is deciding upon a location for a permanent home, one of the most important of which is personal comfort as determined by climatic conditions.

It has been recognized that in the Gulf country the winters are ideal, as evidenced by the large number of visitors who seek our sunshine and balmy breezes during every winter season. Unfortunately, however, the impression that the South is almost unbearably warm during the summer season seems to have much credence in some of the more northern localities, and I wish to go briefly into the actual facts of the case in order that that erroneous conception may be dispelled. A number of interesting tables and charts, showing the climatic characteristics of the Gulf States and also like information for the British Northwestern Provinces and the adjoining Northern States of the Union, have been kindly furnished me by Prof. Charles F. Marvin, Chief of the Weather Bureau. (See Appendix A.) These disclose the facts in the case, which not only emphasize the unquestioned advantage of our winter climate but also explode the popular but erroneous impression regarding the heat conditions in the summer. For example, we find in the latter that the average January temperature in New Orleans is 53 degrees, while in portions of the extreme northern Plains States and the adjoining Canadian provinces it is from zero to about 10 degrees below. On the other hand, portions of the summers are frequently hot in the northern sections, the temperature during the day, in fact, often going higher than along the Gulf coast. These give temperature ranges frequently too great for persons unaccustomed to such variations. At Prince Albert, Saskatchewan, the average temperature for July is about 70 degrees warmer than for January, while in New Orleans the difference in the average January and July temperatures is only 28 degrees.

In North Dakota the temperature each winter, on an average, falls at some time to more than 30 degrees below zero and rises to 100 degrees each summer, making an average annual range of more than 130 degrees. In New Orleans the average of the lowest reached each year is 26 degrees, and the average of the highest 97 degrees, making an annual rang of only 71 degrees, as compared with 130 in the other case. Thus, while the winters are balmy and pleasant in the South and cold, bleak, and disagreeable in the North, the maximum summer heat is frequently greater in the latter than is experienced in the Gulf coast section. In this connection I desire to call special attention to the fact that, while the average lowest winter temperature in Louisiana is 56 degrees higher than in North Dakota, the average highest summer temperature is 3 degrees lower in Louisiana than it is in North Dakota, these figures being from the official Weather Bureau reports.

Mr. President and Senators, are not these figures very striking? Are they not remarkable? It is 56 degrees colder in winter on an average in North Dakota than it is in Louisiana, and 3 degrees warmer in summer in North Dakota than it is in Louisiana. These figures are not mine, for they are taken from the official Weather Bureau reports.

The degree of discomfort experienced in hot weather is determined not only by the air temperature but also by the relative humidity. The actual amount of moisture in the air has but little physical influence on plant or animal life, it being the relation of the amount present to that necessary to cause saturation which affects our sensibilities. Thus, while the atmosphere of the Southern States contains much more actual moisture than the more northern localities previously mentioned, which insures, ordinarily, an abundant rainfall, no such variation is shown in the relative humidity, which does not differ greatly for the two localities, and the physical discomfort due to high humidity is but little more perceptible in the southern country than to the northward.

As still further evidence in refuting assertions that our summer weather is oppressively warm, I wish to call attention to the fact that sunstrokes are almost unknown in the South. During the prevalence of hot waves the daily press of other sections announces numerous cases of heat prostrations, but if you will note the headlines you will find the Southland is conspicuous by the absence of such cases.

Mr. President, I have lived all my life in the South, and I have never known a case of sunstroke in my immediate locality. I have read of a great many cases in the northern and middle portions of this country, and I have heard of a very few in the cities of the South; but in my section of Louisiana I have never known of a single case.

In the winter we read of people perishing from cold in the North, and in the summer of their dying from heat, but throughout the year the South continues to smile and extend a welcome to all who may be far-sighted enough to take advantage of the opportunity to reside where financial and commercial advantages are unlimited and where outdoor life can be enjoyed throughout the year.

HEALTH CONDITIONS IN THE SOUTH.

From the viewpoint of health the South is as fortunate as it is in climate. The greatest change effected in this section during the past decade has been accomplished through sanitation—a change which is perhaps more noticeable in the South than in any other portion of the United States. The South has had a hygienic rehabilitation, and from a condition of sanitary chaos has moved forward to the front rank of the vanguard of modern countries. The work has been performed quietly but thoroughly, until today life expectancy with us is the same as in the Northern States and the incidence of disease is no greater than elsewhere. This is because the South has learned the lesson of disease prevention and has put sanitary principles into actual practice.

In spite of this wonderful advancement—an advancement which is fully confirmed by our mortality tables—much misconception still remains concerning the healthfulness of the South. This misconception is due to a number of causes, fallacies which the general public know nothing about and which they do not thoroughly investigate. Erroneous impressions still prevail as to the healthfulness of this region, and many still suppose that our climate and other natural conditions are conducive to the development of disease, whereas quite the opposite is the case.

Many similar erroneus impressions have arisen, most of which are based upon ignorance of all the facts. It is my desire to invite your attention in a general way to what has been accomplished in the conservation of human life, presenting certain comparative mortality tables and leaving you to draw your own conclusions therefrom.

The fact that epidemics of disease have in years gone by swept over the South is reason enough for many to suppose that those diseases are still present. This is a decided misconception. It is true that the South has been visited in the past by many frightful epidemics—epidemics which the older residents still recall. These visitations of disease often came upon us without warning and we were helpless before them, for we knew nothing of their causes and their means of prevention. Now all this has changed. We have definite knowledge of the means of dissemination of practically all of the infections to which we are subject, and their prevention is based upon the most simple facts—facts which the children master in their lessons at school. These principles have been put into practical and almost universal application, and as a result the South is freer today from the presence of epidemic disease than any other section of our country.

It is true that certain infections still exist, as, for instance, measles, diphtheria, and whooping cough, but their incidence is far less than in many other sections of the United States, and they are not attended with nearly the mortality of the same diseases in colder climates. For example, measles in the South is a comparatively mild and harmless affection, usually unattended with complications, whereas in the colder portions of our country it constitutes one of the most fatal diseases of children. Pneumonia is another disease which with us is not only considerably less virulent but is also far less common than in other climates, this fact being generally recognized by the public.

Influenza, commonly called la grippe, is also rarer. Epidemics of all of these diseases are far less common than in the North, apparently being held in abeyance by the favorable climatic conditions. No better proof of this could be cited than the widespread epidemic of influenza and pneumonia which swept the country during the past winter. Everywhere these infections were reported as unusually virulent and attended with an unprecedented mortality, but south of the Ohio River their severity was much less pronounced and the actual number of cases reported not nearly as great.

Practically all of the infectious diseases indigenous to the South have now been conquered, and yellow fever, malaria, dengue, and hookworm have to a great extent been robbed of their terrors. This is because the essential facts concerning the transmission of these diseases are thoroughly established and our southern communities have adopted simple and effective measures for their control. The diseases which are more prevalent in the North—e. g., pneumonia, influenza, and the acute infections of childhood—continue there with almost unabated sway, because the knowledge concerning their dissemination is incomplete and the methods of their prevention less satisfactory. The figures relating to the presence of the infections mentioned will altogether bear out this statement.

There has not been a case of yellow fever in the South since the infection was eradicated 11 years ago under the leadership of the Public Health Service, and with our knowledge of its dissemination through the medium of the Stegomyia mosquito, an insect which is finding its habitat more and more restricted, there is not the slightest danger of its spread should by any chance an infected person happen to pass through one of the numerous efficient quarantine stations. The disease, as far as the South is concerned, is a matter of history, and as a factor in present-day problems has been relegated by sanitation to the realm of remote possibility. Similarly dengue, a disease also transmitted by a species of mosquito, has almost entirely disappeared. In going over the records for the past 10 years I was unable to find a single instance of an epidemic of this disease in any Southern State, a few isolated cases occurring only during that period. All through the South there are physicians who have been engaged in active practice for a dozen or fifteen years who have never seen a single case of either yellow fever or dengue and who probably never will.

Malaria is being rapidly exterminated and there are sections where it is no more prevalent than in many districts of the West and North. In the early days of Ohio, Illinois, and even of many Eastern States fever and ague was common enough, but as the land was settled and the swamps drained the disease disappeared, although the reason for its disappearance was not at that time recognized, for we then knew nothing of the means of transmission through the Anopheles mosquito. Every fact in connection with the prevention of malaria is now definitely established and in the majority of southern towns and cities put into actual practice. Houses are screened, the land drained, pools oiled, and personal prophylaxis instituted wherever it is necessary, so that the disease in the South is now comparatively rare and in many communities altogether absent.

The incidence of hookworm is rapidly becoming less and less. Whether it was as important a disease to the South as has been made to appear is questionable, certainly under present conditions of life it is relatively inconsequential.

Pellagra still exists, but our knowledge of the disease has rapidly widened and discoveries made within the last year by the Public Health Service lead us to believe that the condition is distinctly curable as well as entirely preventable. With the better dissemination of knowledge concerning its prevention and cure, it is confidently expected that pellagra will soon be relegated to the same position that yellow fever now occupies.

A factor of importance in producing a widespread misconception of the healthfulness of the South on the part of those unfamiliar with conditions has been the presence of the negro. It is well recognized that the mortality among negroes is naturally much higher than among whites, in some instances being more than twice that of the white race, but many people fail to consider this point when making an analysis of health conditions. Were the subject viewed with this fact in mind an entirely different interpretation would be given to the mortality figures of this region and a much more correct opinion would be formed as to the healthfulness of the South. That this is so can, I believe, be demonstrated within a very few moments.

Wherever accurate figures are maintained, the colored death rate in the United States is higher than the white death rate, this being true without exception for every section of the country. During the year 1913, the last period for which we have the complete returns, the death rate among whites for the entire registration area was 13.7 per 1,000 of population, while that among negroes was 21.9, a difference of over 60 per cent. In certain sections of the country the disparity was even more pronounced. Necessarily, then, those areas having a large percentage of negroes will show a high general death rate, the figures for the general population being distorted by those for the negro. For this reason any comparison of crude and uncorrected death rates of northern and southern communities is an unfair comparison. If the people are divided into two classes, the whites and the blacks, the comparison becomes entirely legitimate and should lead to much more correct conclusions.

Comparison of southern cities with northern cities is instructive.

The colored death rate itself is steadily and rapidly falling, another proof of our improved sanitary conditions. In Mobile the colored death rate has been reduced 18 per cent during the past 12 years and in Jacksonville 26 per cent, while similar reductions were made in Atlanta and Louisville. At present the colored death rate is not a whit higher than the general death rate 20 years ago of Boston, New York, and other cities. In the rural sections this improvement in health conditions has been even more pronounced, and the negro rural dweller of the South has today the same life expectancy as the city dweller of Hartford, Conn.; Portland, Me.; or Ashland, Wis.

I cannot leave this subject without referring to the magnificent work which has been done in New Orleans in the eradication of bubonic plague and the way in which that city has gone about making of itself "the city sanitary." The commercial relations of that great port made it natural that plague should be introduced there through the intermediation of shipping. When the disease appeared we did not attempt to hide it. Instead, we announced the fact fearlessly and freely to the whole world. Our State and city governments united in asking that the General Government loan us its expert officers to lead the campaign. The public and the private purse was opened freely, and there occurred a sanitary renaissance which was unexampled in this or any other country. Today New Orleans is clean. Today New Orleans is the most rat-proof city in America, and it will not be long before it is the most sanitary in the United States. The work which has been done has not been spasmodic or temporary in character. It has been built for all time. Stone, concrete, and masonry have been installed, and, while the danger of a great epidemic has long passed, still the work goes forward with unabated vigor to the end that the great gateway of the Mississippi Valley shall be secure against disease. Our people know the lesson of plague, and never again will the dread pestilence menace the people of Louisiana. The example of New Orleans has been followed by many of the other southern cities. Florida, Alabama, Mississippi, and many of the other Southern States have passed and are enforcing rigid anti-plague laws. Even some of the northern cities have profited from this demonstration, and Philadelphia and Baltimore have fallen into line for this much-needed civic improvement.

This whole subject of the sanitary condition of the Southland is of such great importance and so dear to my heart that I could continue to give you examples of the healthfulness of our section of the country, the sanitary intelligence of our people, and the hygienic tenor of their lives. I could tell of the way we teach health and hygiene and sanitation in our schools, academies, and colleges. I could dilate on the way in which we endeavor to throw about all our people, whether they live in crowded city, obscure hamlet, or remote farm, the benefits which have come to us through the application of the principles of modern sanitary science. But the limitations of time forbid. The actual healthfulness of this section of the country is the answer to him who would controvert my statement that the South is the most healthful portion of our great Republic, and he who dwells there is assured of length of life, peace, and security from disease.

But one needs more than good health and a pleasant climate. Hence I must describe some of the other advantages of this region.

THE AGRICULTURAL HEART OF THE NATION.

The South is preeminently an agricultural section, and her strides in this direction are truly amazing. In 1915 the gain in the value of all farm crops in the United States over 1914 was $526,000,000. Of this gain

$317,209,000, or a little over 60 per cent, was in the South. Remember, the South occupies only one-third the total area of the country, and this one-third produced 60 per cent of the agricultural increase. In other words, the South is advancing three times as fast agriculturally as the rest of the Nation. Nor is this increase due to cotton. The 1915 cotton crop was valued at $750,000,000, while the value of diversified crops, such as grain, sugar, hay, tobacco, vegetables, fruits, and so forth, and exclusive of live stock, was $1,957,000,000, or two and one-half times as great as cotton. If we include live stock, the total value of all southern farm products, exclusive of cotton, was $2,850,000,000 in 1915, or nearly four times the value of the cotton crop.

KING COTTON.

Cotton, the monarch of southern agriculture, is too well known to make it necessary for me to say much in regard to it. This crop has ever been, and will continue to be, the principal money crop of the Nation, for, while corn has much greater actual value, it is not converted into money like cotton, but is largely consumed on the farm and sold indirectly. The southern cotton crop last year, including the seed, sold for about $750,000,000, and it is one of the greatest of our national assets.

Cotton is one of the chief instrumentalities through which the United States has attained its dominant commercial position. All the gold and silver produced in the world in any one year in the last 35 would not be sufficient to purchase last year's southern cotton crop. In fact, the value of the world's entire production of gold and silver during the past 35 years is nearly $6,000,000,000 less than the total value of the south's cotton crops for the same period. The cotton crop ranges in value from $750,000,000 to $1,000,000,000 annually, and amounts to 60 per cent of the world's total cotton production.

Raw cotton is the commodity which gives the United States the great balance of trade in its favor. Cotton represents approximately 30 per cent in value of our annual exports, and it is this great southern staple which places the rest of the world in our debt.

But the prospective immigrant may object that cotton is distinctively a crop adapted to negro labor, and that a white man is not well fitted to grow it. This is entirely erroneous. I insert as Appendix B a census table showing the acreage, yield, and value of cotton grown by all farmers, and by colored farmers in 1909. These are the latest available figures.

It will be noted that negroes produced that year only 38 per cent of the cotton yield in bales, and only 32 per cent of its value. In other words, the white farmer grew 62 per cent of the cotton yield and received 68 per cent of the cotton value. Cotton is a crop which the white man can grow most profitably, and the prospective immigrant need have no fear on that score.

The doctrine of diversified farming, epitomized in the phrase "safe farming,'" has been preached and is being practiced in almost every part of Dixie. With what result we shall see. Everything produced in the temperate zone is being raised by our people in ever-increasing quantities and with great profit.

I insert as Appendix C a table showing the total yield of corn, oats, wheat, and hay in the 11 cotton States for the years 1909 to 1915, inclusive. I ask Senators in looking over these tables to bear in mind that while there are a total of 16 Southern States only the 11 that raise cotton are included in these tables. The other five do not raise cotton, or at least only in such small quantities as not to be appreciable.

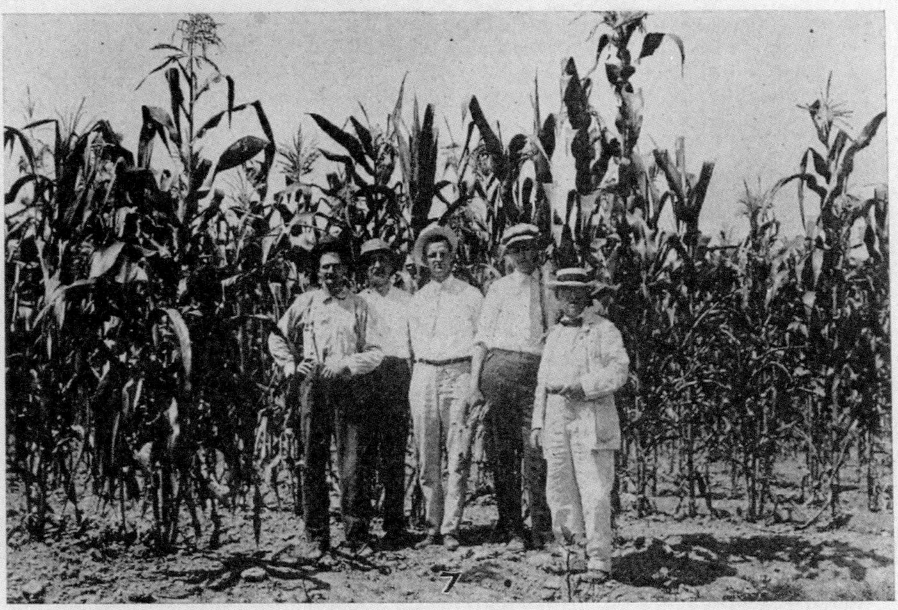

A CORN FIELD IN EAST LOUISIANA.

This table evidences in a striking manner the progress of diversified farming. The corn crop of these cotton States doubled in seven years, increasing from 461,536,000 bushels in 1909 to 812,883,000 bushels in 1915. The oat production trebled, climbing from 51,847,000 in 1909 to 157,714,000 in 1915, while in the same period the wheat crop increased from 28,-662,000 bushels to 88,842,000, and hay kept pace by advancing from 3,108,-000 to 6,269,000 tons. The true significance of these figures is not realized until we remember, for instance, that while the corn production of the cotton States doubled, that of the rest of the country increased only 5 per cent; and while the southern oat crop trebled, the oat crop of the rest of the Nation increased only 40 per cent.

CORN OUTSTRIPPING COTTON.

Corn is a crop which is peculiarly adapted to the South. The 16 Southern States produced in 1915 1,246,945,000 bushels of corn, which was considerably more than one-third of the total crop of the Union.

The truly enormous increase in its growth shows that its value is being appreciated by the southern farmer, and although the average yield per acre is less than in some of the Western States, this is because it has not been given that intensive cultivation so necessary for the best results.

In the grain States of the Central West corn is the money crop, and the most intelligent attention has been given to it, while in the South to within the last few years cotton was king of agriculture and corn was neglected. This, however, is being rapidly remedied, and the statistics of the United States Department of Agriculture show that during the past seven years the average production of corn per acre in the South has increased from 25 to 90 per cent, ranging from 15 bushels per acre in Florida and Georgia to 35 bushels in Maryland. (Appendix D.)

In the light of these figures and from much study of the subject I am convinced that the people of the South are just beginning to raise corn and that the great crop of 1,246,945,000 bushels produced in 1915 by the sixteen Southern States is only a moderate percentage of what may be expected in the future.

It is interesting to note that the estimated value of this corn crop was $786,646,000, or $36,000,000 in excess of the value of the cotton crop of the same year, so that cotton must look to its laurels, or corn will soon be monarch of southern agriculture, as it is unquestionably of the Nation's crops.

The largest yield of corn ever produced on a single acre by a member of a boy's corn club was 232.7 bushels, made by Walker Lee Dunson, of Alabama, at a total cost of only 19.6 cents per bushel.

The work of these boys is so remarkable that I wish to insert the following records from the reports of the Department of Agriculture:

Record of Seven Boys Producing 200 Bushels of Corn per Acre.

Name of club member.	State.	Yield per acre *Bushels.*	Cost of production per bushel. *Cents.*
Jerry Moore	South Carolina	$228\frac{3}{4}$	42.0
Junius Hill	Alabama	$212\frac{1}{2}$	8.6
Eber Kimbrough	...do	$224\frac{3}{4}$	19.8
Ben Leath	Georgia	$214^5/_7$	14.2
J. Jones Polk	Mississippi	$214^9/_{10}$	21.4
Bennie Beeson	...do	$227\frac{1}{3}$	14.0
Walker Lee Dunson	Alabama	$232^7/_{10}$	19.9

Number of corn club members in the Southern States who have raised 100 or more bushels of corn to the acre each year from 1909 to 1914, inclusive:

1909	52
1910	171
1911	327
1912	493
1913	374
1914	354
Total	1,771

I hope the Senators from the corn States are listening to these figures.

The greatest yield of corn per acre in the United States was made in South Carolina by a gentleman who produced 256 bushels on a single acre. However, the table I have read refers to the boys' corn club work. These wonderful yields were made by the young boys to whom I have just alluded.

Mr. President, in the light of these figures and from much study of the subject I am convinced that the people of the South are just beginning to raise corn and that the great crop of 1,246,945,000 bushels produced in 1915 by the sixteen Southern States is only a moderate percentage of what may be expected in the future.

It is interesting to note that the estimated value of this corn crop was $786,646,000, or $36,000,000 in excess of the value of the cotton crop of the same year, so that cotton must look to its laurels or corn will soon be monarch of southern agriculture, as it is unquestionably of the Nation's crops.

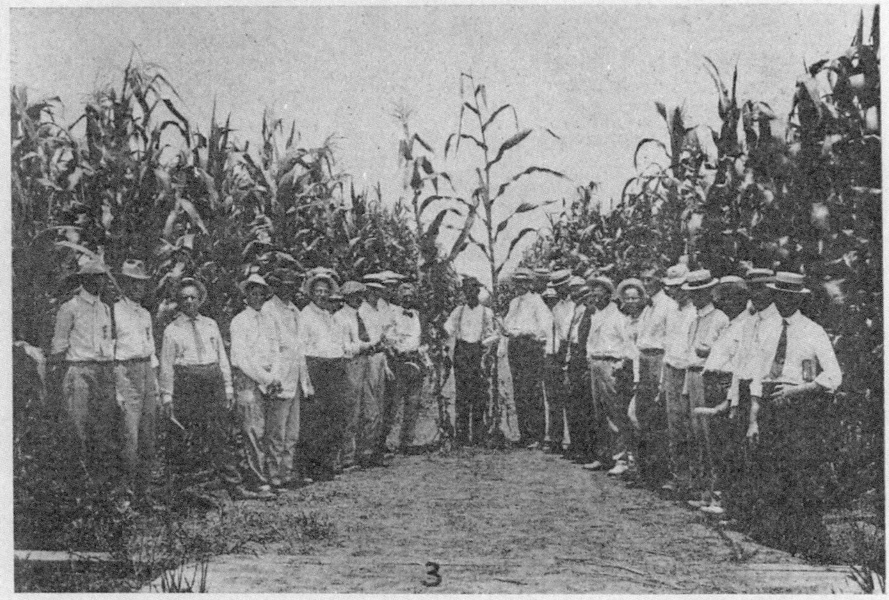

A CORN FIELD NEAR RACELAND.

The largest yield of corn ever produced on a single acre by a member of a boys' corn club was 232.7 bushels, made by Walker Lee Dunson, of Alabama, at a total cost of only 19.6 cents per bushel.

I have already given the figures in regard to this matter in answer to questions, and I shall not now repeat them.

Careful experiments have demonstrated that the greatest yields of corn on small areas have been made in the South, and the best scientists are of the opinion that if the methods of cultivation followed in the corn States are applied in the South our average production will be fully as great, if not greater, than in any part of the Union.

THE SUPERIORITY OF SOUTHERN CORN.

Now, as to the quality of this corn—and, Mr. President, I hope Senators will pay strict attention to this, because I know most people think that, even if we do raise large crops of corn in the South, the corn is not half so good as that produced in the corn States. The opinion has long and widely prevailed that southern corn is inferior to that of the so-called corn States. Not only is this belief erroneous, but I shall show that the corn of Dixie is actually superior to that produced in sections famed for the quality of their grain.

The United States Department of Agriculture has made a series of scientific tests which place the stamp of superiority upon the southern product. I quote from a letter from Dr. William A. Taylor, Chief of the Bureau of Plant Industry of the Department of Agriculture, under date of April 29, 1916. He says: "The moisture content of corn is one of the principal factors determining its commercial grade and value. The following table gives the average moisture content of corn raised in Louisiana compared to the moisture content of corn raised in Virginia and Illinois, in samples submitted by members of the boys' corn clubs, 1915 crop:

State.	Number of samples.	Average moisture content.
Louisiana	7	13.4
Virginia	20	17.8
Illinois	16	19.1

The above table shows that the Louisiana corn was very dry in comparison with that grown in the more northern States.

In the following table is shown a comparison of the moisture content and damaged kernels in samples of corn grown in Louisiana compared to corn grown in Illinois. Both of these factors are important from a commercial point of view, and it will be noticed that the Louisiana corn shows up the best in both factors:

	Number of samples.	Average	
		Moisture content.	Damaged kernels.
NOVEMBER, 1914.		PER CT.	PER CT.
Louisiana corn	70	14.0	5.1
Illinois corn	114	16.3	3.6
DECEMBER, 1914.			
Louisiana corn	110	14.3	2.3
Illinois corn	99	16.6	4.3
JANUARY, 1915.			
Louisiana corn	40	13.8	1.0
Illinois corn	158	17.0	4.1
FEBRUARY, 1915.			
Louisiana corn	20	13.3	.4
Illinois corn	90	17.1	4.4

This is fairly representative of conditions, and indicates that the Louisiana corn usually contains considerably less moisture than corn from the central part of the corn belt and shows a lower percentage of damaged kernels.

In a letter of May 11, 1916, in response to a further inquiry, speaking of the standard Government grades for commercial corn, Dr. Taylor says:

"In the definition of these grades it will be noticed that there is a maximum limit to the amount of both the moisture content and the damaged kernels in each of the grades and that the higher grades allow less moisture and fewer damaged kernels than the lower grades. Commercial corn is sold mostly by grade and the higher grades generally command the highest prices.

"Applying the maximum limits of moisture content and damaged kernels in the corn grades to the data shown in the table previously submitted, it will be seen that so far as the factors of moisture content and damaged kernels are concerned the Louisiana corn, with one exception, would grade higher on an average than the Illinois corn during the period covered in that table.

"In addition to the high commercial grade which corn testing low in moisture content and damaged kernels is entitled to, corn of this nature will stand up better in storage and during transportation than corn testing high in these factors. Enough information is at hand to indicate that southern-grown corn generally tests lower moisture and damaged kernels at the time of harvest than corn grown in the remainder of the country, and as the southern corn matures earlier, it has the additional advantage of an early market."

Mr. President, to resume, these official tests, as given by Dr. Taylor, demonstrate that southern corn has many advantage over that grown in other sections. Why not? I hope the Senator from Kansas will listen to this. In the laboratory of nature more sunshine and rain are available for the production of corn in the Southern States than in the so-called corn belt. The prospective immigrant, therefore, need have no fear if he wishes to settle in a corn country. Dixie is the place for him. His honest toil can produce from her fertile lands corn that will grade better, ship better, and therefore bring higher prices than that grown in the so-called corn belt of the United States.

SUGAR, RICE, TOBACCO, ETC.

Sugar cane also is a very interesting and profitable crop, and, though it is now mainly confined to southern Louisiana, there is no reason why it should not be grown in all the Gulf States and Georgia, especially along the coasts of Texas and Florida.

Perhaps the southern crop that, next to corn and wheat, would appeal most to the northern farmer is rice, which is handled in many respects the same as wheat. This most nutritious cereal grows well on any flat land in the South that can be irrigated, and it has proved very successful in Louisiana, Texas, Arkansas, and South Carolina. It will not be amiss to say a word in regard to the great success with which rice is grown in Louisiana, which leads all other States in its production. In 1915 Louisiana produced 13,714,000 bushels of rough rice, which was 47.4 per cent of the total American crop, and practically 6,000,000 bushels more than its nearest competitor. This crop was worth $12,343,000 on the farm. The yield of 34.2 bushels per acre in Louisiana that year is 1.1 bushels more than the average for the entire country during the past ten years. In 1914 there were forty-one rice mills in Louisiana, which was 55 per cent of all in the United States, while in the city of New Orleans is situated the largest rice mill in the Union. Rice also affords great opportunities to the farmer seeking a change of location.

Tobacco is a very extensive industry in Virginia, Kentucky, and Tennessee, and does well in several other States. Peanuts thrive marvelously, especially on the sandy lands of Virginia and Tennessee, and have proved a big success on the rich bottoms and sandy hills of Louisiana and Mississippi. And wheat can be profitably grown on two-thirds of our southern farms.

Indeed it would take a long time to enumerate the various crops, fruits, and vegetables which can be raised with interest and profit in the South. One can literally take his choice and find suitable conditions for it.

OUR UNEQUALED FORAGE CROPS.

Now, let me say something about our wonderful forage crops, many kinds of which do excellently, the famed blue grass and equally nutritious Bermuda being our best natural grasses. Alfalfa, Lespedeza, the clovers and vetches, cowpeas, soy beans, oats, rye, and so forth, do well in every State in the South.

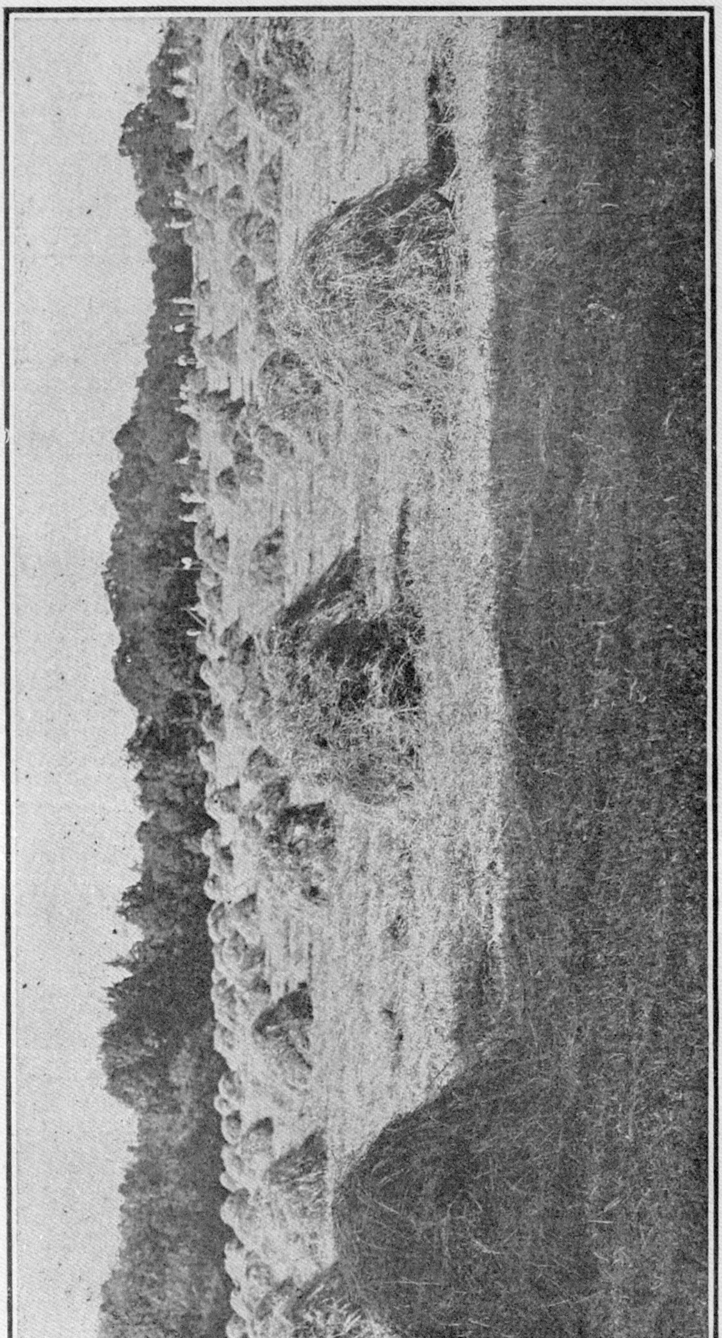

A LESPEDEZA FIELD.

On this subject Dr. Taylor, in a letter to me dated April 29, 1916, says:

"The culture of forage in Louisiana in common with other Southern States has been a relatively unimportant part of the State's agriculture, but in the last few years there has been an enormously increased interest awakened in animal husbandry.

"Notwithstanding the relatively small amount of live stock and consequently of forage production in Louisiana, it is probably true that at least as much forage per acre can be grown on the alluvial lands of Louisiana as in any other portion of the United States."

I should like to call this statement of Dr. Taylor to the attention of Senators from the cattle States, if there are any within the sound of my voice:

"On these alluvial lands Bermuda grass and Japan clover combined form a permanent pasture which will easily carry two head of stock per acre for eight months in the year, and in some cases double this amount. When it is borne in mind that the best blue-grass pastures of the North will carry only one head of cattle to two acres for about six months of the year the extraordinary productiveness of the alluvial land pastures is evident."

Senators, this is not my statement. It was made by Dr. Taylor, chief of the Bureau of Plant Industry of the Department of Agriculture.

This disinterested testimony is the voice of truth. No section of the United States is more favored by nature for the production of forage crops, and our possibilities in this direction are so vast that a splendid future awaits the South as the principal cattle section of the Union. With corn and forage crops naturally goes animal industry, and our recent successes in this new field speak with prophetic voice for the future.

HOGS, THE, MORTGAGE LIFTER.

There are no enemies to hogs, sheep, horses, and mules in the Southern States which do not exist everywhere, and all of these animals succeed well. Our winters are so mild that with a proper variety of crops grazing can be secured every day in the year, and animals require much less dry food and close attention than in the North. Conditions with us are especially favorable to hogs, and no State in the Republic has as many advantages for the lowly porker, called the "mortgage lifter," in the great agricultural States of Iowa and Illinois, as my own Louisiana, which is the natural home of the hog. Food crops of every kind grow in great profusion throughout the year, no housing is necessary, and the health of the pigs is fine whenever properly cared for.

The mild climatic conditions in the South make it unnecessary to invest any large amount of capital in equipment, and it is possible to raise two litters per year from mature sows much more successfully than in the so-called corn belt. In 1915 there were 20,481,000 hogs in the South, representing a total farm value of $161,111,000. The breeding of swine is an excellent investment for the farmer with small capital, for hogs multiply rapidly and give quick returns upon the money expended. No hog diseases exist in the South which are not also prevalent in the great hog States, and southern hogs are practically immune to pulmonary and bone troubles, such as pneumonia and rheumatism, and so forth, which are very common in the colder States. Beyond question, southern hogs are more healthy than their northern brethren, and hog raising in the South can be made more profitable than in any other part of the Union.

Equally favorable conditions exist as to mules, horses, and sheep. Kentucky, Tennessee, and Missouri are justly famous for the best horses and mules on the continent, but I have seen as good animals raised in Louisiana as ever trod the ground, and Texas has become very noted in recent years for its horses and mules.

RAPIDLY GROWING CATTLE INDUSTRY.

The South is naturally and otherwise adapted for live stock production, especially cattle for beef and dairying, and her farmers who have made the attempt have settled into this type of farming with an ease and grace befitting the best of our corn-belt farmers. Why should not they? There is no limit to the diversity or production of their grain and forage crops. There may be a few crops that do not thrive as well in our Southern States as in colder climates, but their places are more than filled by the hundreds of varieties of grain, forage, and pasture crops farmed in this section. While the so-called corn-belt and northern farms are locked in ice and snow the South is green with winter pastures. Southern cattle, unhoused and with little attention, make gains on pasture during the winter months that are unheard of without heavy grain feeding on northern farms.

To those who have watched southern agricultural development closely during the past few years the stride she has taken is phenomenal. This is especially true in the case of the development of the cattle industry. Pure-bred herds and flocks are springing up everywhere. Almost every county has its "better live stock associations." Nearly every State has its corps of specialists who are fostering their particular branch of agricultural development. The work of these specialists is concerted and organized, and branches through the county agents and farmers on one side and back through the State colleges and the Department of Agriculture on the other.

The change from straight cotton to diversified and live stock farming has not been exactly "a bed of roses" for the planters of the South. The difficulties which they are overcoming, while few in number, are large in

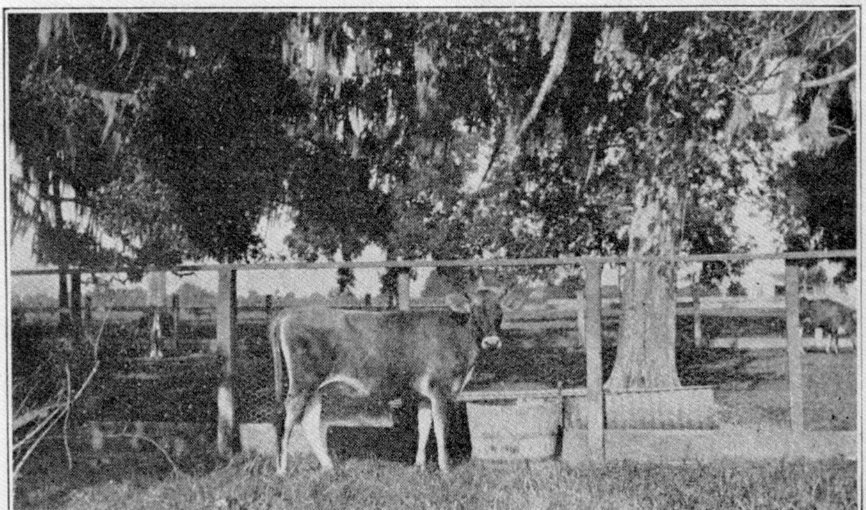

A COMING BEAUTY.

size. The greatest drawback in the way of cattle production the South has is the Texas fever tick. The Government specialist has landed on the work of eradicating this destroyer with a vim. During the few years in which the work has been in progress about one-third of the total ticky area has been cleaned of this pest. That this work is of great value to the southern cattle industry is indicated by the following figures. The average weight of cattle in the States of Florida, Georgia, Louisiana, Alabama, and Mississippi in 1915 were 340, 419, 471, 500, and 550 pounds per head, respectively.

The cattle of Wyoming, Idaho, and Montana, which are tick-free States, averaged 985, 966, and 938 pounds, respectively, in weight. The average values of cattle in these ticky States are: Georgia, $18; Florida, $18; Alabama, $20; Mississippi, $22. In a few of the tick-free States the average values of all cattle are as follows: Wyoming, $64; Montana, $60; Ohio, $56; Illinois, $56; Indiana, $54. Not only are the prices and values of beef cattle in ticky areas reduced, but it is estimated that milk production in such areas is reduced about 40 per cent because of the blood-sucking tick. When the work of tick eradication was first taken up it moved slowly, but at the present time southern farmers are making heroic efforts toward cleaning up their respective States. It is estimated that in from five to seven years the work will be completed.

It gives me much pleasure to state that the Legislature of Louisiana passed a law last week requiring all its citizens, under heavy penalties, to eradicate the cattle tick, and I have no doubt that my State will soon be free from the pest.

Following rapidly in the wake of tick eradication is the introduction of pure-bred beef animals. The beef cattle sales which have been held in the South during the past two years are numbered among the hundreds. Southern farmers appreciate good cattle and are paying good prices for them. At the Hereford sale held in Atlanta last November 46 head of pure-bred cattle were sold at an average price of $371 per head. One bull in this sale sold for $800; several went at $600. The best feature of this sale was the fact that most of these cattle went to southern breeders.

Another sale is that of the Lespedeza farm at Hickory Valley, Tenn. In this sale 60 head of pure-bred Shorthorn cattle sold at an average of $228. The bulls in this sale averaged $318, and one bull sold for $1,600. These were southern cattle and sold largely to southern breeders.

At the Davis Hereford sale at Jackson, Miss., in March of this year, some forty-odd cattle sold for an average price of $511. More than one-half of these cattle were sold to southern breeders, which in itself shows how rapidly the southern farmers are becoming accustomed to diversified and live stock farming. In recent sales in North Carolina, South Carolina, Georgia, Alabama, Tennessee, Arkansas, Oklahoma, and Louisiana cattle have sold at excellent prices.

More cattle have been taken into Southern States during the months since January 1 of this year than during any months previous. If this record keeps up the year 1916 will mean a great deal to southern live stock improvement. Already cattle coming from these States are beginning to show the results of breeding, and a few good bulls scattered here and there in counties of the South will go a long way toward the establishment of a better type of cattle.

The boys' pig and baby beef clubs should also be given due credit for the part they have played in the development of southern live stock conditions. The pig club idea originated a few years ago in Louisiana. Since that time it has grown to such an extent that the mere supervision of the work necessitates the employment of several hundred specialists. Some of the specialists devote all their time to the work, while others only give part of their time. The baby beef club work, also a southern idea, has not existed as long as the pig club work, but boys everywhere are glad of the opportunity to take up this interesting work. The work at present is going on in Texas, Mississippi, and Georgia, with promise that it will spread over all the South in a few years.

One might ask what has the South to show for all the work which has been done there in the interest of beef cattle during the last five years. It is difficult to answer the question with justice to the work, because the data and information which we have at hand are so small and so poorly representative of the real good that has been done.

That new institution, the Atlanta Live Stock Show, is a good example of what the South has produced and can do when called upon. This Atlanta show, because of certain factors, was devoted entirely to Hereford cattle last year. Hereford breeders are responsible for the statement that this was the biggest show of their breed ever held. Over $5000 was offered in prize money, and the best of Hereford cattle from all over the United States were in the competition. One cow imported from England, the place where Herefords are supposed to be really good, was not good enough at Atlanta to win over some of her competitors. This show was reputed to have been better than the Hereford show at the Panama-Pacific Exposition, and several breeders brought their show herds across the continent to get an opportunity at the prize money offered. Every first prize offered by the fair association at Atlanta, as well as the four championships, and last but best of all, the two grand champion animals, were all owned by breeders living below Mason and Dixon line. These southern breeders did not win because of lack of competition, for the strength of this show was without precedent.

Further, southern-bred cattle have won time and again at that great Mecca of all cattlemen, the International at Chicago. It remained for a Mississippi breeder to capture the premier recognition at this show in 1913 on that greatest of all present-day Hereford bulls, Point Comfort XIV. In making this wonderful product of the South a grand champion, the greatest possible honor was bestowed on southern farmers.

The offspring of this great bull, as well as those of many others, are being scattered over all the Southern States. Already their influence is being felt in the improvement of and the better prices received for the steers that are being marketed.

The South, with her cheap feeds and her wonderful variety of winter and summer pastures, can not be equaled for cheapness of the gains made by cattle fattened there. Bermuda grass, lespedeza, bur and other clovers, paspalum, and alfalfa are a few of the many grasses which are furnishing the basis of very economic beef production. Any one given section in our Northern States may boast of one or two standard pasture crops. In some sections of the South as many as 20 pasture grasses have been found growing in one pasture. Any one of these grasses alone would have been successful as a grazing proposition. With such a variety of resources at her command, one can appreciate how easily the South meets any and all conditions.

All that I have said in regard to beef cattle applies with equal force to dairy cattle. Although as yet there are but few creameries in the South, every branch of the dairying industry has been making rapid strides. Probably no one feature represents this development more definitely than the number of silos that have been built in the South recently. A report from the United States Department of Agriculture shows that during the past nine years the department has given advice, and so forth, in the building of 1,200 silos, which represent only a very small fraction, probably about one-sixth, of those actually built. Ten years ago a silo in the Southern States was almost unknown, but today there is hardly a county in the whole South in which silos are not in use.

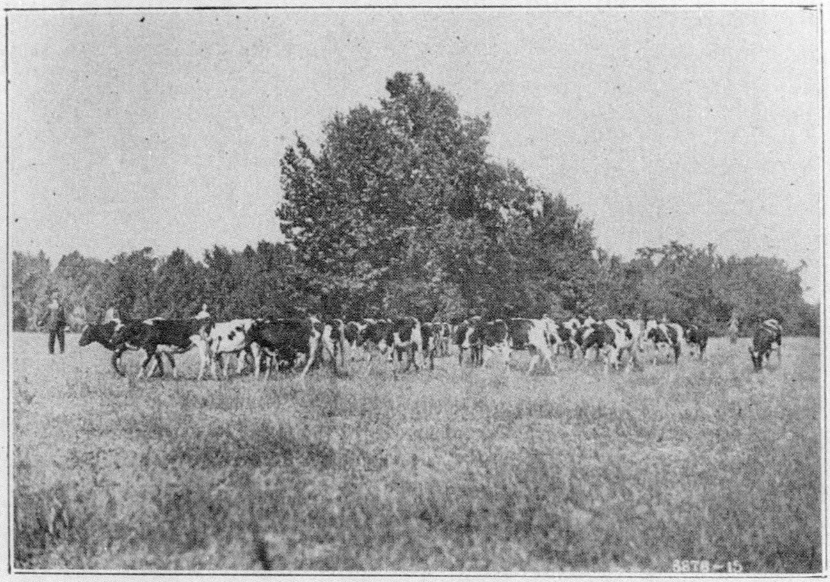

HOLSTEIN CATTLE.

THE SOUTH A MINERAL EMPIRE.

Rapid, however, as has been the South's agricultural progress, it has been fully equaled and even surpassed by her strides in the mineral world. In 1882 the total southern mineral production was valued at only $38,000,000, and amounted to 8 per cent of the mineral output of the country; in 1890 it was 14 per cent of the Nation's production, and its value was $87,000,000; in 1900 it was 16 per cent and brought $177,000,000; in 1910 it rose to 19 per cent and was valued at $370,000,000, while in 1914 the South's output brought $467,000,000 and constituted 22 per cent of the total production of the United States.

The increase in value of mineral production for the whole country from 1882 to 1914 was from $452,000,000 to $2,115,000,000, or about 370 per cent; for the South the increase was from $38,000,000 to $465,000,000, or 1,100 per cent. In other words, while during the generation from 1882 to 1914 the country, as a whole, was increasing the value of its mineral output not quite five-fold, the South increased the value of its mineral production about twelve-fold. And what minerals made up this grand total of nearly half a billion dollars—more than one-half as much in value as the great cotton crop of which the South is so justly proud? Of the 57 useful minerals mined in the United States every one is produced in the South except borax and platinum, and to make up for these two not produced, nine, namely, phosphate, bauxite, manganese, sulphur, monzonite, zircon, barite, fuller's earth, and nearly all the mica and pyrite are produced nowhere outside the South. The South is indeed a mineral empire. I insert as Appendix E some statistics as to the South's mineral wealth.

SULPHUR LOUISIANA'S MONOPOLY.

Louisiana produces practically all the sulphur in the United States. Fifteen years ago the United States produced only 3,000 tons of sulphur and imported 167,000 tons. Then what are probably the largest sulphur deposits in the world were made available in Calcasieu Parish, La., and the deficit was turned into a surplus—the import into an export. In 1914 our Nation mined 327,000 tons of sulphur, of which 98,000 tons were exported. Of this, more than 300,000 tons, valued at over $5,000,000, came from the South. Louisiana had put the United States on the sulphur map of the world.

In the production of petroleum, now so important in our marvelous industrial development, the South stands to the front. Her output was 52 per cent of our national production and amounted to 118,000,000 barrels in 1915. This was nearly twice as much as the total produced by any other country in the world. Oklahoma is second in the United States in the production of petroleum, and I have but to mention the Cushing field to recall to your minds its phenomenal output. Louisiana has the great Jennings and Caddo oil fields and ranks fifth in the production of oil. Geologists tell us that the central South from Oklahoma to Louisiana is underlain with what are probably the greatest oil deposits in the world.

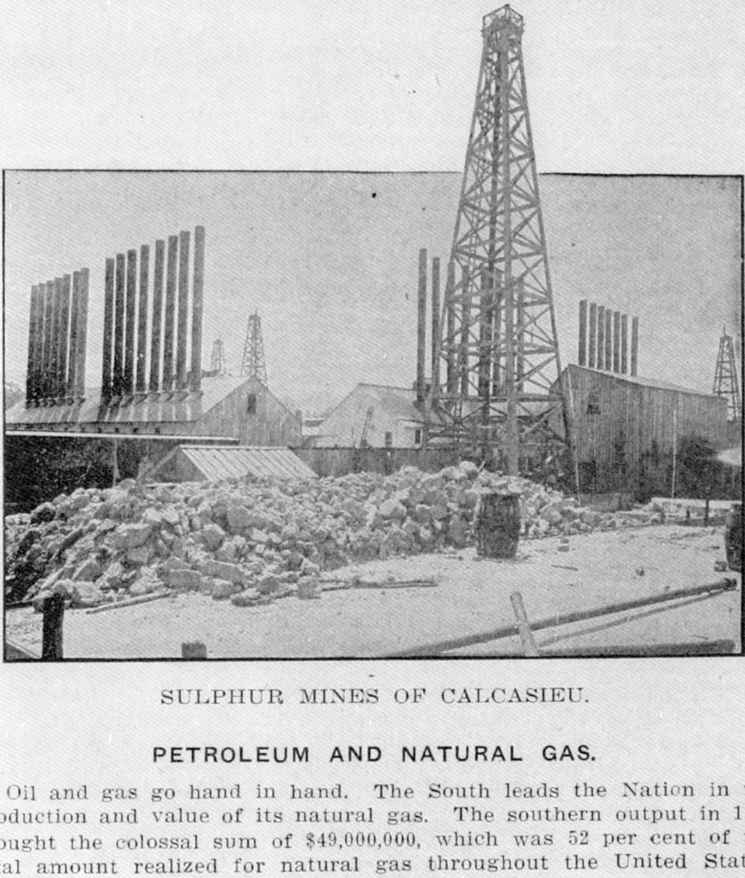

SULPHUR MINES OF CALCASIEU.

PETROLEUM AND NATURAL GAS.

Oil and gas go hand in hand. The South leads the Nation in the production and value of its natural gas. The southern output in 1915 brought the colossal sum of $49,000,000, which was 52 per cent of the total amount realized for natural gas throughout the United States.

Oklahoma produces more than any other State, and next to her is Louisiana. Three hundred and thirty-four thousand domestic consumers and more than 5,000 industrial consumers are supplied with natural gas from southern fields. Louisiana, Oklahoma, Texas, Virginia, and West Virginia have large deposits of salt, the annual production of which runs into the millions. The Louisiana output is only limited by the demand, for mother nature has given her salt enough to supply the world for centuries.

The South mines nearly half of all the lead and zinc produced in the United States, and these deposits bid fair to do even better in the future. The southern output of these metals was valued in 1915 at $63,000,000.

The limits of this address do not permit more than a mere naming of our other minerals. Fuller's earth, bauxite, phosphates, cement, marble, clays, building stones, and health-giving mineral waters abound in many parts of Dixie. The Newcomb pottery made at New Orleans is justly famed and has taken prizes in many exhibits.

GOLDEN OPPORTUNITIES.

My discussion of this portion of my subject would be very incomplete if I did not call attention to the magnificent opportunities to which the marvelous advantages of the South give birth. The proximity of almost every known mineral makes no prophecy as to future manufacturing industries of the South improbable.

Dr. David T. Day, formerly of the United States Geological Survey, speaks of a conspicuous instance of this in the Manufacturers' Record of February 22, 1912:

"Certain classes of chemicals should be produced in the South at least to the full limit of the southern demand.

These include products coming from southern minerals shipped frequently long distances away from home to be manufactured and transported back to the South for consumption. Equally obvious are the cases where the proximity of various raw materials admit of a product cheaper than anywhere else. Attention can not too often be called to the most prominent case of the latter kind, the production of soda salts. Everyone is familiar with the vast beds of pure rock salt in southern Louisiana, as well as the brines accompanying oil and gas to the north. In close proximity to this is found the cheapest sulphur production in the world—at the sulphur mines of Calcasieu Parish, in Louisiana. With abundant cheap fuel, oil, gas, and wood, with transportation in all directions by rail and water, no one can dispute the South's claim to supremacy as to location."

Dr. Day told me several years ago that the gas fields near Shreveport, La., were the largest known to science, and would generate more electrical power than all the waters of Niagara Falls, and a great deal cheaper, although subsequently he said that, owing to later discoveries, he thought there were greater supplies of gas in Oklahoma than in Louisiana. He said that Shreveport and other localities in my State were ideal for many enterprises requiring cheap fuel, especially in view of the proximity of sulphur, salt, gypsum, and sand. He also mentioned that bauxite, the mineral base of aluminum, is found in great quantity in America only in Arkansas, near Shreveport, whence it is carried thousands of miles to the cheap electricity of Niagara, whereas an enormous saving might be effected if the Arkansas and Louisiana products, bauxite and gas, lying side by side could be worked in cooperative unison. This is a great opportunity for men of brains and capital, and many others are offered by this wonderful gas field.

Our whole nation has aroused on the subject of conserving our natural resources. Location and ownership of water-power sites out West cause the fiercest controversy. Cabinets tremble at the mere mention of "conservation." Captains of finance and industry are searching the world for profitable investment, and yet this marvelous wealth of gas in Louisiana and Oklahoma, better than a dozen power sites in the West for superior electrical productivity to the mighty flow of Niagara's cataract, is actually going begging for some one to conserve and use it.

The West, however, is not alone in the possession of streams with water-power potentialities. It has been estimated that there is a minimum of over 5,000,000 primary horsepower in southern streams. This potential energy is sufficient for the creation of an industrial empire. Already these giant forces of nature have been partially harnessed, and over 1,000,000 horsepower are annually developed from southern streams; and I need but mention Mussel Shoals to call to your mind 600,000 horsepower in the Tennessee River at one place, which the National Government may utilize in the production of nitrates from the air.

SOUTH'S REMARKABLE MANUFACTURING GROWTH.

The South is not generally known as a manufacturing section, but her growth in this sphere is fully keeping pace with her advancement along other lines. In 1900 the value of all manufactured products in the South was $1,289,000,000, about 11 per cent of that estimated for the entire country, while the value of her farm products was $1,354,000,000. In other words, in 1900 the farm products of the South brought about $70,000,000 more than her manufactured products.

In 1910 a marvelous change had taken place. The South's manufactured output had more than doubled in value, amounting to $2,637,000,000, or 13 per cent of the total for the United States, while her farm products were valued at $1,927,000,000. In 1910 the manufactured products of the South brought $700,000,000 more than all her agricultural products.

The Department of Commerce estimates that last year Dixie manufactures aggregated over $4,000,000,000, which was 18 per cent of that produced by the entire country, while our farm products were valued at $3,600,000,000. The South now manufactures more than half of all the cotton it grows, and there is hardly a line of industrial activity that can be mentioned in which the South is not advancing faster than the rest of the Nation. Of 262 different lines of manufacture in the entire Union, 236 are already being carried on in the South. For a long time the South was considered purely an agricultural section, but that is true no longer. Agriculture is still of the greatest importance, reaching in value every year considerably more than one-third of the total agricultural wealth of the Nation, and being over $3,600,000,000 last year; but manufactures have grown far more rapidly than agriculture, and last year reached the colossal total of $4,000,000,000, which clearly gives the palm to manufacturing rather than agriculture.

SOUTHERN BANKS.

In natural cooperation with the South's marvelous growth in agriculture, mining, and manufacturing, her banking facilities have expanded enormously. In 1900 there were only 713 national banks in the South with total deposits of $456,000,000, while on March 7, 1916, 2,147 national banks, with total deposits amounting to $1,636,000,000, were doing business. In 1900 the South had 1,589 State banks with deposits of $333,000,000, while in 1915 she boasted of 6,865, whose deposits totaled the colossal sum of $1,355,000,000. To put it in another way, in fifteen years the number of southern banks qudrapuled, while their deposits increased from about three-quarters of a billion to nearly three billions. These figures show that the South now has banking resources as great as the entire country had as late as 1884. Truly, Dixie is the land of opportunities, for, although her growth was retarded for a while by various circumstances, she is now going forward with startling rapidity.

OUR SPLENDID TIMBER WEALTH.

Of vast importance to the South as well as to the entire United States are the timber resources, which have contributed much to the prosperity of the region and which will continue to add to its wealth for several generations. Lumbering—a term broad enough to embrace the cutting of the timber in the woods until it has gone through a refining process and is ready for consumption as boards, planks, or timber—has always been a part of the activities of the South; it was not, however, until the 90's that it began to grow with strides that quickly outdistanced the older producing regions. The exploitation has increased year after year and the end is not yet in sight.

As indicative of the economic importance of the forests to the States of Virginia, North and South Carolina, Georgia, Florida, Alabama, Mississippi, Louisiana, Arkansas, and Texas, the following estimate of timber remaining after several decades of heavy cutting is made, the figures being those of the Forest Service:

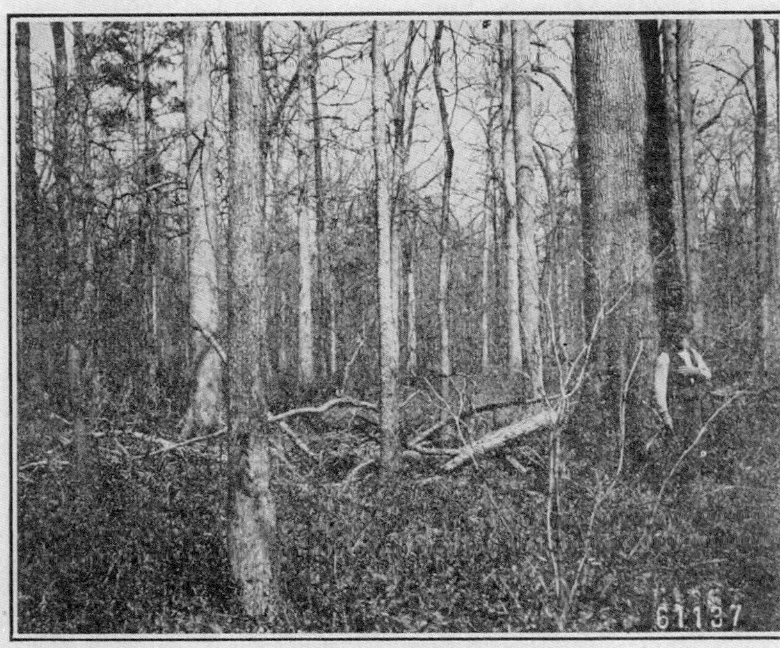

A HARDWOOD FOREST.

	Billions of feet b. m.
Virginia	14.5
North Carolina	42.9
South Carolina	30.7
Georgia	46.0
Florida	74.1
Alabama	56.3
Mississippi	92.7
Louisiana	119.8
Arkansas	81.5
Texas	66.0
	624.5

The South, as shown in the preceding tabulation, has a total estimated remaining stand of 624,500,000,000 feet of timber—Louisiana's 119,800,000,000 feet alone representing nearly one-fifth of the aggregate timber remaining uncut. The value of this timber it is difficult to even fairly approximate, much less to make a close estimate of its real worth. If its value is placed at the very low price of $2 per thousand feet, the potential value of the forests is a billion and a half dollars. This represents but about one-sixth of the aggregate value of the resource by the time the timber is manufactured into lumber and ready for distribution. All of this money goes to the South—to labor and to the producers of other products of the region.

The South has produced in the way of lumber in the last ten years—1905 to 1914, inclusive—more than 160,000,000,000 feet of lumber. Its yellow pine is known almost everywhere that lumber is used; it dominates the markets of the great Central West and the Eastern States; from the Gulf and South Atlantic ports it is shipped in cargo lots in normal times to practically all of the countries of Europe, in addition to the Republics of South America. In 1914 an aggregate cut of 17,500,000,000 feet was reported by nearly 12,000 mills. It is not difficult for the mind to picture what the operation of these 12,000 mills means in the way of prosperity.

Louisiana in 1904 ranked fourth in the list of lumber-producing States in the Union in the volume of lumber cut. By 1907 this Commonwealth had advanced to second place and maintained that position until 1914, when the production reported exceeded that of any other individual State. Participating in that cut were 428 sawmills, which reported the quantity of lumber manufactured. Louisiana can boast of not only some of the most modern equipped sawmill operations, but can with pride point to the single largest mill in the United States, a mill at Bogalusa, La., with a capacity of 1,000,000 feet of lumber a day.

Some idea of the extent of the lumber industry in the South may be gained from the fact that this industry employs 281,704 wage earners and that the capital invested amounts to the colossal sum of $364,852,000. In this again Louisiana leads, with 46,072 wage earners and $88,973,000 of capital invested.

Not only have the forests of the South given much to the upbuilding of the country as a whole through the volume of lumber cut each year, but the returns from the naval stores industry are enormous. The value of these products—28,988,000 gallons of turpentine and 3,263,000 barrels of rosin—was $25,295,000.

The South's economic condition has been doubly benefited through exploitation of the forests. Not only has the timber cut brought many millions of dollars into the several States, given employment to hundreds of thousands, resulted in the construction of tens of thousands of miles of railroads, and afforded to the existing railroads millions of dollars' worth of freight traffic, but it has necessitated the building of many communities, now grown into thriving towns, and at the same time afforded a market for the products of the field and factory.

EXCELLENT TRANSPORTATION FACILITIES.

Mr. President, we have noted in a hasty and inadequate manner the varied and valuable products of southern forests, mines, and farms. A study of our production, however, necessitates brief mention of the great transportation problem, and of its three agencies—road, rail, and river.

There seems to be quite widespread belief that the South is woefully lacking in improved roads. This is entirely erroneous, for, while it is true that the South did not take up State-aid highway improvement as early as New Jersey or Massachusetts, it may be pointed out that Maryland was the first to practically complete a comprehensive system of State roads built entirely at State expense and reaching every county and important city in the State.

While the good roads movement was a few years late in getting under way in the South, as compared with some other sections, the movement since that time has been, if anything, more rapid there than in any other section of equal extent. Furthermore, it may be well to note that, with the exception of the period of great railroad expansion, when every section of the country came to regard the public road as merely a local utility, the South has always been at the very front in the movement for better roads.

It was during the last ten or twelve years, however, that the South made special progress in the improvement of its highways. This was accomplished through State aid, the utilization of convict labor, and the skillful adaptation of local materials to road improvement in a way equaled by no other section of the Union. In 1904 the sixteen Southern States had a total road mileage of 790,274 miles, of which only 29,853 miles, or 3.8 per cent, were improved, as compared with 7.1 per cent of improved roads for the entire United States. The total cash road and bridge expenditures for these States amounted to only $12,636,959, or an average of only $16 per mile of road, as compared with $28 of average cash road expenditure per mile of road for the Nation. (Appendix G.) The ten years following 1904, however, worked a wonderful transformation. At the close of 1914 the Southern States had a total road mileage of 954,671 miles, of which 84,155 miles, or 8.9 per cent, were improved. This is practically three times the mileage which was improved in 1904, while the cash road and bridge expenditures in 1914 amounted to $61,-680,956, or about five times the total road and bridge expenditures in 1904. In comparison with the entire United States we note that the improved roads of the South amounted to 8.9 per cent of the total in those States, with a cash road and bridge expenditure of $64 per mile, while for the Union as a whole the improved road mileage was 10.9 per cent of the total, with a cash expenditure of about $100 per mile. Thus, while in 1904 the percentage of the improved mileage in the South was only one-half of the average for the country at large, in 1914 it was almost equal to the average for the entire United States. (See Appendix G.)

The above will serve to show how erroneous is the idea that the South is far behind in the improvement of its public roads. The work is by no means as yet complete, but when we stop to consider that at the present time about 8.9 per cent of its public roads have been improved, and most of this in the short period of ten years, and when we recall that 15 or 20 per cent of the roads of any section carry at least 80 per cent of the traffic, we see that the South is well on its way toward completion of a system of improved roads which will answer all its needs. In the wisdom shown in financing its road improvements, in utilizing convict labor, and adapting local materials so as to answer the needs of the particular traffic requirements, no section of the United States has made as great progress as have the sixteen Southern States. The people know what

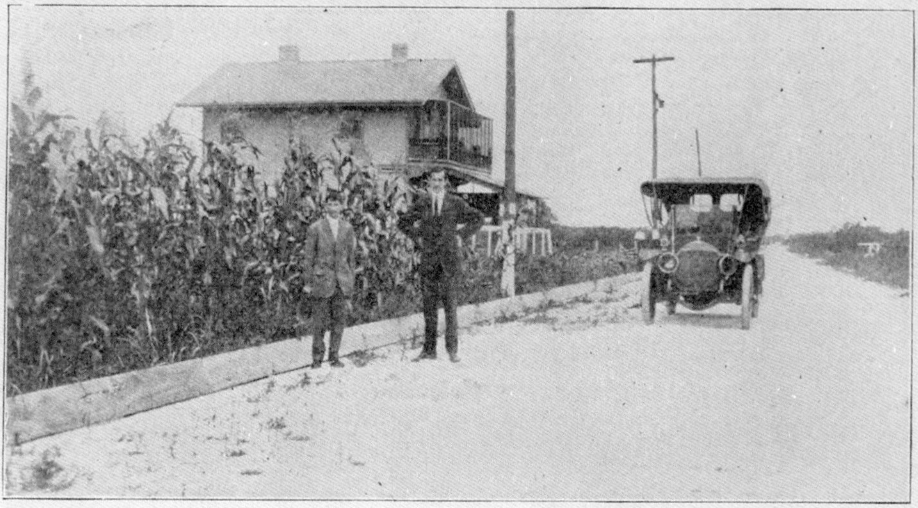

A SAMPLE OF LOUISIANA GOOD ROADS.

good roads mean and have set about to secure them. While the work has in no instance been as spectacular as that of some other States, it has been no less effective in securing actual results; that is, roads adapted to the needs and traffic requirements of each of the several States.

In the South, however, as throughout the United States, the principal means of transportation is by rail, and we are very well supplied in this respect. The United States has a total of 252,000 miles of railroads, of which the South, constituting less than one-third of the country in area, has 92,000 miles, or more than one-third of the railroad mileage. The average southern mileage is more than three times that of many of the Western States, and the enormous growth of the southern region is forcing a rapid increase in these great arteries of commerce. Our railroad officials are as enterprising and energetic as those in any section of the country, and their persevering and untiring labor is bringing our railways to a very high degree of efficiency.

In regard to waterways, the South has been unusually blessed. Taken as a whole, the Southern States have a greater per cent of navigable rivers than any other part of the Union. The mighty Father of Waters sweeps through the heart of the Southland, and the Ohio, the Missouri, the Tennessee, the Cumberland, the Arkansas, the White, the St. Francis, the Red, and the Yazoo are worthy tributaries to this great parent. Pouring into the Atlantic and the Gulf are many fine streams, and my own Louisiana has nearly 5,000 miles of navigable waters. The South can boast of the second largest shipping port in the United States—New Orleans, the Queen City of the Gulf—whose commerce last year was second only to New York, while Galveston ranks third among the ports of the Union. The opening of the Panama Canal has brought to our very doors the great markets on the west coast of South and Central America, where the products of the South are in active demand.

In transportation, then, as in production, the South stands in the front rank.

I fear, however, that the facts recited above, showing the limitless resources of the South, are not as widely known as they should be and I trust that the press of the United States will call to the attention of our people the opportunities offered by this section. In no portion of the United States is the public better served by its press than in the South. This refers to the rural as well as metropolitan newspapers. The large number of wide-awake periodicals is an indication of the progressive spirit that is sweeping Dixie from the Ohio to the Gulf, and I know that the press, not only of the South but of the entire country, will assist in giving these facts the publicity that their importance merits.

COME TO THE SOUTHLAND.

Mr. President, in a hasty and imperfect manner I have pointed out a few of the myriad advantages that should lure men and money to the Southland, and hope my feeble words will meet with some response. I trust that many of our fine people now pouring into Canada, and the boys and girls who are leaving northern and eastern farms and villages for the exciting but dangerous life of great cities, will make their homes in the South. I cordially invite capital and labor in every branch of human endeavor to invest in Dixie and become citizens of that favored country. We will gladly welcome all who wish to come—millions of them—for the South needs 50,000,000 additional people and fifty billions of wealth to assist in developing her marvelous resources. The lure of the Southland is calling and the response will be all she desires.

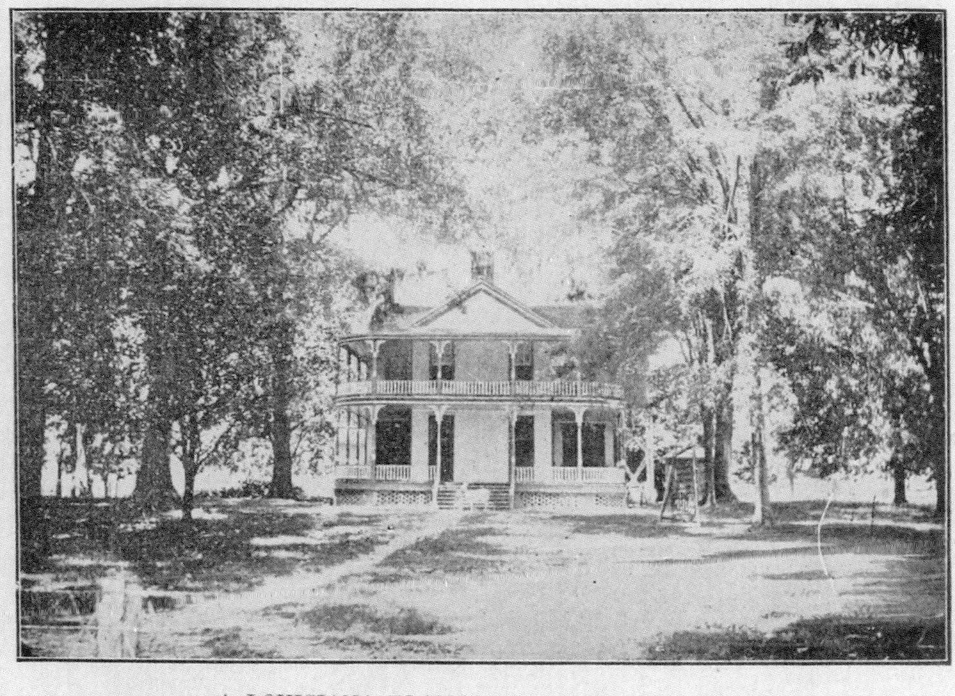

A LOUISIANA PLANTATION HOME OF TODAY.

APPENDIX A.

MEAN TEMPERATURE.

Stations.	January	February	March	April	May	June	July	August	September	October	November	December	Annual
Edmonton, British Northwest	1.8	8.3	24.2	39.9	50.8	56.9	60.6	58.8	49.3	41.1	22.9	13.1	35.6
Prince Albert, Saskatchewan	—8.4	—3.0	12.0	36.1	47.6	57.7	61.9	58.9	48.4	37.1	15.4	2.8	30.5
Swift Current, Saskatchewan	3.1	8.0	22.0	41.3	50.7	60.0	66.5	64.0	53.1	42.1	23.2	10.0	37.5
Winnipeg, Manitobia	—6.8	—1.6	12.3	35.9	51.6	62.2	66.0	63.4	52.5	39.1	18.0	4.1	33.1
White River, Ontario	—0.4	0.2	12.2	33.0	45.7	58.7	59.5	56.4	50.3	37.1	20.5	9.7	32.1
Ottawa, Ontario	9.6	11.7	21.5	40.0	54.9	65.3	69.5	64.8	57.4	43.8	31.7	17.0	40.6
Bismarck, N. Dak.	6.7	8.3	22.1	42.6	55.2	64.2	70.2	68.1	57.1	44.1	26.0	15.0	40.0
St. Paul, Minn.	11.6	15.0	28.2	45.7	58.2	67.4	72.1	69.5	60.3	48.1	30.9	19.3	43.9
Des Moines, Iowa.	20.4	24.1	35.7	50.6	61.6	70.4	75.5	73.0	65.0	52.5	36.8	25.7	49.3
Boston, Mass.	27.0	28.0	35.0	45.3	56.6	65.8	71.3	68.9	62.7	52.3	41.2	31.6	48.8
Albany, N. Y.	22.5	23.6	32.1	45.8	58.9	67.9	72.0	69.5	62.3	50.4	38.4	27.5	47.6
Buffalo, N. Y.	24.7	24.0	31.2	42.3	54.5	65.1	70.2	68.8	62.9	51.5	39.3	30.1	47.0
Chicago, Ill.	23.7	25.4	34.4	45.9	56.5	66.3	72.4	71.2	64.6	53.2	39.2	29.3	48.5
Little Rock, Ark.	40.6	44.1	52.7	62.7	70.4	77.2	80.6	79.2	73.1	62.9	51.5	43.5	61.5
Atlanta, Ga.	42.2	45.2	52.4	61.1	69.5	75.6	77.6	76.1	72.1	62.4	51.9	44.6	60.9
Shreveport, La.	46.2	50.0	58.2	65.8	73.2	79.6	82.1	81.4	75.7	65.6	55.3	48.9	65.2
Charleston, S. C.	49.3	51.7	57.2	63.8	72.4	78.5	81.3	80.3	76.2	67.1	58.1	51.3	65.6
Jacksonville, Fla.	53.9	56.9	61.9	67.6	74.2	79.0	80.9	80.1	77.3	69.6	61.3	55.2	68.2
Mobile, Ala.	49.8	53.2	59.1	66.0	73.6	79.1	80.5	79.7	76.5	67.1	57.5	51.5	66.1
New Orleans, La.	53.0	56.3	62.0	67.9	74.5	79.6	81.3	81.0	78.0	69.5	60.6	54.4	68.2
Galveston, Tex.	52.7	55.6	62.3	68.7	75.4	80.9	83.0	82.6	79.4	72.4	62.9	56.3	69.4
San Antonio, Tex.	51.1	54.4	62.1	69.0	74.8	80.4	82.4	82.0	77.1	69.2	59.2	53.1	67.9

DAILY MEAN MAXIMUM TEMPERATURE.

Stations.	January	February	March	April	May	June	July	August	September	October	November	December	Annual
Edmonton	23	22	34	56	65	69	74	71	60	55	34	26	49
Prince Albert	12	12	27	51	64	69	73	71	58	50	29	16	44
Swift Current	23	19	33	56	65	71	78	77	64	56	36	27	50
Winnipeg	13	12	28	54	68	73	78	76	66	54	33	16	48
Montreal, Province of Quebec	21	23	31	49	64	74	77	75	66	53	39	26	50
Toronto, Ontario	29	30	36	49	61	72	77	76	68	54	42	32	52
Bismarck	18	20	34	54	66	75	82	80	71	58	38	25	51
St. Paul	21	24	37	56	68	77	82	80	71	57	39	27	53
Des Moines	29	32	45	61	71	80	85	83	75	64	47	34	59
Boston	36	36	43	54	66	75	80	78	71	60	49	39	57
Albany	31	32	41	56	69	78	82	80	73	60	46	35	57
Buffalo	31	31	38	50	62	72	76	76	70	58	45	35	54
Chicago	31	33	42	54	64	74	80	78	72	60	46	36	56
Little Rock	50	53	63	72	79	86	90	89	83	73	61	52	71
Atlanta	50	53	62	70	79	85	87	85	81	71	61	52	70
Shreveport	56	59	69	76	83	90	92	92	87	77	66	58	75
Charleston	58	59	66	72	80	86	88	87	83	74	66	59	73
Jacksonville	64	66	72	78	84	88	90	90	86	78	71	65	78
Mobile	59	62	68	75	82	88	90	89	86	77	66	61	75
New Orleans	62	64	71	76	83	88	89	89	86	78	69	63	76
Galveston	59	61	68	74	80	86	88	88	84	78	69	62	75
San Antonio	63	66	74	80	85	92	94	94	89	81	71	64	79

APPENDIX A—Continued.

DAILY MEAN MINIMUM TEMPERATURE.

Stations.	January	February	March	April	May	June	July	August	September	October	November	December	Annual
Edmonton	4	1	10	31	39	45	50	47	38	32	17	9	27
Prince Albert	—10	—11	4	26	35	46	50	48	38	30	12	—3	22
Swift Current	4	— 1	14	30	41	59	52	50	40	33	19	10	29
Winnipeg	— 9	—11	7	29	40	49	54	52	42	32	16	—2	25
Montreal, Province of Quebec	4	7	17	33	46	56	61	59	51	39	27	12	34
Toronto, Ontario	15	14	21	33	43	53	58	57	50	39	30	20	36
Bismarck	— 3	— 1	13	31	42	52	57	55	45	33	17	5	29
St. Paul	3	7	20	36	48	58	62	60	51	40	24	11	35
Des Moines	11	14	27	40	51	60	65	63	55	43	29	18	40
Boston	20	20	28	38	48	58	64	62	55	45	34	24	41
Albany	15	16	25	38	50	59	63	61	54	43	32	21	40
Buffalo	19	17	24	35	46	57	63	61	55	44	34	24	40
Chicago	17	18	28	39	49	59	65	65	58	46	33	73	42
Little Rock	34	35	45	53	61	68	72	71	65	54	43	36	53
Atlanta	35	37	44	51	60	67	70	69	64	53	44	36	52
Shreveport	39	41	49	56	64	70	73	72	67	56	46	41	56
Charleston	43	44	50	57	66	72	75	75	71	60	51	44	59
Jacksonville	46	49	54	59	66	72	74	74	71	63	54	47	61
Mobile	43	46	52	59	66	72	74	73	70	59	49	44	59
New Orleans	47	49	56	61	68	74	76	75	72	63	54	48	62
Galveston	48	50	58	65	71	77	79	78	75	68	58	51	65
San Antonio	42	44	52	59	66	71	73	73	68	59	50	44	59

HIGHEST TEMPERATURE OF RECORD.

Stations.	January	February	March	April	May	June	July	August	September	October	'ovember	December	Annual
Edmonton	48	56	61	84	90	86	94	92	87	78	74	59	94
Prince Albert	53	52	62	79	90	93	87	88	84	75	66	52	93
Swift Current	59	58	70	86	92	104	102	101	90	83	77	54	104
Winnipeg	42	44	58	81	92	100	94	93	99	82	71	41	100
Montreal, Province of Quebec	52	50	57	77	92	98	94	90	91	68	78	59	98
Toronto, Ontario	58	54	70	90	93	93	103	99	94	81	67	61	103
Bismarck	60	64	81	90	96	103	107	105	102	91	73	64	107
St. Paul	51	61	83	87	94	98	104	100	96	87	74	58	104
Des Moines	64	70	88	92	96	101	109	103	99	91	79	69	109
Boston	70	64	78	87	97	98	104	97	102	90	76	69	104
Albany	64	63	79	91	97	99	104	98	97	90	71	66	104
Buffalo	70	67	79	84	94	93	95	95	95	86	71	64	95
Chicago	65	63	81	88	94	99	103	98	98	87	75	68	103
Little Rock	78	80	89	94	94	102	106	105	101	93	84	78	106
Atlanta	75	78	87	89	97	100	100	98	97	94	82	73	100
Shreveport	83	82	90	96	101	104	107	110	101	95	86	79	110
Charleston	80	80	94	90	98	101	104	100	100	93	83	78	104
Jacksonville	81	86	91	92	98	101	104	101	99	95	86	82	104
Mobile	78	80	91	90	98	101	102	101	97	95	83	80	102
New Orleans	82	82	86	90	96	102	102	100	98	94	89	83	102
Galveston	75	76	85	85	93	97	99	98	94	91	85	77	99
San Antonio	87	90	97	99	104	105	106	108	103	99	89	86	108

APPENDIX A—Continued.

LOWEST TEMPERATURE OF RECORD.

Stations.	January	February	March	April	May	June	July	August	September	October	November	December	Annual
Edmonton	—50	—43	—31	— 5	15	29	36	29	12	2	—27	—36	—50
Prince Albert	—50	—48	—37	—14	2	30	36	32	18	— 4	—28	—40	—50
Swift Current	—41	—41	—22	— 2	12	32	38	32	18	4	—22	—27	—41
Winnipeg	—45	—39	—24	2	11	28	36	32	22	6	—29	—34	—45
Montreal, Quebec	—26	—24	—15	8	25	38	40	45	33	22	— 1	—21	—26
Toronto, Ontario	—26	—25	—16	6	25	28	39	40	28	16	— 5	—21	—26
Bismarck	—44	—43	—46	— 3	13	31	32	32	10	— 2	—28	—38	—44
St. Paul	—41	—33	—22	7	23	36	45	40	28	12	—24	—39	—41
Des Moines	—30	—26	— 8	11	26	37	46	40	26	14	—10	—20	—30
Boston	—13	—11	— 8	11	31	42	46	47	34	25	— 2	—12	—13
Albany	—24	—18	— 8	13	29	40	48	43	32	23	—10	—17	—24
Buffalo	—14	—13	— 4	11	28	39	47	44	35	24	2	— 9	—14
Chicago	—20	—21	—12	17	27	40	50	47	32	14	— 2	—23	—23
Little Rock	— 5	—12	16	28	39	51	60	52	41	31	10	6	—12
Atlanta	— 2	— 8	8	25	38	39	58	55	43	30	14	1	— 8
Shreveport	1	— 5	22	32	42	53	62	54	44	31	18	10	— 5
Charleston	10	7	24	32	45	51	64	62	49	37	26	13	7
Jacksonville	15	10	26	34	46	54	66	64	49	40	26	14	10
Mobile	11	— 1	25	32	46	50	64	57	49	34	25	14	— 1
New Orleans	15	7	30	38	52	58	66	63	55	40	29	20	7
Galveston	11	8	30	43	52	57	66	68	54	44	26	18	8
San Antonio	6	4	21	35	44	53	58	57	46	36	21	10	4

MEAN MONTHLY PRECIPITATION (INCHES).

Stations.	January	February	March	April	May	June	July	August	September	October	November	December	Annual
Edmonton	0.68	0.67	0.72	0.88	1.55	2.86	3.03	2.13	1.33	0.70	0.58	0.70	15.83
Prince Albert	.97	.69	.77	.83	1.26	2.51	2.05	2.15	1.28	.83	.83	.74	14.91
Swift Current	.64	.74	.81	.93	1.76	2.67	2.44	1.91	1.22	.88	.69	.78	15.47
Winnipeg	.88	.98	1.03	1.05	2.28	3.29	3.08	2.67	2.03	1.70	1.08	.91	20.98
White River	1.69	1.52	1.38	1.25	1.95	2.22	2.80	3.30	2.77	2.35	1.85	1.71	24.79
Ottawa	2.99	2.69	2.72	1.50	2.59	2.92	3.47	3.03	2.69	2.55	2.54	2.91	32.60
Bismarck	.54	.50	1.04	1.88	2.50	3.54	2.14	1.98	1.19	1.03	.68	.62	17.64
St. Paul	.90	.84	1.60	2.33	3.62	4.41	3.40	3.46	3.42	2.34	1.30	1.06	28.68
Des Moines	1.21	1.08	1.65	2.98	4.56	4.96	3.86	3.61	3.07	2.68	1.48	1.31	32.45
Boston	3.82	3.44	4.08	3.55	3.51	3.03	3.36	4.03	3.19	3.86	4.10	3.41	43.38
Albany	2.59	2.52	2.74	2.39	2.98	3.76	3.90	3.96	3.18	2.99	2.80	2.57	36.38
Buffalo	3.30	2.85	2.62	2.45	3.10	3.14	3.40	2.99	3.18	3.53	3.35	3.37	37.28
Chicago	2.00	2.16	2.55	2.88	3.37	3.66	3.64	2.88	3.02	2.55	2.50	2.07	33.28
Little Rock	4.79	4.18	4.94	4.51	5.10	4.09	3.99	3.65	3.26	2.55	4.59	4.24	49.89
Atlanta	5.31	4.65	5.78	3.63	3.09	3.88	4.73	4.48	3.53	2.34	3.40	4.54	49.36
Shreveport	4.42	3.61	4.52	4.58	4.16	3.58	3.72	2.24	3.22	3.18	4.08	4.37	45.68
Charleston	3.45	3.41	3.72	2.99	3.47	5.39	7.26	6.97	5.46	3.93	2.87	3.15	52.07
Jacksonville	3.12	3.43	3.52	2.72	4.25	5.53	6.20	6.21	8.03	5.06	2.19	2.99	53.25
Mobile	4.85	5.36	7.17	4.35	4.00	5.95	7.04	6.81	5.02	3.18	3.74	4.57	62.04
New Orleans	4.63	4.47	5.30	4.91	3.88	6.16	6.47	5.61	4.81	2.93	3.79	4.46	57.42
Galveston	3.62	3.10	2.90	3.13	3.23	4.75	3.98	5.01	5.41	4.18	4.02	3.73	47.06
San Antonio	1.68	1.78	1.68	2.94	2.96	3.11	2.22	2.69	2.94	1.49	1.78	1.56	26.83

APPENDIX A—Continued.

PERCENTAGES OF SUNSHINE.

Stations.	January	February	March	April	May	June	July	August	September	October	November	December	Annual
Battleford, Saskatchewan	40	49	50	52	44	47	52	54	44	44	34	31	45
Winnipeg, Manitoba	41	48	49	50	54	52	59	59	47	37	34	34	47
Toronto, Ontario	27	37	40	47	48	56	60	60	55	44	29	24	44
Ottawa, Ontario	30	38	40	46	48	50	53	56	45	39	28	22	41
Quebec, Province of Quebec	30	36	41	40	41	44	46	50	42	37	24	27	38
Bismarck	56	62	56	64	56	60	71	66	59	59	50	49	59
St. Paul	50	62	62	63	59	66	75	70	62	58	48	44	60
Des Moines	46	47	59	58	60	65	70	70	60	62	54	52	59
Boston	44	57	60	62	61	69	72	67	58	60	48	46	59
Albany	38	47	51	51	49	56	59	54	47	48	34	34	47
Buffalo	23	40	48	49	55	61	67	62	57	49	30	25	46
Chicago	37	47	55	58	65	73	71	69	65	61	52	42	58
Little Rock	48	55	57	57	64	69	68	70	74	71	61	49	62
Atlanta	46	51	60	59	62	66	58	60	62	63	62	44	58
Shreveport †	48	51	57	53	65	71	66	75	79	70	56	47	63
Charleston	61	62	69	70	69	69	63	67	68	68	70	56	66
Jacksonville	56	58	69	68	69	68	64	63	61	60	59	53	62
Mobile	54	60	63	67	75	70	59	62	63	70	69	48	63
New Orleans	52	51	60	56	62	63	54	58	53	61	56	42	56
Galveston	60	59	63	63	71	83	74	73	71	71	61	51	67
San Antonio	48	50	49	48	54	68	67	67	68	60	45	45	56

† Interpolated percentages of sunshine.

MEAN RELATIVE HUMIDITY (PERCENTAGES).

(8 a. m. and 8 p. m., 75th meridian time.)

Stations.		January	February	March	April	May	June	July	August	September	October	November	December	Annual
Bismarck	a. m.	80	80	80	76	77	81	80	81	81	81	81	80	80
	p. m.	69	69	65	53	53	58	52	50	53	60	69	69	61
St. Paul	a. m.	83	84	80	74	74	78	79	83	83	80	80	83	80
	p. m.	75	74	66	54	52	56	54	56	60	62	69	75	63
Des Moines	a. m.	82	82	79	76	76	79	79	81	83	80	79	82	80
	p. m.	76	73	65	55	56	59	56	59	63	59	65	74	63
Boston	a. m.	73	71	70	68	70	72	71	75	77	75	75	73	73
	p. m.	70	67	68	67	70	71	71	74	76	72	71	69	70
Albany	a. m.	82	81	79	73	72	74	75	78	81	82	82	82	78
	p. m.	78	77	72	64	64	67	66	69	73	73	75	75	72
Buffalo	a. m.	80	79	77	73	74	76	75	75	77	76	77	79	77
	p. m.	78	79	75	71	71	71	70	69	72	72	75	77	73
Chicago	a. m.	84	83	79	75	75	75	74	78	76	77	79	82	78
	p. m.	79	78	75	70	68	69	66	69	68	67	73	78	71
Little Rock	a. m.	80	79	77	77	81	81	84	85	84	83	80	80	81
	p. m.	66	62	59	58	62	64	65	65	65	60	59	64	63
Atlanta	a. m.	81	78	78	74	74	78	83	85	82	77	77	80	79
	p. m.	70	65	62	59	59	63	70	72	60	61	63	70	65
Shreveport	a. m.	81	79	80	81	84	84	86	86	86	85	83	82	83
	p. m.	65	61	58	59	62	63	65	64	63	59	60	61	62
Charleston	a. m.	81	80	81	75	76	78	79	82	83	80	80	80	79
	p. m.	76	76	76	74	76	78	79	80	80	76	75	75	77
Jacksonville	a. m.	86	84	83	78	79	81	83	85	86	84	85	87	83
	p. m.	77	74	72	69	73	78	79	81	82	79	78	77	77
Mobile	a. m.	85	83	85	82	81	81	84	86	85	83	84	85	84
	p. m.	75	74	75	72	71	73	77	78	75	70	73	76	74
New Orleans	a. m.	85	84	85	83	81	81	83	84	84	81	83	84	83
	p. m.	73	72	71	68	68	71	74	75	74	69	73	74	72
Galveston	a. m.	86	87	88	86	82	82	81	82	81	80	83	85	84
	p. m.	83	83	83	81	78	76	74	75	73	72	78	80	78
San Antonio	a. m.	76	76	77	81	84	84	85	85	84	80	79	77	81
	p. m.	56	54	50	54	56	51	50	49	53	52	56	57	53

AVERAGE DATE OF FIRST KILLING FROST IN AUTUMN.

Edmonton, September 9. (Not much data available.)
Prince Albert, September 9. (Not much data available.)
Swift Current, September 11. (Not much data available.)
Winnipeg, September 14. (Not much data available.)
Bismarck, September 19.
St. Paul, October 3.
Des Moines, October 11.
Boston, October 22.
Albany, October 17.
Buffalo, October 16.
Chicago, October 18.
Little Rock, November 13.
Atlanta, November 3.
Shreveport, November 11.
Charleston, December 11.
Jacksonville, December 6.
Mobile, December 4.
New Orleans, December 10.
Galveston, December 24.
San Antonio, November 26.

AVERAGE DATE OF LAST KILLING FROST IN SPRING.

Edmonton, May 17. (Not much data available.)
Prince Albert, May 17. (Not much data available.)
Swift Current, May 15. (Not much data available.)
Winnipeg, May 15. (Not much data available.)
Bismarck, May 12.
St. Paul, April 27.
Des Moines, April 22.
Boston, April 20.
Albany, April 23.
Buffalo, April 26.
Chicago, April 18.
Little Rock, March 18.
Atlanta, March 23.
Shreveport, March 4.
Charleston, February 19.
Jacksonville, February 11.
Mobile, February 16.
New Orleans, February 3.
Galveston, January 27.
San Antonio, February 23.

EARLIEST DATE OF KILLING FROST IN AUTUMN.

Edmonton, August 25. (Not much data available.)
Prince Albert, August 25. (Not much data available.)
Bismarck, August 23.
St. Paul, September 8.
Des Moines, September 13.
Boston, September 21.
Albany, September 15.
Buffalo, September 23.
Chicago, September 20.
Little Rock, October 22.
Atlanta, October 11.
Shreveport, October 28.
Charleston, November 17.
Jacksonville, November 12.
Mobile, October 31.
New Orleans, November 11.
Galveston, November 30.
San Antonio, November 9.

LATEST DATE OF KILLING FROST IN SPRING.

Edmonton, May 31. (Not much data available.)
Prince Albert, May 31. (Not much data available.)
Bismarck, June 7.
St. Paul, May 23.

Des Moines, May 31.
Boston, May 16.
Albany, May 30.
Buffalo, May 25.
Chicago, May 29.
Little Rock, April 26.
Atlanta, April 17.
Shreveport, March 27.
Charleston, April 2.
Jacksonville, April 6.
Mobile, April 6.
New Orleans, March 27.
Galveston, March 1.
San Antonio, March 27.

LENGTH OF THE CROP-GROWING SEASON.

	Days.
Edmonton (approximately)	114
Prince Albert (approximately)	114
Swift Current (approximately)	118
Winnipeg (approximately)	121
Bismarck	130
St. Paul	159
Des Moines	172
Boston	185
Albany	177
Buffalo	173
Chicago	183
Little Rock	240
Atlanta	225
Shreveport	252
Charleston	295
Jacksonville	298
Mobile	291
New Orleans	310
Galveston	331
San Antonio	276

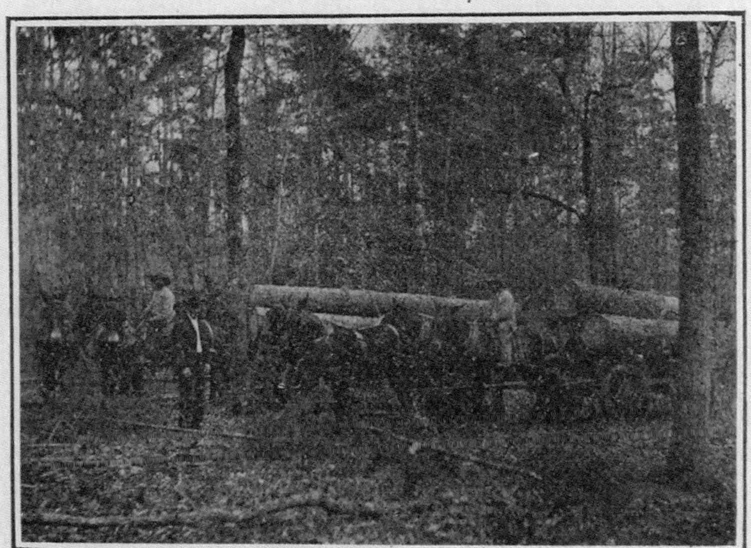

SCENE NEAR MANY, SABINE PARISH.

APPENDIX B.

Acreage, yield, and value of cotton grown by all farmers and by colored farmers, 1909.

Division and State.	Farms Reporting Cotton, 1910.											
	Number of farms.			Acreage in cotton.			Yield of cotton (bales).			Value of crops.		
	Total	Operated by colored farmers.		All farms.	Farms operated by colored farmers.		All farms. (bales)	Farms operated by colored farmers.		All farms	Farms operated by colored farmers.	
		Number	Per cent		Acreage	Per cent		Yield	Per cent		Value	Per cent
Southern States	1,706,767	684,721	4.01	31,946,142	12,096.638	52.7	10,594,360	4,065,978	38.4	$700,199,244	$269,868,346	32.4
South Atlantic	556,504	253,286	45.5	9,002,776	4,442,773	49.3	4,012,942	1,806,026	45.0	254,636,958	113,311,266	44.5
East South Central	522,735	266,450	51.0	7,926,019	4,614,339	58.2	2,524,714	1,356,813	53.7	175,543,582	95,717,387	54.5
West South Central	627,528	164,985	26.3	15,017,347	3,039,526	20.2	4,056,704	903,139	22.3	270,018,704	60,839,693	22.5
SOUTH ATLANTIC.												
Virginia	5,283	3,102	58.7	25,147	13,362	53.1	10,480	5,051	48.2	695,721	334,465	48.0
North Carolina	129,704	44,256	34.1	1,274,404	474,889	37.3	665,132	232,536	35.0	42,066,099	14,551,099	34.6
South Carolina	158,167	88,904	56.2	2,556,467	1,364,375	53.4	1,279,866	612,953	47.9	80,337,945	38,248,916	47.6
Georgia	242,673	108,115	44.6	4,883,304	2,468,242	50.5	1,992,408	927,162	46.5	126,695,612	58,195,483	45.9
Florida	20,677	8,909	43.1	263,454	121,905	46.3	65,056	28,324	43.5	4,841,581	1,981,303	40.9
EAST SOUTH CENTRAL.												
Kentucky	504	155	30.8	7,811	2,937	37.6	3,469	1,478	42.6	223,024	96,247	43.1
Tennessee	67,663	24,740	36.6	787,516	387,527	49.2	264,562	116,874	44.2	17,966,517	8,062,110	44.9
Alabama	224,871	100,506	44.7	3,730,482	1,960,709	52.6	1,129,527	510,465	45.2	74,205,236	33,261,538	44.8
Mississippi	229,697	141,049	61.4	3,400,210	2,263,166	66.6	1,127,156	727,996	64.6	83,148,805	54,297,492	65.3
WEST SOUTH CENTRAL.												
Arkansas	148,311	54,296	36.6	2,153,222	949,734	44.1	776,879	348,635	44.9	54,559,503	25,262,870	46.3
Louisiana	74,373	40,607	54.6	957,011	514,352	53.7	268,909	141,882	52.8	17,324,804	9,203,157	53.1
Oklahoma †	88,140	11,270	12.8	1,976,935	217,231	11.0	555,742	70,738	12.7	35,399,356	4,314,200	12.2
Texas	316,704	58,812	18.6	9,930,179	1,358,209	13.7	2,455,174	341,884	13.9	162,735,041	22,059,466	13.5

† A small percentage of the crop in Oklahoma was produced by Indians, who are included with negroes in the census classification "Colored."

APPENDIX C.

Table showing total yield of corn, oats, wheat, and hay in the 11 cotton States of Alabama, Arkansas, Florida, Georgia, Louisiana, Mississippi, North Carolina, Oklahoma, South Carolina, Tennessee, and Texas, for the years 1909-1915, inclusive.

Year	Bushels of corn.	Bushels of corn. †	Bushels of oats.	Bushels of wheat.	Tons of hay.
1909.....	461,536,000	291,755,000	51,847,000	28,622,000	3,108,000
1910.....	664,752,000	432,912,000	96,577,000	55,120,000	3,428,000
1911.....	539,136,000	432,898,000	65,506,000	34,619,000	2,611,000
1912.....	685,333,000	430,155,000	90,659,000	46,829,000	4,295,000
1913.....	658,252,000	442,802,000	97,237,000	51,009,000	4,214,000
1914.....	610,851,000	436,051,000	102,685,000	85,188,000	4,577,000
1915.....	812,883,000	513,908,000	157,714,000	88,842,000	6,269,000

† Total production of corn for States named above, other than Texas and Oklahoma.

APPENDIX D.

Yield per acre in bushels and 10-year averages for 15 Southern States.

CORN.

State.	10-year average.				1909	1910	1911	1912	1913	1914	1915†
	1870–1879	1880–1889	1890–1899	1900–1909							
Alabama	13.9	12.6	12.8	13.5	11.9	18.0	18.0	17.2	17.3	17.0	17.0
Arkansas........	24.4	19.8	18.2	18.7	14.8	24.0	20.8	20.4	19.0	17.5	23.0
Florida	10.2	9.6	9.7	10.2	11.6	13.0	14.6	13.0	15.0	16.0	15.0
Georgia.........	11.2	10.4	11.1	11.5	11.6	14.5	16.0	13.8	15.5	14.0	15.0
Kentucky	29.7	23.8	25.7	26.7	24.3	29.0	26.0	30.4	20.5	25.0	30.0
Louisiana.........	17.2	16.0	16.3	17.5	16.4	23.6	18.5	18.0	22.0	19.3	20.5
Maryland	25.2	24.2	27.0	32.7	27.7	33.5	36.5	36.5	33.0	37.0	35.0
Mississippi	15.4	14.3	15.0	15.2	13.1	20.5	19.0	18.3	20.0	18.5	19.0
North Carolina...	14.7	12.2	13.0	14.8	13.8	18.6	18.4	18.2	19.5	20.3	21.0
Oklahoma	.....	.....	.....	24.2	15.9	16.0	6.5	18.7	11.0	12.5	29.5
South Carolina...	9.4	9.4	9.9	11.6	13.3	18.5	18.2	17.9	19.5	18.5	16.5
Tennessee	24.2	20.5	22.0	23.0	21.5	25.9	26.8	26.5	20.5	24.0	27.0
Texas	21.7	18.1	19.0	19.0	14.7	20.6	9.5	21.0	24.0	19.5	23.5
Virginia	20.1	16.8	19.1	22.7	20.6	25.5	24.0	24.0	26.0	20.5	28.5
West Virginia....	28.3	23.4	24.4	27.5	25.3	26.0	25.7	33.8	31.0	31.0	31.5

† December, 1915, "Crop Reporter."

APPENDIX E.

TABLE I.—Mineral products of Southern States compared with United States, 1913-1915.

	1913	1914	1915
Southern States..................	$505,363,082	$467,044,946	$490,600,000
United States.....................	$2,439,159,728	$2,114,946,024	$2,373,280,000
Southern States, per cent of United States......................	21	22	20

In the above totals pig iron is used as the basis of iron valuation. (United States Geological Survey.)

TABLE II.—Mineral products of Southern States and United States, 1914 and 1915.

Product.	1914		1915	
	Southern States.	United States.	Southern States.	United States.
Cement	$13,434,833	$80,533,203	$12,796,395	$75,155,102
Coal (bituminous) †	155,464,036	493,300,244	155,860,000	504,500,000
Coke ‡	14,852,047	88,334,217	15,737,403	105,503,868
Copper	2,524,017	152,968,246	3,245,039	242,900,000
Iron:				
Ore ‡	7,252,338	71,905,079	8,308,548	101,288,984
Pig	27,398,597	298,777,429	36,970,059	401,409,604
Lead	15,633,268	39,997,932	20,529,619	47,660,000
Petroleum	104,051,228	214,125,215	88,000,000	172,000,000
Phosphate rock	9,592,553	9,608,041	5,400,836	5,413,449
Zinc	13,416,185	35,028,636	42,734,129	113,617,500
All other minerals	125,530,229	790,598,078	125,064,000	810,624,000
Total	467,044,946	2,114,946,024	490,600,000	2,373,280,000

† Exclusive of Pennsylvania anthracite.

‡ Value not included in total value, as such inclusion would duplicate coal and pig iron values.

TABLE III.—Mineral products of Southern States by States, 1913 to 1915.

State.	1913	1914	1915
Alabama	$34,660,545	$30,879,288	$29,500,000
Arkansas	6,780,760	5,785,199	6,580,000
Florida	10,508,016	8,497,688	4,863,000
Georgia	6,525,792	5,695,084	5,354,000
Kentucky	26,845,579	26,668,474	27,460,000
Louisiana	21,011,828	21,89[illegible],025	18,650,000
Maryland	11,292,723	10,587,564	10,570,000
Mississippi	1,143,472	1,104,197	662,000
Missouri	54,001,088	48,597,593	74,500,000
North Carolina	3,739,696	3,519,245	3,458,000
Oklahoma	80,168,820	78,744,447	72,400,000
South Carolina	1,464,150	1,414,294	1,010,000
Tennessee	21,008,938	19,615,213	22,175,000
Texas	31,666,910	30,363,426	29,157,000
Virginia	17,178,580	16,400,347	16,895,000
West Virginia	143,591,272	134,071,803	134,100,000

In the above States totals iron ore is used as the basis of iron valuation. (United States Geological Survey.)

APPENDIX F.

Manufacturers' Record,
Baltimore, June 28, 1916.

Hon. Joseph E. Ransdell,
United States Senate, Washington, D. C.

My Dear Senator Ransdell: As I understand you intend to make an address shortly touching on the agricultural development of the South, permit me to call your attention to a few facts that bear directly on the agricultural prosperity of this section and the general prosperity of the Nation.

Until the people of the whole country come to realize that the South is the Nation's greatest undeveloped asset they will never fully realize how its development will enrich the Nation and how everything that helps to advance the progress of the South safeguards the business interests as well as the actual life of the Nation.

In this section, where iron ore and coal are in vast abundance, furnishing unsurpassed advantages for the production of iron and steel, and all of the products of iron and steel, which produces three-fourths of the sulphur of the world, and which has many other natural advantages unequaled in this or in any other country, industrial development is limited as compared with that of other sections.

There are many reasons for this, and one of them is that the Nation as a whole has concentrated its thought and energy, through Government circles and in other ways, upon the development of the North and the West to the exclusion of the South. Let me illustrate:

Over 90 per cent of the steel made in the United States is made out of ores that are mined in the Lake Superior district, immediately contiguous to Canada, a region which could easily be overrun and captured at any moment by an enemy assailing us through Canada. But more than that, these ores to the extent of more than 50,000,000 tons a year pass through the Soo Canal, only about one and one-quarter miles long. I am reliably informed by some of the best engineers in the country that two or three sticks of dynamite could be exploded in such a way as to completely block this canal. Instantaneously, the entire iron and steel industry of the country to the extent of 90 per cent of our output would collapse. A few million tons of foreign ores are imported, and, of course, all importations of ore would be instantaneously shut off by war unless we had the complete command of the sea, and that is hardly possible any time in the near future.

We are thus staking the business interests of the country and national life itself upon one ore supply, the capture of which or the blocking of the canal through which the ore passes, would make impossible the production of armor plate or of munitions of war. Along the Atlantic coast, say from Boston to Newport News, stretching back anywhere from 10 to 100 miles, but covering in the aggregate probably not over 2 per cent or 3 per cent of the Nation's area, is centered the entire munition-making business of the United States. All of this munition-making business would have to be instantaneously stopped if the Lake Superior ore supply were cut off by capture of the district or by the blocking of the Soo Canal. In such an event any effort to oppose invasion would be useless, and any army or naval officer familiar with the situation will confirm this statement.

This mighty Nation—mighty in population and in wealth—would under such conditions be as helpless as an infant against a giant. The South is the only section of the country which can possibly provide a remedy for this situation. In the South and Southwest, back of the mountain ranges which would afford protection against invasion, there are vast stores of iron ore and coal and manganese, lead, and zinc, and all other materials needed for the making of war supplies, explosives included. The South has about three-fifths of the Nation's coast line; it produces all of the Nation's cotton and more than one-fourth of the Nation's grain; but neither the Government nor the great financial and metallurgical leaders of the country have given heed to the supreme necessity of utilizing this situation by the development of great iron and steel and munition-making interests in the South and Southwest, far away from the coast and from the Lakes, and not dependent upon Lake Superior or foreign ores.

Until this is done all talk of preparedness is largely a visionary dream. I suggest, therefore, that you bring to the attention of the Senate and of the country this danger, which is so vital, and which can be removed in no other possible way than by the prompt development on a large scale of munition-making and kindred industries in the South and Southwest. To permit existing conditions in iron and steel and munition making to last any longer would be as criminal on the part of national legislation and on the part of our business men as would be the failure to enlarge our Navy and Army.

The South supplies every possible material for the making of explosives, the building of ships, the construction of armor, and the creation of great steel industries, all far from the dangers which confront these interests along the Atlantic coast or on the Lakes, dependent as they are upon supplies which could be cut off without a moment's warning.

I trust you will appeal to the patriotism of the Senate to study this situation and realize its danger before it is too late.

Sincerely yours, RICHARD H. EDMONDS, Editor.

APPENDIX G.

Public road mileages and cash expenditures in the Southern States, 1904, Office of Public Roads and Rural Engineering.

State.	Total mileage.	Improved mileage.	Total cash road and bridge expenditures in 1904.
Alabama	50,089	1,720	$378,040
Arkansas	36,445	236	681,934
Florida	17,374	886	437,184
Georgia	57,203	1,634	894,936
Kentucky	57,137	9,486	1,161,194
Louisiana	24,897	34	345,452
Maryland	16,773	1,570	873,470
Mississippi	38,698	149	339,699
Missouri	108,133	2,733	1,570,801
North Carolina	49,763	1,259	624,381
Oklahoma	43,554	....	447,320
South Carolina	41,830	1,878	334,082
Tennessee	48,989	4,285	729,232
Texas	121,409	2,128	2,543,613
Virginia	51,812	1,600	687,751
West Virginia	26,178	255	587,870
Total	790,284	29,853	12,636,959

Per cent improved 3. 8
Cash expenditure per mile of road $16
For the entire United States:
Per cent improved 7. 1
Cash expenditure per mile of road $28

Public road mileage and cash expenditures in the Southern States, 1914.
(Data approximate.)

OFFICE OF PUBLIC ROADS AND RURAL ENGINEERING.

State.	Total mileage.	Surfaced mileage.	Total cash road and bridge expenditures in 1914.
Alabama	57,895	6,295	$3,125,925
Arkansas	47,485	5,095	2,447,368
Florida	17,607	3,246	3,450,000
Georgia	95,926	12,657	2,500,000
Kentucky	63,510	12,063	1,718,000
Louisiana	24,962	1,000	4,461,506
Maryland	16,459	2,482	6,997,458
Mississippi	44,072	1,800	2,850,000
Missouri	120,000	8,000	8,277,253
North Carolina	50,958	6,223	3,925,000
Oklahoma	107,736	500	3,375,000
South Carolina	47,787	4,513	1,000,000
Tennessee	45,913	5,554	2,500,000
Texas	128,971	9,790	8,750,000
Virginia	53,366	3,568	3,915,446
West Virginia	32,024	1,369	2,388,000
Total	954,671	84,155	61,680,956

Per cent improved 8.9
Cash expenditures per mile of road $64
For the entire United States:
Per cent improved 10.9
Cash expenditure per mile $100

THE PARISHES OF LOUISIANA

THE STATE OF LOUISIANA is divided into sixty-four parishes, or counties, the word "parishes" being strictly a localism and has exactly the same meaning as county. Of these sixty-four parishes, fifty-five are reached by navigable streams, which are open nearly all of the year, and furnish means of transportation by this cheapest of all methods. They also create great competition among the railroad lines, and thus it is that Louisiana enjoys unusually low freight rates. These parishes are naturally divided into certain classes, which classification is based on the character of soil found in different sections of the State. Starting with the north Louisiana parishes, we find the first great agricultural division known as the Good Uplands. These lands are from 300 to 500 feet above the level of the sea. The soil is gray or yellow sandy loam, and very fertile. It washes easily, however, unless cultivated by horizontal plowing or embankments. The subsoil is a deep, sandy clay, and retains fertilizers well. Under this classification we find the parishes of Caddo, DeSoto, Sabine, Bossier, Webster, Red River, Claiborne, Bienville, Union, Jackson, Ouachita, Morehouse, and parts of Caldwell and East and West Feliciana.

The red lands are on high ridges, but are very tenacious, and are not easily washed. They are very fine cotton and corn lands, but are especially adapted to small grain. The natural forest growth of these lands are oaks of different varieties, dogwood, beech, sassafras, gum, ash, maple and short-leaf pine. Most of the parishes placed under this head are of heavy alluvial land bordering on the streams which intersect them.

The alluvial region comprises the most fertile agricultural lands of the State. They are those parishes which border on the Mississippi River, the Red River, the Ouachita, and their tributaries, the Gulf Coast and lakes. This region occupies about 18,000 square miles, and its vast possibilities are inconceivable.

ALL THE PARISHES were requested to write their own descriptions, but only a few responded, and hence a general outline of the locations and characteristics of the others are all that can be presented.

Below will be found the assessments for 1910, given in alphabetical order, followed by the populations as given by the United States Census of that year:

TOTAL ASSESSMENT STATE OF LOUISIANA FOR THE YEAR 1910.

Parishes—	
Acadia	$ 7,419,900
Ascension	4,150,613
Assumption	3,738,250
Avoyelles	4,641,320
Bienville	4,108,282
Bossier	3,406,449
Caddo	20,457,065
Calcasieu	29,907,880
Caldwell	1,820,340
Cameron	1,395,640
Catahoula	2,108,045
Claiborne	2,530,460
Concordia	2,009,540
DeSoto	4,193,570
East Baton Rouge	8,921,161
East Carroll	1,918,620
East Feliciana	2,499,908
Franklin	2,783,156
Grant	4,148,648
Iberia	7,669,228
Iberville	4,442,192
Jackson	2,259,036
Jefferson	5,682,378
Lafayette	5,564,105
Lafourche	4,966,770
LaSalle	3,731,926
Lincoln	2,656,601
Livingston	3,095,920
Madison	2,779,560
Morehouse	3,944,560
Natchitoches	7,344,570
Orleans	231,045,937

Parishes—	
Ouachita	7,811,155
Plaquemines	2,555,235
Pointe Coupee	3,093,523
Rapides	10,695,730
Red River	1,510,491
Richland	2,914,325
Sabine	3,939,580
St. Bernard	3,661,121
St. Charles	2,980,676
St. Helena	1,381,265
St. James	4,964,790
St. John	3,554,703
St. Landry	11,195,820
St. Martin	3,720,570
St. Mary	7,959,245
St. Tammany	5,985,950
Tangipahoa	8,558,290
Tensas	2,087,590
Terrebonne	4,927,981
Union	2,704,275
Vermilion	4,873,970
Vernon	10,182,820
Washington	4,544,870
Webster	3,393,263
West Baton Rouge	2,251,861
West Carroll	1,935,900
West Feliciana	2,044,961
Winn	5,002,360
Grand total	$527,773,950

POPULATION OF PARISHES.

The population of the State of Louisiana is 1,656,388, as compared with 1,381,625 in 1900, and 1, 118,587 in 1890. The increase from 1900 to 1910, therefore, is 274,763, or 19.9 per cent, as compared with an increase for the preceding decade of 263,038, or 23.5 per cent.

The distribution of the population of the State by parishes is shown by the following table:

	1910	1900	1890
The State	1,656,388	1,381,625	1,118,587
Parishes—			
Acadia	31,847	23,483	13,231
Ascension	23,887	24,142	19,545
Assumption	24,128	21,620	19,629
Avoyelles	34,102	29,701	25,112
Bienville	21,776	17,588	14,108
Bossier	21,738	24,153	20,330
Caddo	58,200	44,499	31,555
Calcasieu	62,767	30,428	20,176
Caldwell	8,593	6,917	5,814
Cameron	4,288	3,952	2,828

	1910	1900	1890
Catahoula	10,415	16,351	12,002
Claiborne	25,050	23,029	23,312
Concordia	14,278	13,559	14,871
DeSoto	27,689	25,063	19,860
East Baton Rouge	34,580	31,153	25,922
East Carroll	11,637	11,373	12,362
East Feliciana	20,055	20,443	17,903
Franklin	11,989	8,890	6,900
Grant	15,958	12,902	8,270
Iberia	31,262	29,015	20,997
Iberville	30,954	27,006	21,848
Jackson	13,818	9,119	7,453
Jefferson	18,247	15,321	13,221
LaSalle	9,402	.....	.....
Lafayette	28,733	22,825	15,966
Lafourche	33,111	28,882	22,095
Lincoln	18,485	15,898	14,753
Livingston	10,627	8,100	5,769
Madison	10,676	12,322	14,135
Morehouse	18,786	16,634	16,786
Natchitoches	36,455	33,216	25,836
Orleans	339,075	287,104	242,039
Ouachita	25,830	20,947	17,985
Plaquemines	12,524	13,039	12,541
Pointe Coupee	25,289	25,777	19,613
Rapides	44,545	39,578	27,642
Red River	11,402	11,548	11,318
Richland	15,769	11,116	10,230
Sabine	19,874	15,421	9,390
St. Bernard	5,277	5,031	4,326
St. Charles	11,207	9,072	7,737
St. Helena	9,172	8,479	8,062
St. James	23,009	20,197	15,715
St. John the Baptist	14,338	12,330	11,359
St. Landry	66,661	52,906	40,250
St. Martin	23,070	18,940	14,884
St. Mary	39,368	34,145	22,416
St. Tammany	18,917	13,335	10,160
Tangipahoa	29,160	17,625	12,655
Tensas	17,060	19,070	16,647
Terrebonne	28,320	24,464	20,167
Union	20,451	18,520	17,304
Vermilion	26,390	20,705	14,234
Vernon	17,384	10,327	5,903
Washington	18,886	9,628	6,700
Webster	19,186	15,125	12,466
West Baton Rouge	12,636	10,285	8,363
West Carroll	6,249	3,685	3,748
West Feliciana	13,449	15,994	15,062
Winn	18,357	9,648	7,082

ESTIMATED POPULATION FOR 1916.

	Estimated Population July 1, 1916.
Louisiana	1,829,130
Acadia	37,106
†Ascension	23,887
Assumption	25,705
Avoyelles	36,869
Bienville	24,409
†Bossier	21,738
Caddo	66,812
‡Calcasieu	83,098
Caldwell	9,646
Cameron	4,500
¶Catahoula	21,997
Claiborne	26,320
Concordia	14,730
De Soto	29,340
East Baton Rouge	36,735
East Carroll	11,804
†East Feliciana	20,055
Franklin	13,937
Grant	17,878
Iberia	32,673
Iberville	33,436
Jackson	16,772
Jefferson	20,086
¶La Salle	......
Lafayette	32,447
Lafourche	35,769
Lincoln	20,113
Livingston	12,215
†Madison	10,676
Morehouse	20,139
Natchitoches	38,492
Orleans	371,747
Ouachita	28,899
†Plaquemines	12,524
†Pointe Coupee	25,289
Rapides	47,669
†Red River	11,402
Richland	18,694
Sabine	22,675
St Bernard	5,433
St. Charles	12,549
St. Helena	9,608
St. James	24,776
St. John the Baptist	15,598
§St. Landry	75,309
St. Martin	25,665
St. Mary	42,652
St. Tammany	22,425
Tangipahoa	36,411
†Tensas	17,060
Terrebonne	30,742

	Estimated Population July 1, 1916.
Union	21,664
Vermilion	29,962
Vernon	21,819
Washington	24,705
Webster	21,738
West Baton Rouge	14,114
West Carroll	7,860
†West Feliciana	13,449
Winn	23,832

† Population April 15, 1910. Decrease since 1900; no estimate made.

‡ Includes population of Allen, Beauregard and Jefferson Davis parishes, organized from parts of Calcasieu in 1913. Impossible to estimate.

¶ LaSalle Parish organized from part of Catahoula Parish in 1910. Population included with that of Catahoula; no estimate made.

§ Includes population of Evangeline Parish, organized from part of St. Landry Parish in 1911; no estimate made.

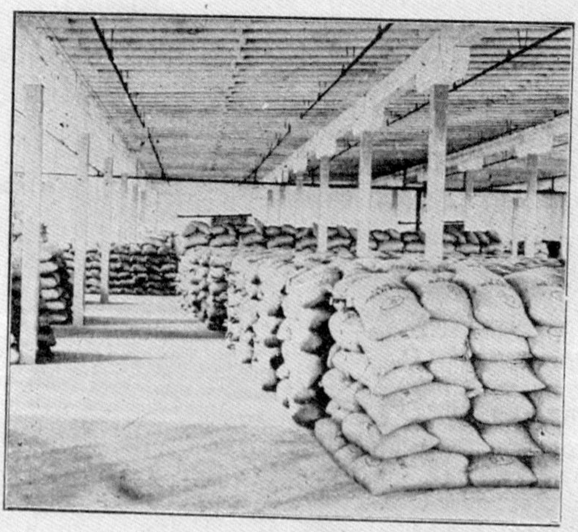

RICE IN A WAREHOUSE.

ACADIA PARISH.

Acadia Parish is situated in the southwestern part of the State, and contains 394,240 acres of land.

The formation is prairie; soil fertile and productive. It is drained by Bayou Nezique to the west, and Queue de Tortue on the south, and through its central portions by Bayous Cannes and Plaquemines Brulee.

Water is plentiful and good throughout the parish.

Oil has been discovered in paying quantities. The Mamou field has furnished several gushers of considerable magnitude.

The Southern Pacific Railroad and branches pass through the parish; Crowley, situated on this line, is the parish seat, and one of the most prosperous cities of the State.

Rice and sugar are the principal crop productions. The largest rice producing parish in the State; corn, cotton, hay, oats, sweet and Irish potatoes, and cowpeas are also produced.

The fruits and nuts are the orange, grape, pear, prune, peach, fig, pomegranate and pecan. Timber is found along the bayous and coulees, suitable for building and fencing, embracing the varieties of oak, cypress, cottonwood, elm, gum, ash, sugarwood, sycamore, persimmon and willow. The raising of live stock is a profitable industry, and sheep, cattle, horses and hogs thrive and increase remarkably well here; many of the farmers being largely interested in wool growing.

Game is found, such as rice birds, partridges, plovers, becasine and jacksnipe, and papabot and doves.

ALLEN PARISH.

A southwestern parish; contains 478,510 acres. Principal agricultural products are rice, cotton, corn and sweet potatoes, etc. Stock is much improved. Dipping vats one of the greatest causes of improvement. Hogs, too, with cholera serum available, are becoming quite an industry. Lumber a great industry; four large sawmills at Oakdale. Schools in fine condition; four high schools; one has a commercial and three domestic science departments; one an agricultural and one a manual training department—between 3,500 and 4,000 pupils, one school with 21 teachers has already enrolled 700. Buildings are nearly all new, three brick and modern. Both Catholic and protestant churches in the parish. One ward just voted $150,000.00 for a gravel road. The fruits are peaches, pears, a few apples and Satsuma oranges. There are corn, pig and poultry clubs.

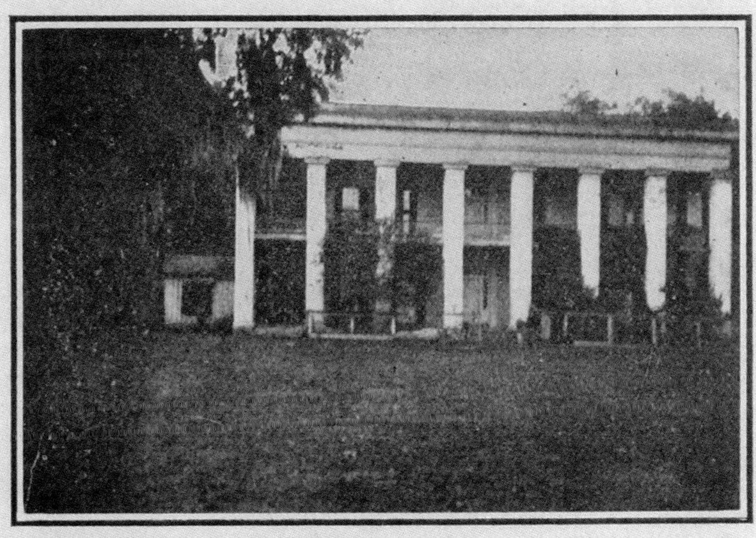

THE OLD HOME OF DUNCAN F. KENNER.

ASCENSION PARISH.

This parish, in the southeastern part of Louisiana, about forty miles northwest of New Orleans, with a population of about 28,000, is unequally bisected by the Mississippi, that section east of the river being larger.

Climatic and health conditions are excellent. Its level, incomparably fertile land, protected by a perfect levee system, is intersected by good roads.

The railroads of the Yazoo & Mississippi Valley, the Louisiana Railway & Navigation Company and the Frisco lines over the same road, on the east bank—on the west the Texas & Pacific, with its two branches, together with the Mississippi and Amite Rivers, transport her products to the great markets. Two privately owned roads enable many farmers of the eastern section to ship cane to the factories of the railroad owners.

The chief product is cane, converted by six factories into sugar, which averages 160 pounds to the ton.

Rice is extensively grown, yielding about fourteen bags to the acre.

The rental system obtains partly.

Corn and hay are raised for home use.

Cotton, once the principal crop of the New River and Brusle sections, has, because of the boll weevil, given place to cane, corn and hogs. Stock does well, but is not extensively raised. The mild climate and variety of forage plants should promote a large dairy industry. Two crops of many vegetables may be grown the same year. Blackberries and figs abound. Trucking and canning will pay farmers and promoters when organized according to western methods.

Loquat and Kumquat oranges, Japanese persimmons and quinces and certain varieties of peaches and pears thrive if tended.

Poultry thrives, and the industry is capable of indefinite expansion.

Shrimp abound and would justify canneries.

One immense sawmill and six smaller ones convert into lumber the hardwoods, cypress, oak, ash and gum.

Catfish, buffalo, sardines, trout, bream, bass, perch and sacalait swim in river and stream—deer, quail, plover, snipe, dove, papabotte and poule d'eau run in field and forest.

Donaldsonville, fronting the Mississippi, is the parish seat. Her mercantile business is large.

ASSUMPTION PARISH.

This parish is situated in the southern part of the State, and contains 227,200 acres of land. The formation is composed of alluvial land and wooded swamp; soil rich and highly productive.

It is drained by Bayous Lafourche, Grant and Vincent, and Grand River and Grand Lake.

The Southern Pacific (main line) runs through its extreme southern sections, and has a branch line, running from Napoleonville, south, connecting with the main line at Schriever Junction. The Texas and Pacific Railway also has a branch line, traversing the parish north and south, along the east bank of Bayou Lafourche, connecting with the main line at Donaldsonville.

Napoleonville, cituated on Bayou Lafourche, is the parish seat.

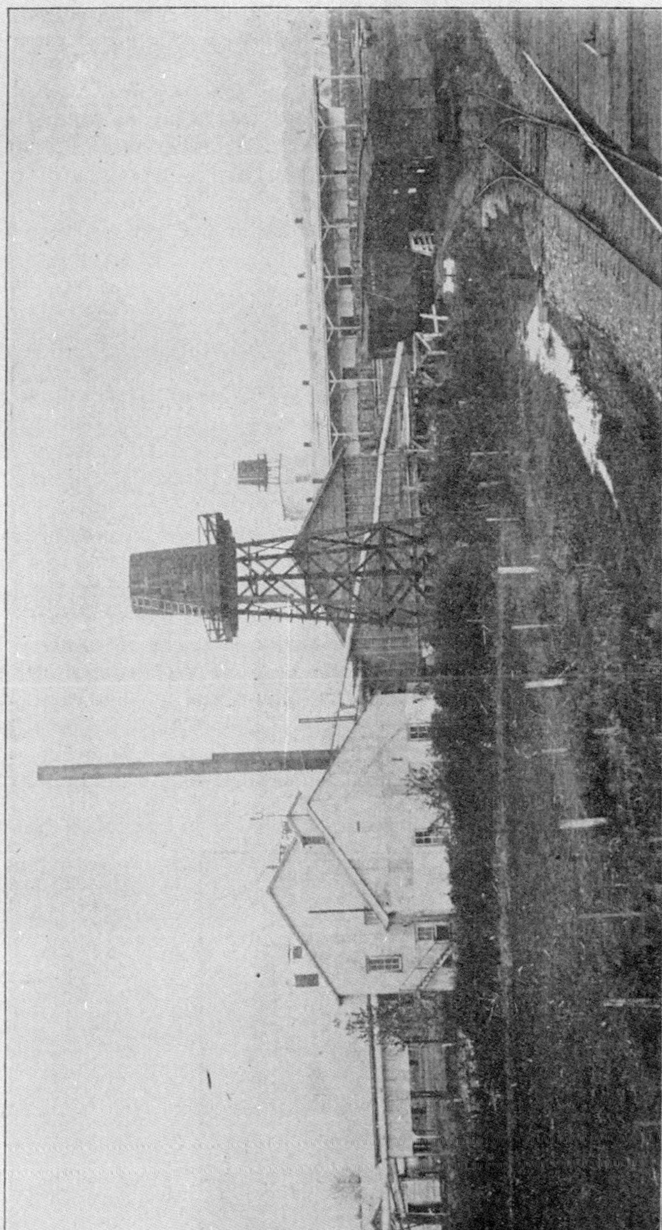

COTTON COMPRESS AT LAFAYETTE

Sugar is the chief crop, and rice, corn, hay, oats, sweet and Irish potatoes, peas, tobacco and the garden varieties are produced. The fruits and nuts are the orange, fig, pear, plum, peach, persimmon, pomegranate and grape, pecans and English walnuts.

The timber is chiefly cypress, oak, gum and persimmon, with some cottonwood, willow and sycamore. Some live stock is raised, mostly cattle and hogs. There is such game as partridges, rice birds, plovers, snipe and becasine, coons, opossums, mink and squirrels; also, in season, wild ducks, wild geese and woodcock.

The bayous and lakes furnish varieties of fish, among them trout, black bass, and white perch.

AVOYELLES PARISH.

Avoyelles Parish is situated near the central part of the State, and contains 539,520 acres of land.

The formation is of several varieties; alluvial land, prairie, bluff land and wooded swamp, the latter predominating. The soil is fertile and productive. It is drained by the Red, Saline and Atchafalaya Rivers, and Bayous Long, Natchitoches, Avoyelles, Des Glaizes and Rouge.

Water is plentiful and of good quality.

The main line of the Texas and Pacific Railroad passes through its southwestern section, and has two branch lines traversing the parish east and west and a portion of the northern central part of the parish. The Louisiana Railway and Navigation Company's line crosses the parish from northeast to southwest. Marksville is the parish seat.

The products are chiefly cotton and corn; sugar cane, alfalfa, oats, hay, peas, sweet and Irish potatoes, sorghum and garden varieties are also produced.

The fruits and nuts succeed well here, such as peaches, pears, pecans, apples, figs, plums, quinces, grapes, pomegranates, persimmons and the smaller kinds.

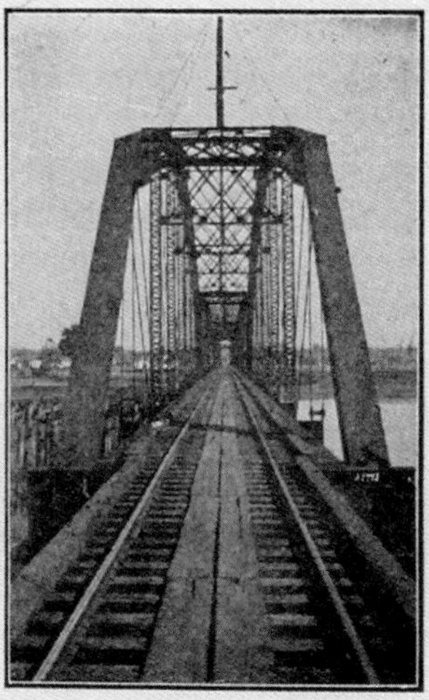

TEXAS & PACIFIC BRIDGE ACROSS THE ATCHAFALAYA.

The live stock industry is profitable and cattle, sheep, hogs, horses and mules are raised in abundance.

Game is plentiful, such as bear, deer, foxes, coons, opossums, squirrels, rabbits and wild turkeys, partridges, rice birds, robins, snipe, woodcock, wild ducks, wild geese, pheasants and plovers. Fish of excellent quality and large quantities abound in the lakes and streams. The timber of this parish is very extensive, comprising oak, ash, cypress, gum, elm, cottonwood, poplar, pine, locust beech, maple, hickory, holly, magnolia, walnut, hackberry, sycamore, persimmon and willow.

BEAUREGARD PARISH.

One of the new parishes, in southwestern Louisiana, with 732,000 acres. Corn is the principal agricultural product, but cotton and potatoes are also produced.

Stock raising, that was once upon the old range system, is giving away and high grades are developing much interest. Besides cattle, horses, mules, hogs and sheep are being raised. Lumber is still the greatest industry of the parish. Twelve large sawmills with an output of from 50,000 to 300,000 feet per day are in operation.

The experimental farm at Bon Ami is a great aid in the development of fruit culture. Figs and oranges do well. A farm demonstrator is doing good work, especially in corn and pig clubs, while a lady is developing the home clubs—poultry, canning, etc.

There are two high schools with agricultural and domestic science departments, besides four other five-room schools that teach domestic science.

Churches of different denominations throughout the parish.

Great interest developing in good roads. A recent vote of 3 to 1 majority has ordered a $500,000 bond issue for road purposes.

BIENVILLE PARISH.

This parish is situated in the northwestern part of the State and contains 547,840 acres of land. Its formation is good upland, red, sandy clays, the soil being fertile and productive.

It is drained by Lake Bisteneau on the west, and by Bayous Blacklake, Saline, and the headwaters of the Dugdemona River in other sections.

The Vicksburg, Shreveport and Pacific Railroad passes through the northern portion of the parish. The Louisiana and Northwestern Railroad runs north and south, from Gibsland, on the Vicksburg, Shreveport and Pacific Railroad, connecting on the north with the Cotton Belt, and on the south with the Texas & Pacific and the Louisiana Railway and Navigation Company.

Water is abundant and good. Many springs, creeks and branches.

Arcadia, situated on the Vicksburg, Shreveport and Pacific Railroad, is the parish seat, and has a cotton compress, cotton oil mill, ice factory, electric light plant and other industries.

The timber is oak, pine, ash, cypress, persimmon, gum, beech, elm, holly, hickory, sycamore, poplar and cottonwood.

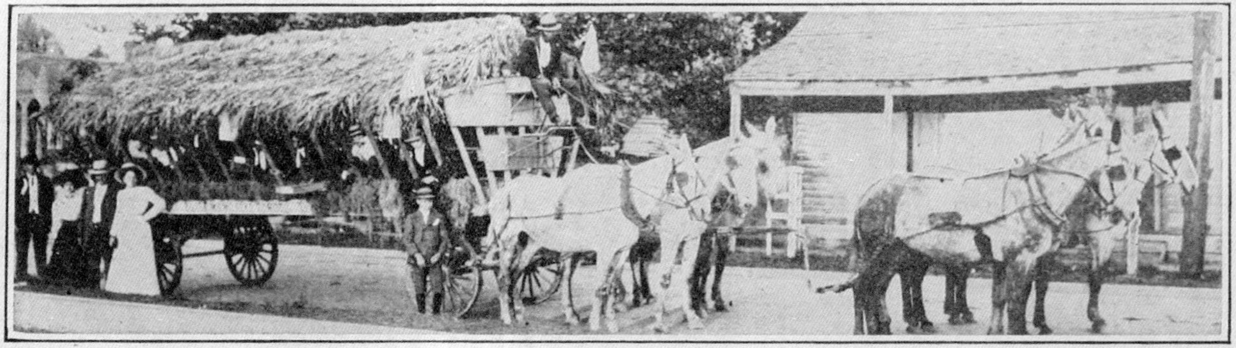

SCHOOL CHILDREN OFF FOR A PICNIC.

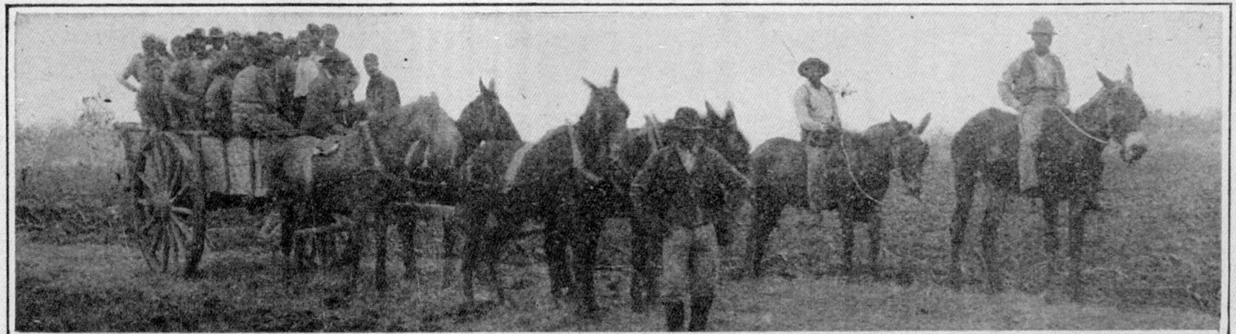

GOING IN TO DINNER ON A SUGAR PLANTATION.

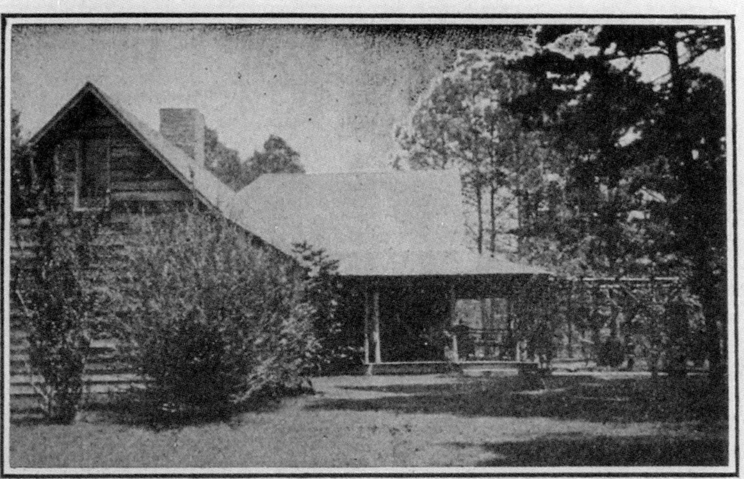

A FARMER'S BUNGALOW IN NORTH LOUISIANA.

Cotton is the chief crop product; corn, hay, oats, peas, sugar cane, sweet and Irish potatoes, sorghum and the garden vegetables all do well. A diversified farming section.

The fruits and nuts are apples, pears, peaches, pecans, plums, quinces, grapes and figs.

Cattle, hogs, sheep and horses are raised and thrive well.

Game is found, such as deer, coons, opossums, foxes, squirrels, rabbits, mink, wild turkeys, wild ducks and geese, partridges, snipe, and woodcock. Fish of good quality are found in the lakes and streams, among them bar fish, trout, bass and perch. There are deposits of salt, fireclay, potters' clay, marl and green sand.

BOSSIER PARISH.

Bossier parish is located in the northwest corner of the State. Along Red River there is a belt of alluvial bottom lands, consisting of 120,000 acres; back from the river lie the rolling hill lands amounting to 385,000 acres.

Good water is found at a depth of from 20 to 80 feet, and there are springs throughout the hills.

This section of the country is equal for truck, fruit and other farming to many of the more widely advertised parts of the South; such pasture grasses as Bermuda grass, Carpet grass, Japan clover, etc., make live stock a profitable industry.

The great attraction this section has for the northern farmer is the climate; it is practicable to farm eleven months in the year; freezing weather will not occur more than twenty or thirty days in the winter season, nor last more than a day or two at a time.

Good material for the building of roadways, a disintegrated iron rock, is abundant, and some very satisfactory results have been attained.

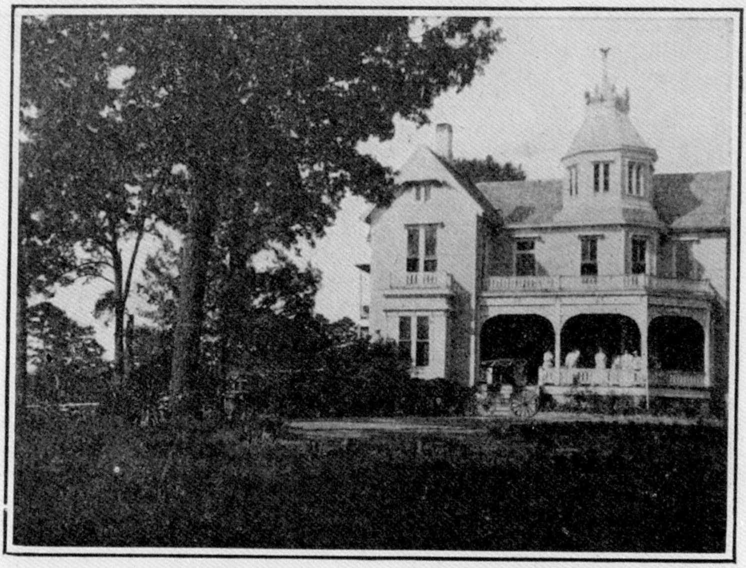

A FARM HOUSE IN BOSSIER PARISH.

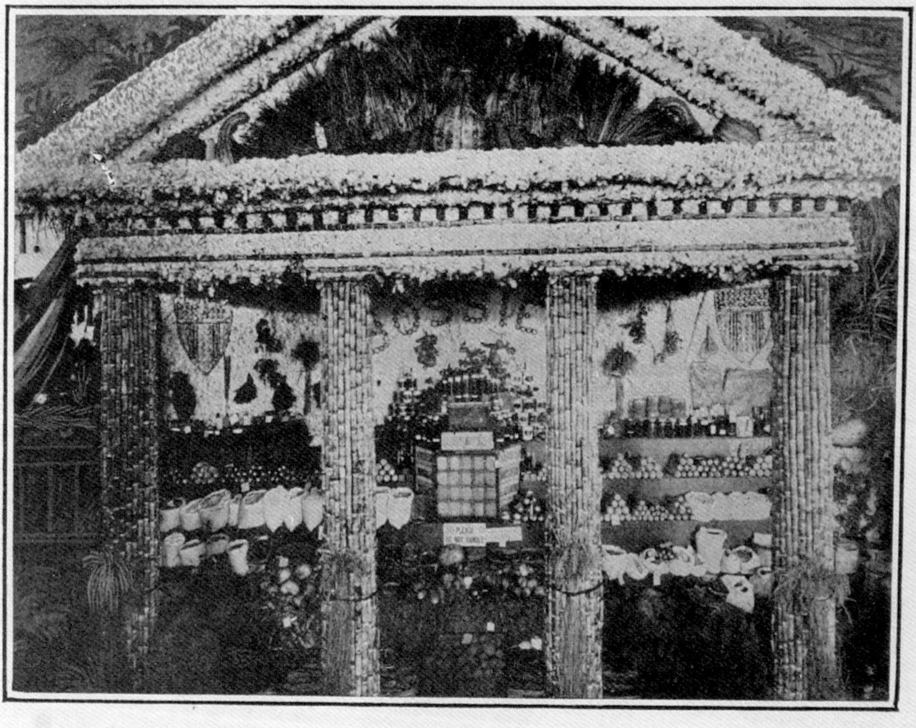

A BOSSIER PARISH EXHIBIT.

Schools consisting of the usual primary and high school grades are conveniently located throughout the parish.

Churches of all the different denominations are represented both in town and country.

Agriculture is the main occupation of the people; cotton, corn and hay are the staple crops.

Alfalfa grows luxuriantly in the bottom lands, and is a finer quality than that of the North or West, producing about four tons to the acre.

Oats are a paying crop in this section, when planted in the fall affording a fine winter pasture, and are ready to harvest the last of May.

The early production of truck for the northern markets has been found profitable.

All fruits and nuts of standard and semi-tropical type grow in abundance.

CADDO PARISH.

Caddo is located in the extreme northwest corner of the State. The parish has an area of 545,280 acres of land, which is characterized as upland and alluvial.

Shreveport is a city of 30,000 souls. The city as a whole is supported by the surrounding fertile lands and the lumber industry, though the gas and oil business is a rapidly increasing feature of the city's commercial life.

Comparison of the weather records of Shreveport, Fort Worth and Dallas will show that on unusually cold days it is from 5 to 10 degrees warmer in Shreveport, while during the hot weather the records here show a temperature 5 to 10 degrees cooler. Yet the Texas cities are practically on the same longitude as Shreveport and Caddo Parish.

Caddo is equipped with one of the best school systems in the State. Shreveport's school system is unexcelled, while in the country districts the parish is being redistricted and graded schools installed. School vans are furnished by the parish board to haul the children to and from school.

A movement is now on foot for better roads throughout the parish, while this will not only better the country schools but will enable the planters to bring their crops to market with much less expense.

In addition to its agricultural wealth Caddo also has one of the greatest oil fields in the South, and the greatest gas field in the world. Gas wells making 50,000,000 cubic feet of the best of all heating and illuminating gas are a matter of every day occurrence in the Caddo field. These are the things which Caddo can claim with all truth: Shreveport, one of the greatest cities of the State, whose death rate is the lowest in the entire nation. A city of excellent schools, of many churches, more paved streets than any other city of the same population in the United States. A city which is the home of the State Fair, a Charity Hospital (State institution), two orphan asylums, one Old Ladies' Home, five colleges, all church institutions, and two business colleges.

Caddo contains excellent cotton-producing soil, makes corn equal to any in the country, produces potatoes and other truck to an extent unexcelled by any other section of the South. Lands are cheap and the new homeseeker will find Caddo one of the best places on earth to which he may bring his family and an ambition to build a new home and a fortune.

CALCASIEU PARISH.

Its formation embraces prairie, pine hill, pine flat, coast marsh, and a little alluvial and wooded swamp land.

It is drained by Bayous Nezpique and the Sabine, Mermentau, and Calcasieu River, with its many tributary streams. Water is plentiful and of good quality.

The Southern Pacific, the St. Louis, Watkins and Gulf, and the Kansas City Southern Railroads traverse the parish. Lake Charles, situated on Lake Charles, is the parish seat.

The crop productions are principally rice and sugar, corn, cotton, sweet and Irish potatoes, peas, hay and oats; garden crops are also raised.

The fruits and nuts are the orange, grape, peach, pear, plum, pecan, guava, pomegranate, prune and fig.

The timber is pine, oak, gum, elm, sugarwood, cottonwood, willow, locust and persimmon. The lumber interests, long-leaf yellow pine, are extensive, and millions are here invested. Live stock raising is a profitable industry, and sheep, cattle, hogs and horses are extensively raised. Game is found, such as deer, foxes, coons, rabbits, squirrels, snipe, becasine, partridges, rice birds, plovers, robins, wild ducks and geese, woodcock, pheasants and papabotte. Fishing is good in the streams and lakes; bass, trout and carp are found.

Inexhaustive deposits of sulphur are found, and gypsum exists in great quantities. Petroleum oil of a high grade has been found in paying quantities.

CALDWELL PARISH.

This parish is situated in the north central part of the State, and contains 348,800 acres of land. Its formation is alluvial, pine hills and good uplands. Its physical outline or topographic features are very rugged and broken in the upland portions of the parish, but the soil is fertile and productive.

It is drained by the Ouachita and Boeuf Rivers, and Bayous Castor, Lafourche and Marengo.

The St. Louis, Iron Mountain and Southern Railway runs through the parish north and south. Columbia, situated on the Ouachita River, is the parish seat. Water is plentiful and of good quality. The timber consists of pine, oak, ash, beech, hickory, cottonwood, gum, elm, poplar, magnolia, locust, holly, maple, walnut, persimmon and willow. The principal crop is cotton; corn, oats, hay, peas, sweet and Irish potatoes, sorghum, sugar cane, tobacco and garden products are raised.

Live stock are raised, consisting of cattle, hogs and sheep, in large quantity. Game abounds, such as deer, foxes, coons, oppossums, squirrels, rabbits, wild turkeys, partridges, wild ducks, geese and woodcocks.

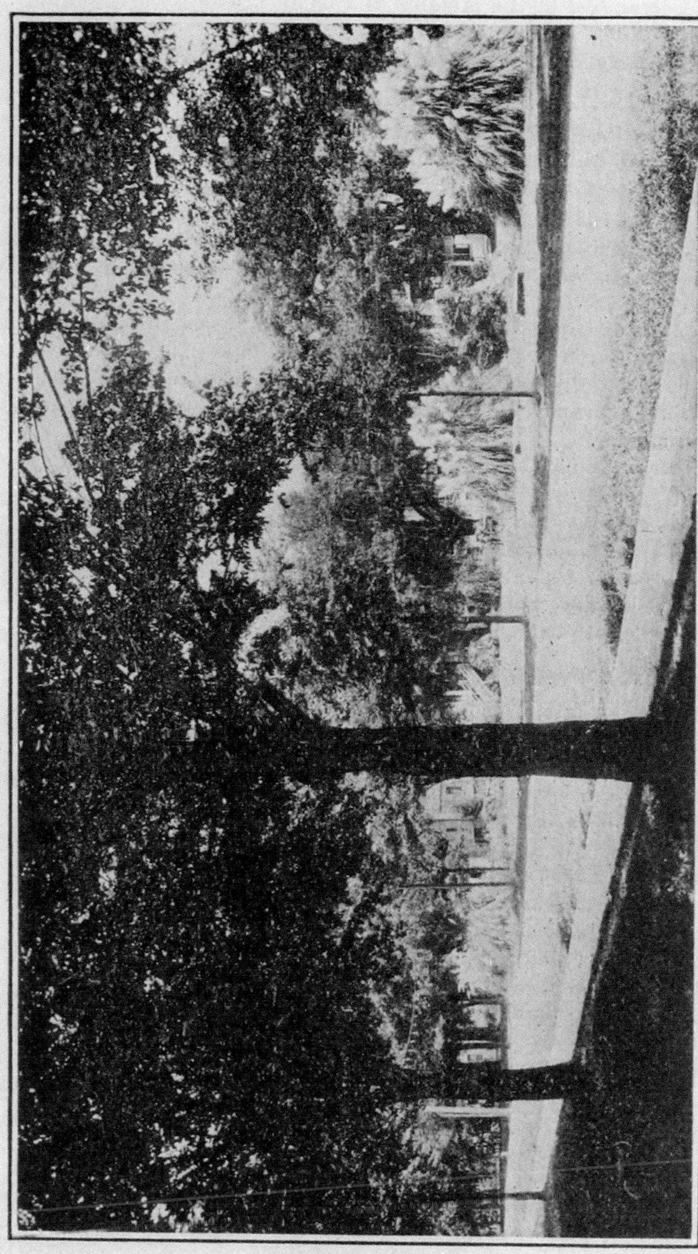

A LOUISIANA GOOD ROAD.

Fish are plentiful in the streams and bayous, where bass, bar fish and trout are found.

There are deposits of chalk, kaolin, fire clay, potters' clay, iron and marl in the parish.

CAMERON PARISH.

This parish is situated in the southwestern corner of the State, and contains 998,400 acres of land. The formation is largely coast marsh, with some prairie and alluvial land, the soil being extremely rich and highly productive. It is drained in part by the Mermentau, Calcasieu and Sabine Rivers. Lakes Sabine, Grand and Calcasieu lie in its confines.

The Kansas City, Watkins & Gulf Railroad passes through the parish. Cameron, situated at the mouth of Calcasieu Pass, is the parish seat.

Cistern water is chiefly used. The timber is cypress, oak and willow. The fruits are orange, lemon, olive, fig, grape, banana, guava, prune, plum and mandarin.

The crop productions are rice and sugar, while garden truck succeeds well.

Game, such as wild duck and geese, becasine, jack snipe, papabot and rice birds are abundant. Fishing is extensive and excellent; Sheepshead, red fish, pompano, salt water trout, Spanish mackerel, carp, shrimp and crabs abound, and the oyster and diamond-back terrapin exist in extensive quantities.

CATAHOULA PARISH.

This parish is situated near the central part of the State, and contained 864,000 acres of land before LaSalle was taken off. The formation is pine hills, wooded swamp, alluvial land, good upland and bluff land; the alluvial lands being very rich and productive, and the good uplands and bluff lands being of a superior quality and very fertile. The parish is drained by the Ouachita, Tensas, Black and Little Rivers, Bayous Louis, Saline and Castor, and Gastons, Fords, Brushley, Hemp Hill and Funny Louis Creeks. The New Orleans and Northwestern Railroad passes through the eastern portion of the parish, and the St. Louis, Iron Mountain and Southern Railroad through its northwestern corner. Harrisonburg, situated on the Ouachita River, is the parish seat. The water supply throughout the parish is abundant, and generally of good quality. There are valuable mineral waters at the White Sulphur Springs, the Castor Springs, Gaston's Creek, Harrisonburg and other points, of very superior qualities. There are deposits of kaolin, bauxite, limestone, grindstone, Ouachita limestone, flintstone, potters' clay, lignite, marl, green sand and iron.

The timber is very extensive and various, with pine in the lead; the other varieties being oak, cypress, ash, cottonwood, willow, maple, gum, elm, hickory, locust, mulberry, sassafras, maple, walnut, poplar, sycamore, holly, beech, magnolia and persimmon.

The fruits and nuts are peaches, pears, pecans, apples, plums, grapes, figs and quinces. The wild mahaw grows abundantly throughout the western portion of the parish, and this fruit has no superior, and, in fact, no equal, for jellying purposes, having a peculiar and delicate flavor possessed by no other fruit. A factory for preserving this fruit (which is allowed to waste and rot), in the form of jellies, would be a very paying investment. The bluff lands of Sicily Island are of superior quality. The chief crop product is cotton, while corn, oats, hay, sweet and Irish potatoes, tobacco, sorghum and sugar cane yield abundantly. The live stock are hogs, sheep and horses; a large industry being developed in raising hogs for shipment.

Game is found, such as deer, bear, foxes, coons, oppossum, squirrels, rabbits, wild turkeys, wild ducks and geese, partridges, robins, rice birds and woodcock. Fish are plentiful in the creeks, bayous and lakes; among them are found trout, bass, bar fish and white perch.

CLAIBORNE PARISH.

This parish is situated in the northwestern part of the State, and contains 497,920 acres of land. The formation is good uplands, red sandy clays, the soil being fertile and productive. It is drained by the headwaters of Bayou D'Arbonne and numerous small streams.

Homer, situated near the center, is the parish seat, and is on the line of the Louisiana and Northwestern Railroad. This railroad runs through the parish north and south, and has direct connections with the Cotton Belt, the Vicksburg, Shreveport and Pacific, the Louisiana Railway and Navigation Company, and the Texas and Pacific railroads. Water is plentiful and of excellent quality.

Cotton is the chief product; corn, oats, hay, peas, sweet and Irish potatoes, tobacco, hemp, wheat, buckwheat, sugar-cane and sorghum all yield good crops.

The fruits and nuts are peaches, apples, pears, plums, pecans, quinces, pomegranates and grapes. The soil and climate of this parish have been found especially adapted to peach growing, the fruit being very highly esteemed on the market for both its size and flavor.

The timber is oak, pine, poplar, hickory, beech, holly, elm, walnut, maple and locust. Live stock raised here are cattle, sheep, hogs and horses. Game is found, such as deer, coons, opossums, foxes, squirrels, rabbits, wild turkeys, partridges, woodcock and robins.

The streams are mostly small, but fine varieties of fish are found in their waters, among them trout, bar fish, perch, and blue and spotted cat.

Deposits of marl, green sand, potters' clay, fire clay, iron and lignite are found.

CONCORDIA PARISH.

This parish is situated in the east central part of the State, contains 425,000 acres of land. Its formation is alluvial land and wooded swamp; soil highly fertile and productive. It is drained by the Mississippi, Tensas, Black and Red Rivers.

Vidalia, on the Mississippi River, is the parish seat.

The New Orleans and Northwestern Railroad runs through the northeastern part of the parish, and there is also a line extending from Concordia Station to Trinity, on the Tensas River.

The timber is oak, cypress, ash, gum, elm, cottonwood, hackberry, persimmon and willow. The chief crop product is cotton, corn, rice, hay, oats, sweet and Irish potatoes, peas, sorghum, sugar cane and tobacco are raised. Live stock raised are chiefly cattle and hogs.

The fruits and nuts are pears, peaches, pecans, grapes, figs, apples and plums. Game abounds, such as deer, bear, coons, opossums, squirrels, rabbits, wild turkeys, wild ducks and geese, partridges and woodcock, also rice birds. Fish are plentiful in the lakes and rivers, among which are bass, blue cat, white perch and pike.

DE SOTO PARISH.

The Parish of De Soto is situated in the northwest part of the State, and contains 547,840 acres of land. The formation is chiefly good uplands, with a little alluvial land along the Sabine River and Bayou Pierre. It is drained by these two streams and their numerous small affluents. The soil is of good quality, fertile and productive.

The Texas and Pacific Railroad and the Shreveport and Houston, Kansas City Southern Railroads extend through the parish. Mansfield, situated near the center, is the parish seat. It is on the Kansas City Southern Railroad, and has a short tap line connecting it with the Texas and Pacific Railroad. Water is abundant and of good quality.

The chief product is cotton; corn, hay, oats, sweet and Irish potatoes, peas, sorghum, tobacco and sugar cane all thrive well. The fruits are peaches, pears, apples, plums, figs, pomegranates, quinces and grapes.

The timber is chiefly pine, oak, poplar, beech, holly, gum, magnolia, elm, maple, locust, mulberry, hickory, and some walnut is found.

Game, such as deer, coons, opossums, foxes, rabbits, squirrels, wild turkeys, partridges, wild ducks, wild geese, woodcock and rice birds are found. Fish of various kinds abound in the streams and lakes. Live stock raised are cattle, hogs, sheep, and some horses. Deposits of potters' clay, fire clay, kaolin, iron, marl and green sand are found; also extensive beds of lignite, producing a high grade coal. The commercial value of these beds has only been recently demonstrated, and in the opinion of experts the quality and extent of the deposits promise to make this industry quite an important factor in the development of north Louisiana.

Among her great assets of today are the gas and oil wells.

EAST BATON ROUGE.

The Parish of East Baton Rouge, area 272,000 acres, fronts on the Mississippi River, 130 miles above New Orleans.

The city of Baton Rouge, eighty miles from New Orleans by rail, is the parish seat and the capital of the State, and is built on the extreme southern point of bluff land that touches the Mississippi River.

The lands along the Mississippi River south of Baton Rouge are alluvial, of which about one-third are in cultivation, the remainder being pasturage and woodland. The timber found here is principally cypress, gum, oak, and many small varieties of trees. The other portion, about nine-tenths, of the parish, called the highlands or bluff, is not subject to inundation by the Mississippi River. The forest growth is of great variety, comprising all kinds of oak, gum, magnolia, poplar and beech, interspersed with much undergrowth. The soil is as various as the forest growth, ranging from poor to very fertile; but under the energetic manipulation of the progressive farmer will yield a rich reward to the husbandman.

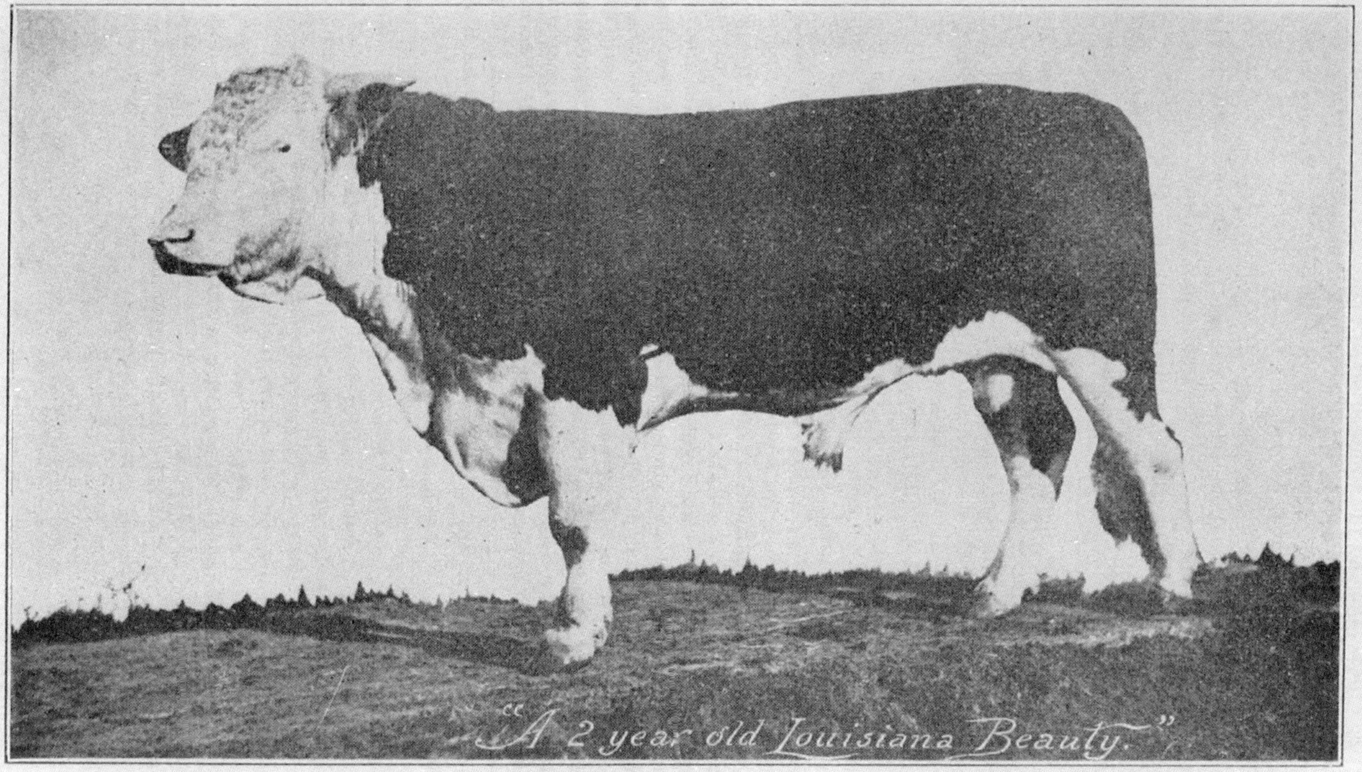

THE HEREFORD BULL.

Upon these lands all the staple crops are cultivated successfully, viz.: cotton, cane, corn, potatoes, truck products, fruits, etc. The city of Baton Rouge affords an excellent distributing point for the products of the parish to the principal markets of New Orleans, St. Louis, Chicago and western cities.

There are many small streams passing through and bordering on the parish, which afford sufficient drainage to all its lands. They are the Amite, Comite, Manchac, Bayou Fountain, Ward's Creek, Montecino, White's Bayou, Redwood, Blackwater, Sandy Creek, and many other minor water courses. In these streams are to be found many kinds of fish and water fowl.

The health of East Baton Rouge Parish has always been good, that of the city of Baton Rouge being 12 per 1000. The military post, formerly located at Baton Rouge, showed the best health record of any post in the Southwest. The thermometer rarely rises above 90 degrees, or falls below 20 degrees F., and when either extreme is reached, it lasts but a few days. The leading nationalities of the world are represented in the population, the English, French and German languages being spoken principally. Educational facilities are very good. The State University and Agricultural and Mechanical College is located at Baton Rouge. There is also a Catholic convent for girls, a Catholic college for boys, and several other private schools. Public schools are in a progressive condition. In addition to this, there are two institutions that deserve notice, viz.: the Institute for the Blind and the Institution for the Deaf and Dumb. The State Penitentiary is also located in Baton Rouge. The facilities for reaching market with manufactured and agricultural products are unsurpassed. The parish lies for nearly forty miles upon the Mississippi River, affording daily communication with New Orleans and the western cities. The Texas and Pacific, Frisco, Southern Pacific and L. R. & N. Co. give connections with all points to west and southwest. The Yazoo and Mississippi Valley, Frisco, Illinois Central, via the Baton Rouge, Hammond and Eastern, and the Louisiana Railway and Navigation Company give connections to all points east of the Mississippi River.

Since the advent of the boll weevil the agricultural conditions of the parish are changing rapidly. The raising of cotton has not been abandoned, but carried on under intensified cultivation. Stock and diversified crops and dairying are proving very profitable. Figs and pecans are being extensively planted. Flowing artesian wells, with water 99 per cent pure, are numerous throughout the parish. Springs of valuable medicinal properties are located here. This parish, with its wonderful agricultural resources, its parish seat being a port of entry and a railroad center, capital of the State, with the largest southern oil refinery for supplying oil for fuel for manufacturing its raw material, and the good roads campaign being waged, has the prospects of a very bright and prosperous future.

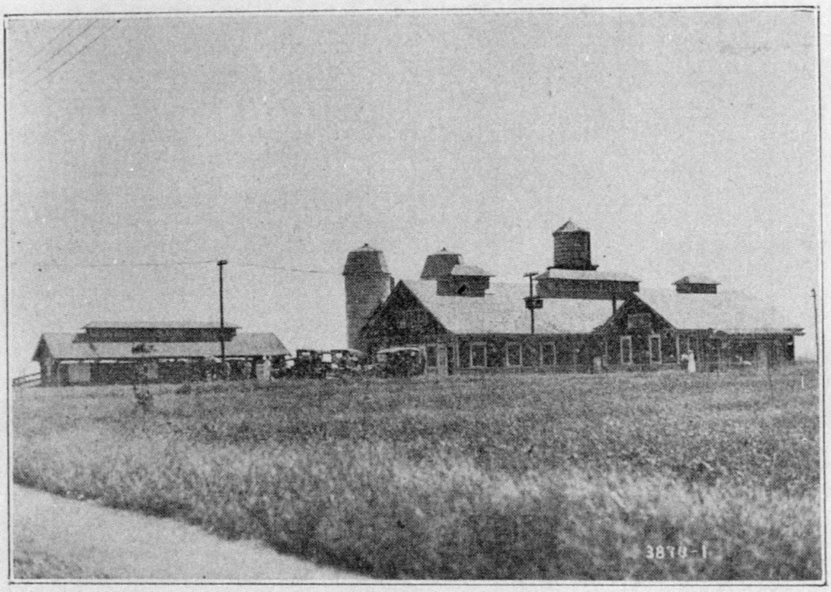

AN UP-TO-DATE DAIRY.

EAST CARROLL PARISH.

East Carroll is the extreme northeastern parish of Louisiana, bounded by the Mississippi River on the east and extending west to Bayou Mason, which divides it from the Parish of West Carroll. It contains 238,436 acres of land, about 60,000 of which are open and in cultivation and pasturage, and the remainder in timber land. Other things than cotton are produced in East Carroll. Corn, hay, oats and fruits and vegetables of all kinds can be grown abundantly and most profitably. Rice is becoming one of the leading crops. Sweet and Irish potatoes yield handsome profits and are marketed in time to admit of a crop of cotton being grown on the same land. Tomatoes, cabbages, peanuts, peas, beans, carrots, melons, strawberries, radishes, etc., are also successfully grown. All kinds of fruit do well, but the best success has been made in apples, peaches, figs and persimmons. The pecan is indiginous. In the truck industry yields of from $75 to $1,000 per acre have been made every year, and, as the profit on truck is usually 35 to 55 per cent, it can be seen that there is good money in the business. Stock can be kept through the winter without scarcely any feeding. Cases are on record of stock being marketed at top prices which never received a mouthful of food other than that which grows wild. In fact, it has been demonstrated that here on the rich natural grasses can be produced larger and stronger horses in the same length of time than can be done on the famous Kentucky blue grass.

In cattle, hogs, sheep and goats the improvement is marked. The time was when only the most common kinds of chickens, turkeys, ducks and geese could be found. Now, no matter which way one goes, there will be seen the best strains, and the best of their kind, on the farms and plantations, as well as in the homes of the townspeople.

You will find good schools and churches all over the parish. And last, but not least, you will find a hospitable class of neighbors who will welcome you with open arms.

The great Mississippi, the "Father of Waters," and the Memphis, Helena and Louisiana Railroad, a branch of the Gould system, afford easy and quick access to the markets of the world for all products and insure cheap competitive freight rates.

Large portions of East Carroll are heavily timbered, much of it cypress, white, red and black oak, ash, white and red gum, sycamore, hickory, locust and cottonwood are plentiful in the virgin state. The parish is also well watered, there being many bayous and lakes.

Fish and game abound in great quantities. Bass and other varieties of game fish furnish excellent sport for the angler, and the huntsman finds plenty of birds, ducks, geese, turkeys, squirrels, opossums, deer and bear.

EAST FELICIANA PARISH.

This parish is situated in the southeastern part of the State, and contains 298,240 acres of land. The formation is good upland, bluff and pine hills; the soil being very fertile and productive. It is drained by the Comite and Amite Rivers, Pretty Creek, Redwood, Thompson's, Beaver, Sandy and Black Creeks. The Yazoo and Mississippi Valley Railroad extends through the parish, having branch lines from Slaughter to Woodville, Mississippi; from Ethel to Clinton, the parish seat, and there is also a short private railroad line from McManus to Jackson, a town of 2,012 inhabitants, where the State Insane Asylum is located. The Louisiana Railway & Navigation Company's line passes through the lower part of the parish at Port Hudson, on to Alexandria, Shreveport, etc. Water throughout the parish is abundant, and of excellent quality. The chief crop product is cotton, while corn, oats, hay, peas, sweet and Irish potatoes, sorghum, sugar cane, tobacco, and the garden varieties thrive exceedingly well. The fruits and nuts are apples, pears, peaches, pecans, figs, plums, quinces, pomegranates, grapes and the smaller varieties.

Game is plentiful, such as coons, opossums, foxes, rabbits, squirrels, beavers, mink, wild turkeys, wild ducks, woodcocks, partridges, jack snipe, robins and rice birds. Fish of good quality abound in the streams; trout, bass, bar fish, perch, and blue and speckled cat are found. The live stock industry is successfully conducted and numbers of fine blooded cattle, horses and jacks are bred, while sheep and hogs thrive remarkably well. Since the advent of the boll weevil stock raising and dairying has been largely increased and corn, peanuts and other feed crops have about doubled the former yields.

The timber is oak, beech, pine, gum, elm, poplar, hickory, magnolia, holly, cottonwood, willow, cypress, walnut and sycamore.

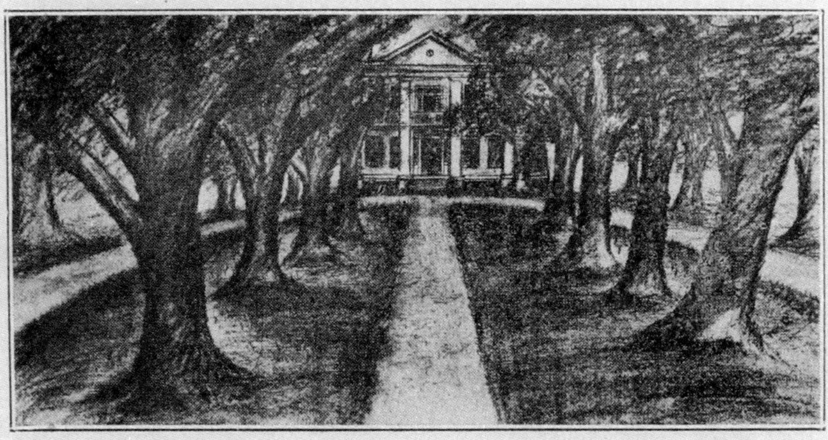

OLD-TIME SUGAR PLANTATION HOME.

EVANGELINE PARISH.

One of the south-central parishes of the State containing 504,620 acres, most of which is in cultivation. Corn, cotton, rice and sugar cane are the principal products. Cattle, hogs and sheep are much thought of. Lumber is quite an industry. Hardwoods, long-leaf pine, etc. Peaches, pears and figs do well. Satsuma oranges are being planted and experiments in them justify the hope that they will soon be one of the great fruits of the parish. Game, such as quail, papabot and snipe abound, and some wild turkeys and deer. Fishing good, such as trout and sacalait. Schools up to date. High schools with agricultural and domestic science additions. Churches, both Catholic and Protestant, are in the parish. Ville Platte is the principal town, and is becoming a great shipping point for poultry and eggs. Banks are sufficient, and orders like the F. and A. M., W. O. W. and K. C. Good gravel roads and good bridges are provided for in a three-mill tax and also a per capita tax.

FRANKLIN PARISH.

Franklin Parish is situated in the northeastern part of the State, and contains 392,960 acres of land.

The formation is chiefly bluff land, with some alluvial land, wooded swamp and a little of prairie. The soil is very fertile and productive. It is drained by Boeuf River, Bayou Macon, Turkey and Deer Creeks, and Turkey Lake.

The New Orleans and Northwestern Railroad passes through the parish.

Winnsboro, situated on Turkey Creek, is the parish seat. Water is plentiful and fairly good. Cotton is the chief crop for export; corn, oats, hay, sugar cane, sweet and Irish potatoes, peas and sorghum are produced. The fruits and nuts are peaches, pears, pecans, apples, plums, quinces, grapes, figs and pomegranates. The timber is oak, pine, gum, elm, beech, holly, magnolia, hickory, poplar, cottonwood, willow, mulberry, maple, ash, and walnut.

The live stock are cattle, hogs, sheep and horses, of which large numbers are raised.

Game abounds, such as deer, bear, foxes, coons, opossums, beavers, mink, squirrels, rabbits, wild turkeys, wild ducks and geese, partridges, snipe, woodcock and rice birds.

Varieties of fish abound in the streams and lakes, among which are trout, bass, white perch and pike.

GRANT PARISH.

This parish is situated near the center of the State, and contains 407,040 acres of land. The formation is pine hills, with some alluvial land bordering Red River. It is drained by Red and Little Rivers, Bayou Jatt, the Rigolet du Bon Dieu, and smaller streams.

Colfax, on the Louisiana Railway and Navigation Company's line, is the parish seat.

The chief product is cotton, while corn, oats, hay, sugar cane, sweet and Irish potatoes, sorghum, tobacco, and peas are raised. The fruits and nuts are peaches, plums, apples, pears, pecans, grapes, figs, pomegranates and quinces. The timber is long-leaf pine, oak, gum, cottonwood, willow, elm, hickory, and sycamore, with some magnolia and poplar. Live stock are raised, such as cattle, sheep, hogs and horses.

Game is found, consisting of deer, foxes, coons, opossums, squirrels, rabbits, mink, wild turkeys, wild ducks and geese, woodcock, partridges and rice birds. Fish are found in the streams and lakes, the choice varieties of which are trout, bass, pike and white perch.

Deposits of marble, limestone, kaolin, marl, lignite, fire clay, potters' clay, iron, and gypsum exist.

IBERIA PARISH.

This parish is situated in the southern part of the State, and contains 426,880 acres. The formation is prairie, coast marsh, alluvial land, wooded swamp and bluff land; the soil being very rich and highly productive. It is drained by Bayous Teche, Petit Anse and Coulee du Portage.

The Southern Pacific Railroad, with branch lines, extends through the parish. New Iberia, situated on Bayou Teche, is the parish seat. Water is good, cistern water being chiefly used.

The general crop production is sugar; rice, corn, oats, hay, peas, sweet and Irish potatoes and garden varieties are all grown extensively, and are very profitable.

The fruits and nuts are the orange, lemon, mandarin, fig, pomegranate, guava, olive, plum, pear, pecan, grape, banana, peach and prune. The timber is composed of cypress, oak, gum, elm, cottonwood, willow, sugarwood and sycamore.

Live stock raised are horses, cattle, sheep and hogs. Game exists, such as deer, coons, opossums, squirrels, rabbits, wild ducks, wild geese, woodcock, papabots, becasine, partridges, rice birds, snipe and pheasants. Fish abounds in the streams, lakes and inlets, among which are red fish, pompano, salt water trout, crabs, trout, bass and sacalait; oysters and terrapin are found in the brackish waters of the coast marsh.

The great salt works of Louisiana are located in this parish.

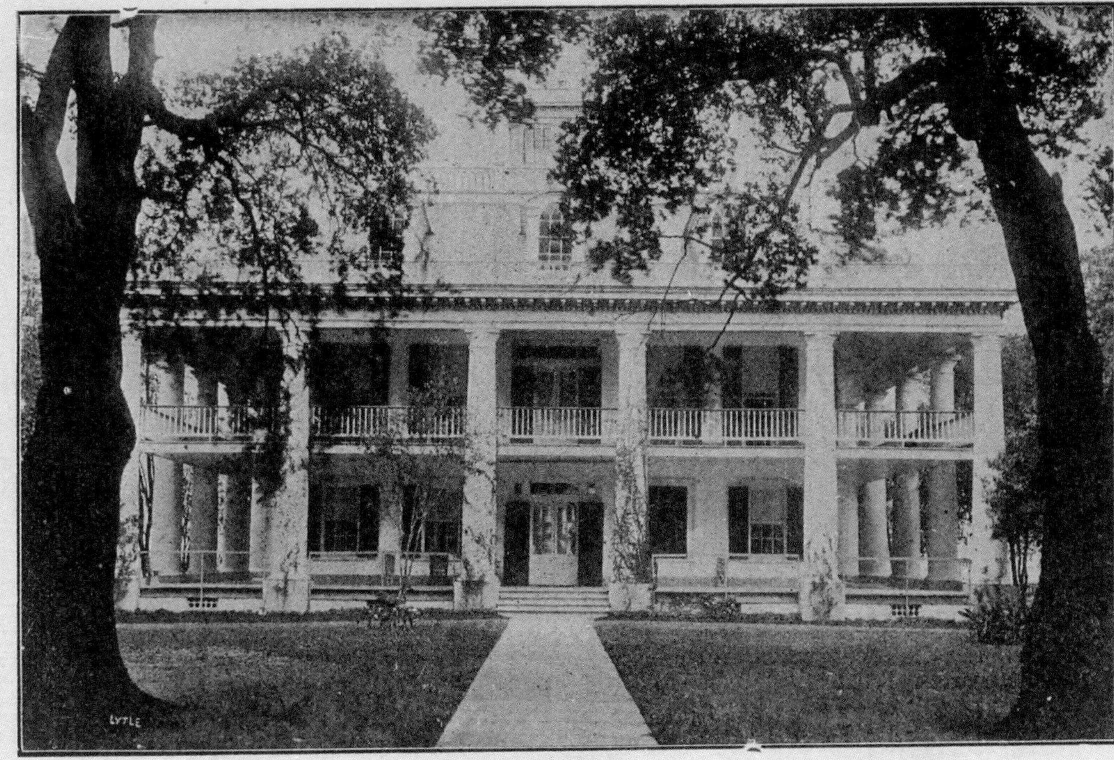

A TYPICAL LOUISIANA ANTEBELLUM HOME.

IBERVILLE PARISH.

This parish is situated in the south central part of the State, and contains 413,440 acres of land. The formation is wooded swamp and alluvial land, the soil of which is extremely rich and productive. It is drained by the Mississippi River—which passes through the eastern portion of the parish—and by Grand River, Bayou Goula, Plaquemine, Maringouin, Grosse Tete, Manchac, and numerous other streams.

The Texas and Pacific Railroad passes through the parish on the western bank of the Mississippi River, and the Yazoo and Mississippi Valley Railroad, the Frisco and the Louisiana Railway and Navigation Company through the eastern portion. Plaquemine, situated on the western bank of the Missisippi River, on the main line of the Texas and Pacific Railroad, is the parish seat. The famous Plaquemine locks, at the mouth of Bayou Plaquemine, are located here; they were built by the United States Government, and it is one of the largest pieces of masonry ever constructed in this country.

Water is plentiful and good, cistern water being chiefly used. Sugar is the chief crop production, and corn, hay, oats, rice, beans, sweet and Irish potatoes and the garden varieties are extensively raised. The fruits and nuts are pears, peaches, figs, pomegranates, oranges, lemons, mandarins, plums, prunes, pecans and grapes. Live stock are cattle, sheep, hogs and horses. The game found are deer, bear, coons, opossums, mink, squirrels, rabbits, wild ducks and geese, snipe, becasine, partridges and rice birds. Fish are found in the streams, such as bass, pike, white perch and common varieties.

JACKSON PARISH.

This parish is situated in the north-central part of the State, and contains 369,280 acres of land. The formation is good upland and pine hills, red sandy clays; soil generally good and fertile. It is drained by the tributaries of Dugdemona River and Bayou Castor. Water is abundant and good.

The Arkansas Southern Railroad runs through the parish from north to south.

Vernon, situated in the northern part of the parish, is the parish seat. There are many springs, branches and creeks.

Cotton is the chief crop produced for export; corn, hay, oats, sorghum, sweet and Irish potatoes, peas, sugar cane, wheat, rye and barley are also raised. The fruits are peaches, apples, pears, quinces, plums, pomegranates and grapes. Cattle, hogs, sheep and horses are raised in great numbers.

Game is found, such as deer, coons, opossums, squirrels, rabbits, foxes, wild turkeys, partridges and woodcock. Fish of good quality of the smaller varieties are found in streams.

The timber consists of pine, oak, beech, hickory, walnut, elm and maple. Extensive areas of long-leaf pine are in this parish.

JEFFERSON PARISH.

This parish is situated in the southeastern part of the State, and is divided by the Mississippi River, which passes its northern portion. It contains 385,920 acres, the formation being composed largely of coast marsh, while it has a large area of alluvial land and some wooded swamp. The soil is exceedingly rich and productive. It is drained by the Mississippi River, Lake Pontchartrain and Bayous Barataria, Rigolet, Des Familles or Dauphine, St. Denis, Dupont and Grand Bayou.

The Texas and Pacific, Southern Pacific, Gulf and Grand Isle, Illinois Central, Yazoo and Mississippi Valley, Frisco and L. R. & N. railroads pass through the parish.

Gretna, situated on the Mississippi River, is the parish seat. Water is good, cistern water being chiefly used.

Sugar is the principal crop produced, although rice, corn, Irish potatoes, onions and garden truck of all kinds are extensively grown, and shipped to northern markets.

The fruits and nuts are oranges, lemons, mandarins, figs, pomegranates, plums, prunes, pecans, guavas, olives, bananas and grapes. Cattle and hogs are raised.

Game is found, consisting of snipe, becasine, papabots, wild ducks and geese, and rice birds and coons, rabbits and opossums.

The timber is limited to cypress, oak, elm and willow.

Fish abound, and the oyster industry of this parish is the most extensive, and superior, along the Gulf Coast. Terrapin, oysters, crabs, and the varieties of Gulf fish are taken in large number in the inlets, bayous and lakes.

JEFFERSON DAVIS PARISH.

One of the new southwestern parishes. Contains 390,961 acres. The agricultural products are rice, corn, cotton, sugar cane, oats, hay. Fruits are figs, grapefruit, satsuma oranges, pears and grapes. Stock, backed by dipping vats and silos in all directions, with pretty good winter grazing, is developing rapidly. Hogs and sheep do well. Good roads sentiment prevailing; 106 miles of hard surface roads in the next year. New $90,000 courthouse. Fine high school with domestic science and manual training included. Thirty-four white schools and six for negroes in the parish. Both Catholic and Protestant churches.

Oil and Gas.—Output of the former about the same for the last twelve years.

LAFAYETTE PARISH.

This parish is situated in the southern part of the State, and contains 152,960 acres of land, in area it being the third smallest parish in the State. Its formation is chiefly prairie, with considerable alluvial and bluff land. The soil is very fertile and productive. It is drained by Bayous Carencro and Tortue and Vermilion River.

The Southern Pacific Railroad extends through the parish, having a connecting line from Lafayette to Cheneyville, in Rapides parish, and also a line to Baton Rouge. Lafayette, situated on the Southern Pacific Railroad, is the parish seat, and is the home of the Southwestern Industrial Institute. It is only a few miles from the Anse La Butte oil field, which lies almost on the line of Lafayette and St. Martin parishes.

Water is abundant, and of good quality. Rice and sugar are the chief productions, and corn, cotton, oats, sweet and Irish potatoes, peas and hay, are extensively raised; also alfalfa is meeting with some success.

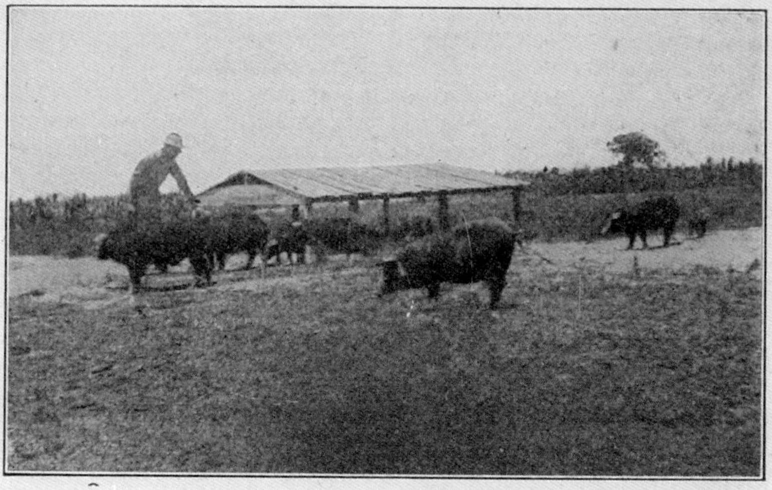

AN ORDINARY MORTGAGE-LIFTER.

The fruits and nuts are the orange, pear, grape, plum, peach and pecan. Cattle, sheep, hogs and horses are raised extensively. Game, such as snipe, becasine, plover, wild ducks, partridges, pheasants and rice birds are found. Some fish are taken from the streams of the parish. The timber is oak, willow, cottonwood, elm, some cypress, sugarwood, gum and sycamore.

Lafayette has a sugar refinery costing $350,000. Some large lumber companies, cotton seed oil mill, a compress and storage plant and other manufacturing interests are also flourishing there.

LAFOURCHE PARISH.

This parish is situated in the southern part of the State, and contains 655,260 acres of land. The formation is alluvial land, wooded swamp and coast marsh. Soil exceedingly rich and productive. It is drained by Bayous Lafourche, Des Allemands and Grand Bayou.

The Southern Pacific Railroad passes through the northern portion of the parish, and the Texas and Pacific runs from Thibodaux north. Thibodaux, situated on Bayou Lafourche, is the parish seat, and is a thrifty, progressive little city, with electric lights, waterworks, foundries, canning factory and many other industries. Water is good, cistern water being generally used. Sugar is the chief product, and rice, corn, hay, oats, peas, jute and garden truck are grown and shipped.

The fruits and nuts are oranges, lemons, mandarins, plums, guavas, olives, figs, pears, grapes, peaches, pecans and bananas. The live stock raised here are mostly cattle and hogs. Game is found, such as snipe, becasine, wild ducks and geese, deer, rice birds, papabots, squirrels, opossums, coons and rabbits. Fishing is very good and oysters, crabs, terrapin and the Gulf fish are found in waters of the coast marsh. The timber is cypress, oak, cottonwood, gum, elm and willow.

LASALLE PARISH.

One of the central parishes of the State. Altitude, about 300 feet above sea level, except small area along upper portion of Little River. Soil, light sandy, with red clay subsoil. Productive and will retain fertilizer. Area, 666,780 acres. Population, 10,000. Chief industry, lumber production. Six mills produce, daily, 600,000 feet, and employ 2300 men. There are two good railroad systems in the parish. Agriculture and stock raising will be the chief industry in a few years, as the timber is not sufficient to run the mills more than six or eight years.

The present acreage in agricultural crops is about 6,000, consisting of cotton, corn, sugar cane, potatoes, oats, truck farming, with corn predominating. Poultry and fruit do well here.

Jena, the parish seat, a town with paved streets and electric lights, has one of the best courthouses and one of the most modern three-story brick high school buildings.

White Sulphur Springs is a summer resort, where fishing is usually good.

The school system is considered progressive and efficient. There are two high schools, one agricultural school, three domestic science schools and a sufficient number of smaller schools to provide for the elementary education of the children.

Urania has a national preserve for elk. There are six young already this year.

Model roads are being built throughout the parish.

There are many automobiles in this parish, the number comparing favorably with any similar parish in the State. Daily mail, rural routes and telephones are to be found in almost all parts of the parish.

In the central and southern portions of the parish the small streams furnish an abundance of pure water. Game, such as ducks in season, squirrels, quails and some few deer and turkeys.

LINCOLN PARISH.

This parish is situated in the northern part of the State, and contains 368,000 acres of land. The formation is good upland, red sandy clay, the soil being fertile and productive. It is drained by Bayou D'Arbonne and smaller streams. Many chalybeate springs, creeks and branches abound.

The Vicksburg, Shreveport and Pacific Railroad passes through the parish. Ruston, situated on this line, is the parish seat. It is a thriving, progressive little city. Here is situated the State Industrial Institute for both sexes. Over 600 pupils are now in attendance. Tuition free. Here is also located the Louisiana Chautauqua. Ruston has a cotton compress, cotton oil mill, ice factory, fertilizer factory and electric light plant. Water is sufficient, and of good quality, from cool springs and wells.

The chief product is cotton; corn, oats, hay, peanuts, sorghum, grasses, wheat, sugar cane, tobacco, sweet and Irish potatoes and peas being also extensively raised. The fruits and nuts are peaches, pears, plums, pecans, apples, quinces, grapes, and all do well. Cattle, hogs, sheep, horses and mules are raised on farms.

Game is found, consisting of deer, coons, foxes, opossums, squirrels, rabbits, wild turkeys, wild ducks, woodcock, partridges and robins. Deposits of marl, potters' clay, fire clay and lignite are found. The timber is pine, oak, poplar, hickory, beech, maple, gum, elm, walnut and persimmon.

LIVINGSTON PARISH.

This parish is situated in the southeastern part of the State, and contains 379,520 acres of land. The formation is bluff land, pine flats, alluvial land and wooded swamps; the soil being generally fertile and productive, some of which is exceedingly rich. It is drained by the Amite and Tickfaw Rivers and Colyell Creek and their branches. Water is abundant and of good quality. Springfield, on the Tickfaw River, is the parish seat.

Cotton is the chief product; corn, hay, oats, sorghum, sugar cane, sweet and Irish potatoes, peas, tobacco and rice are raised. The fruits and nuts are peaches, plums, pears, pecans, apples, grapes, figs, pomegranates and quinces. Cattle, sheep, hogs and horses are raised.

The timber is pine, oak, beech, magnolia, ash, holly, gum, hickory, poplar, persimmon and cypress.

Game is abundant, such as deer, coons, opossums, squirrels, rabbits, wild turkeys, wild ducks, partridges, woodcocks, and robins. Fish are found in the rivers and streams, such as trout, bass, channel catfish and perch.

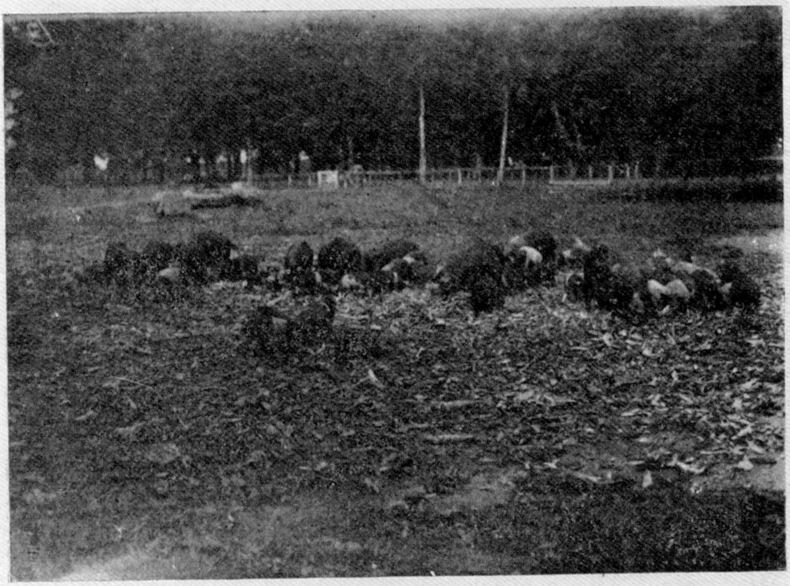

HOGS RUNNING AT LARGE.

MADISON PARISH.

Madison Parish is situated in the northeast portion of the State, East Carroll being the intervening parish between it and the State of Arkansas. The acreage of the parish is placed by the assessor at 397,605 acres. The land is all alluvial, composed of loam and buckshot. It is fertile beyond belief, producing nearly all kinds of crops; especially cotton, rice, corn and truck. The principal streams are the Tensas River, Bayou Macon, Roundaway and its connections known as Walnut and Brushy, Willow Bayou, Little Tensas, Bayou Vidal, etc. Its lakes are Bear Lake, One Eagle Lake, Grassy Lake, Swan Lake, etc. There are two railways which run severally east and west and north and south, to-wit: the Vicksburg, Shreveport and Pacific Railway and the Memphis, Helena and Louisiana Railroad. There is only one incorporated municipality in the parish, the village of Tallulah. Within its limits there is a hoop and stave factory, a cotton oil mill and an ice plant, besides a public ginnery. There is one bank. There are two churches for whites—the M. E. C. S. and the Episcopal. Several negro churches of the Methodist and Baptist faiths. There is one high school building in Tallulah, besides lesser school buildings in the parish. Nearly all kinds of crops can be grown, including fruits of all varieties and pecans. Attention has been given since the advent of the boll weevil to raising stock of all kinds, including hogs, etc., and this departure has become almost universal. Fish of all varieties abound in our lakes. Bear Lake is a noted resort for the sport, where a clubhouse is located. The timber lands are very valuable and little of it has been cut. This consists of all varieties of oak, pecan, willow, cottonwood, gum, hackberry, elm, some cypress, but no pine. The game is also quite plentiful, consisting of deer, bear, squirrel, wild cats, opossoms. The price of land varies according to its location near line of communication.

There are two other villages, Millikens Bend and Delta.

MOREHOUSE PARISH.

This parish is situated in the northeastern part of the State, and contains 486,400 acres of land.

The formation is alluvial land, good upland and wooded swamp; soil rich and productive. It is drained by the Ouachita and Boeuf Rivers and Bayous Bonne Idee, Bartholomew and Gallion. Water is abundant and of good quality. The Vicksburg, Shreveport and Pacific Railroad passes through the extreme southern point; the Iron Mountain Railroad passes through the parish, north and south, while the New Orleans and Northwestern Railroad passes through from southeast to northwest.

Bastrop is the parish seat, located on the uplands. Cotton is the principal crop production for export; corn, oats, hay, tobacco, sweet and Irish potatoes, peas, sorghum and sugar cane are also raised. The fruits and nuts are peaches, pears, pecans, apples, plums, quinces, and grapes. The timber is oak, pine, cottonwood, gum, elm, cypress, poplar, hickory, holly, beech, magnolia, willow and persimmon. Live stock, such as cattle, hogs, sheep and some horses are raised.

Game is found, consisting of deer, coons, foxes, opossums, squirrels, rabbits, wild turkeys, wild ducks, woodcock, snipe, robins, partridges and rice birds. Fish of good quality are found in the streams.

NATCHITOCHES PARISH.

Natchitoches Parish is situated in the west-central part of the State, and contains 825,600 acres of land. The formation is alluvial land, good upland and pine flats; soil generally good, and very productive. It is drained by the Red and Cane Rivers, and Bayous Saline, Pierre and Natchez and the Rigolet Du Bon Dieu. Water is abundant and of good quality.

The main line of the Texas and Pacific Railroad runs through the parish, with branch line to the Red River through the town of Natchitoches; this town is also the terminus of the Louisiana and Northwestern Railroad, and has a branch line of the Louisiana Railway and Navigation Company. It is the parish seat and a thrifty, progressive town. Here is located the State Normal School, with over 700 students.

Cotton is the chief crop raised for export, while corn, oats, tobacco, hay, peas, sorghum, sugar cane and sweet and Irish potatoes are produced. The Natchitoches tobacco enjoys a world-wide reputation.

The fruits are peaches, pears, apples, plums, quinces, pomegranates, figs and grapes. The timber is pine, oak, gum, cottonwood, elm, willow, cypress, holly, magnolia, hickory, walnut, poplar, maple, and persimmon. Cattle, sheep, hogs and horses are raised.

Game, such as deer, coons, foxes, opossums, rabbits, squirrels, wild turkeys and ducks, woodcock, partridges and rice birds, is found. Fish of good quality are found in the streams. Deposits of lignite, marl, marble, limestone, kaolin, iron, fire clay and potters' clay exist. Truffles are also found in this parish.

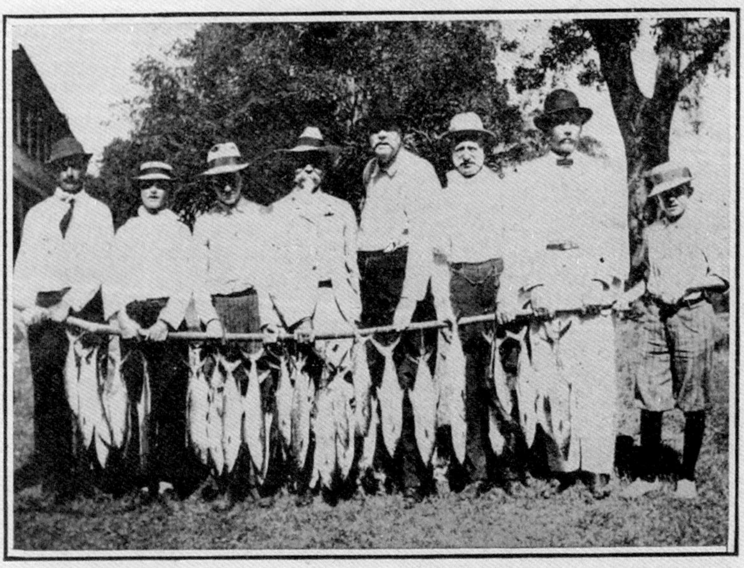

A GOOD CATCH NEAR NEW ORLEANS—150 POUNDS SPANISH MACKEREL IN TWO HOURS.

ORLEANS PARISH.

This parish is situated in the southeastern part of the State, and contains 127,360 acres, it being the smallest parish in area in the State. The formation is alluvial land, coast marshes and wooded swamp. It is drained by the Mississippi River, Lakes Pontchartrain and Borgne, and Bayous St. John and Gentilly. Most of the railroads of the State converge here in the City of New Orleans, which is the parish seat.

The chief crops grown are garden truck, an immense industry; and corn, sugar cane, rice, jute, sweet and Irish potatoes are raised. The fruits are the orange, lemon, mandarin, olive, prune, fig, pomegranate, pear, peach, and the smaller varieties. The timber is cypress, oak, gum, elm, hackberry, cottonwood and willow. Some cattle, hogs and horses are raised here. Very little game is found, though fishing is very good in the lakes and brackish waters, where oysters, crabs, terrapin, and the varieties of Gulf fish are taken.

The city of New Orleans and the Parish of Orleans are practically one and the same thing, as the city now embraces within its limits all of the parish.

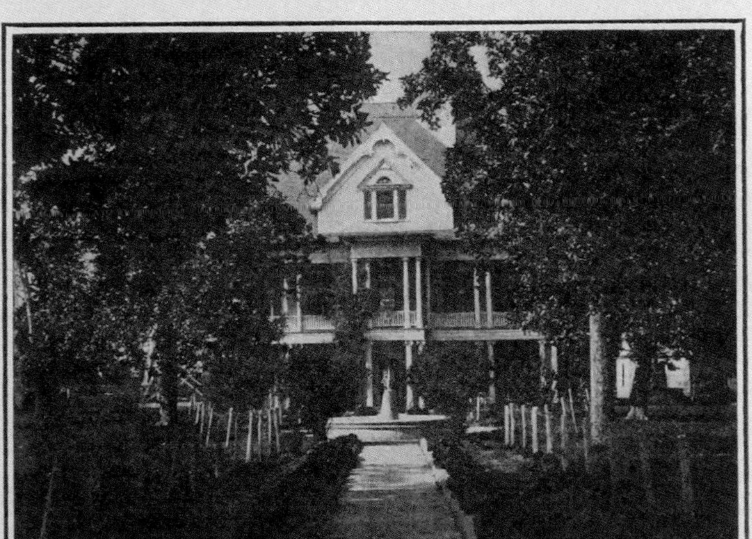

A PLANTATION HOME.

OUACHITA PARISH

Ouachita is in the second tier of parishes from the Arkansas line. It has about 398,720 acres of land.

One of the most beautiful rivers, flowing southward, some quarter of a mile wide, now navigable some nine months of the year, divides the parish, bears the name, and amply justifies its Indian meaning—"Silver-Water." The Ouachita practically never overflows within the parish.

The east side is level and alluvial, with a formation of rich, sandy loams, containing heavy growths of hardwood timber of the finest quality and great variety. The west side, heavily timbered with pine, and also hardwoods, consists of "second bottoms," and so-called "hill lands," generally sandy loams, with heavy clay foundations, productive, and very fertile in the valleys along the numerous streams.

Numerous artesian wells, with abundant limpid waters, flow here as freely as do the multitudinous natural streams, great and small, that are tributary to "the Ouachita."

Ouachita's principal towns are Monroe, the second oldest town in the State, and West Monroe, practically one, only the river divides them, but separately incorporated. Together they constitute a growing, flourishing and progressive modern city. The other towns of the parish are comparatively small—Calhoun, some fifteen miles west, and the seat of the North Louisiana Experiment Station being the next largest.

Large capital is invested in cotton seed oil mills. Numerous sawmills, stave factories, shingle factories, etc., work the wonderful growths of timber—oak, pine, cypress, hickory, ash, gum, etc. The best of brick are made by most modern methods, and concrete is largely used, made from the best of gravels and sands, locally obtained.

Four large, strong banks in Monroe and one in West Monroe are all prosperous and growing. Many churches of all the usual Protestant denominations abound, and there is a large Catholic church and a large synagogue in Monroe. The school system in the parish is of the best.

Practically all kinds of crops and live stock produced on the North American continent can be successfully grown or raised here. It is an excellent fruit country, and the very land of the pecan and other nut-

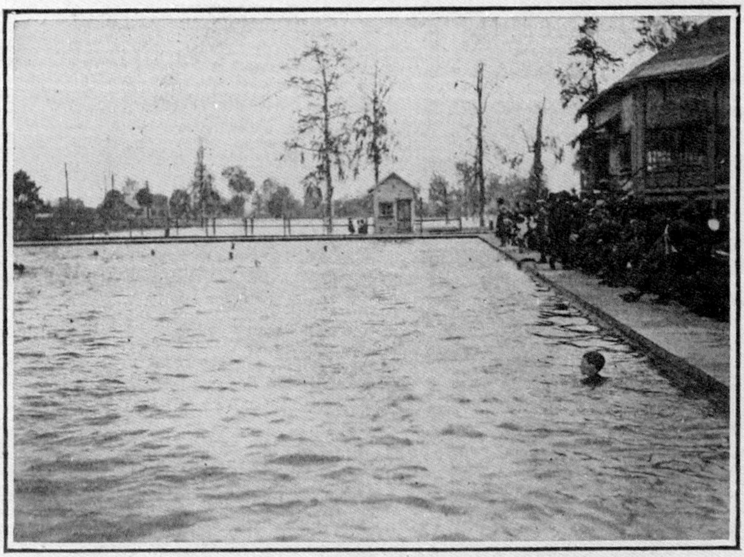

A NATURAL WARM-WATER BATHING POOL AT MONROE. SALT WATER FROM A DEEP WELL AND LIGHTED BY GAS FROM SAME WELL.

bearing trees. The walnut grows wild—the hickory abundant. Figs of the finest never fail. Stock raising is of great and growing importance. Game and fish are plentiful.

This is, pre-eminently, a land of agriculture, and its great partners, live stock and poultry, fruits, nuts and vines. It is a great grass and hay land, and more and more attention is being given to "meadows."

Concrete culverts, constructed from the pure sand gravels of the local deposit, are replacing all small bridges, and even some quite large ones, along the roads.

Louisiana leads all the States in variety of food products, being unique in her combination of sugar, molasses, rice and tropical fruits; also in the amount produced per acre of the world's clothing maker—cotton. Also in the combination of variety, quality and quantity of standing timber; also in extent of navigable waterways. She leads the world in deposits of natural gas,, oil, salt and sulphur. She feeds, clothes, houses, lights and fuels, salts and fumigates "the children of men." Of these things, "Ouachita" does her full quota.

PLAQUEMINES PARISH.

This parish is located in the southeastern part of the State, and is divided by the Mississippi River, which passes through it. The formation is alluvial land and coast marsh; the soil being exceedingly rich and productive.

It is drained by the Mississippi River and Bayous Cheniere, Wilkinson, Long, Terre au Bouef, Vacherie, Dupont and Grand Bayou. The Grand Isle and Gulf Railroad passes down the western coast of the Mississippi, and the Mississippi, Terre au Boeuf and Lake Road down the eastern coast.

Pointe-a-laHache, situated on the Mississippi River, is the parish seat. Cistern water is mostly used. The chief crop productions are sugar and rice; corn and truck varieties are grown and shipped extensively.

Fruits are oranges, lemons, mandarins, olives, figs, bananas, guavas, grapes and prunes. The finest orange groves and lands in the State are here.

Timber is cypress, willow, elm, oak, and cottonwood.

Some cattle are raised, and a few hogs.

Game is becasine, snipe, rice birds, wild ducks, geese and swan, papabots, coon and opossums.

Fishing is excellent, and crab, sheepshead, pompano, red fish, flounder, salt water trout, Spanish mackerel, oysters, terrapin and shrimp abound. The oyster industry is quite extensive in this parish.

POINTE COUPEE PARISH.

Pointe Coupee Parish is situated on the west bank of the Mississippi River, about 22 miles above Baton Rouge. It has an area of 368,000 acres, all of alluvial soil, exceedingly fertile. The parish is especially favored by nature, and it has numerous bayous across and dividing the land into farms of handsome proportions, the bayous affording cheap, efficient and practical drainage.

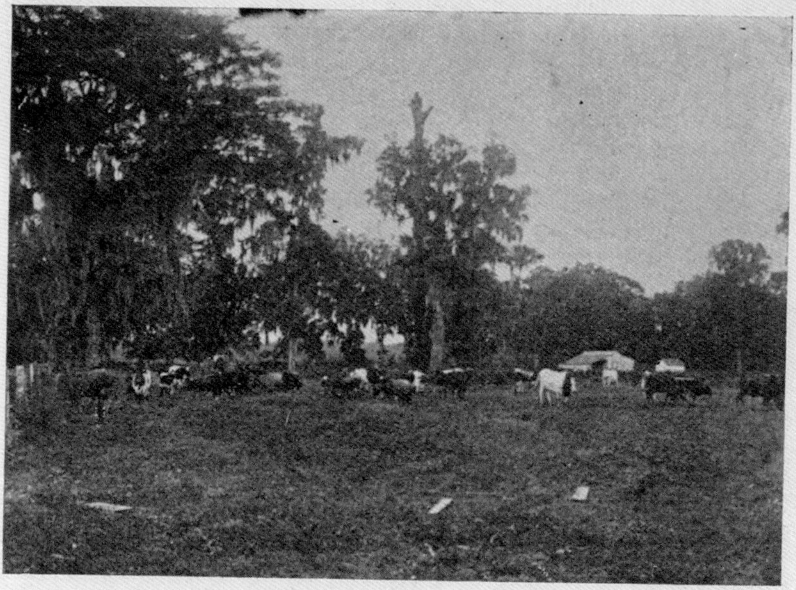

CATTLE IN NORTH LOUISIANA.

The public roads (325 miles in length) which traverse the parish are all in splendid condition, they having a natural drainage, thus keeping them in fine condition. False River, once a branch of the Mississippi, is now a beautiful lake, one mile wide by 24 miles long. As a fishing ground it is surpassed by no stream. It abounds with black bass, sacalait or crappie, perch, catfish, spoonbill catfish, gaspergou, buffalo and numerous other species of the finny tribe.

The lands of Pointe Coupee, exceedingly fertile, can produce all of the various crops possible in the Southern States, such as corn, cotton, cane, peanuts, peas, alfalfa, flax, Irish and sweet potatoes. Cabbage, truck, onions, etc., can be raised in abundance.

Another very easy and handsomely paying crop is that of the pecan tree, which thrives splendidly in this parish. These trees can be found on every farm. The crop is seldom a failure and always finds a ready market. Several thousands of sacks are shipped annually to New Orleans, St. Louis and Chicago markets. Wood is to be found in abundance, the varieties mainly consisting of cypress, oak, persimmon, ash, and gum. Pointe Coupee is belted with two parallel lines of the Texas and Pacific Railroad, and its western section by the Frisco system, and which has just completed an extension to Lakeland, in the southwestern portion of the parish.

Taxation is reasonable and consistent with the needs of the development and management of the parish. There are several towns—New Roads, Morganza, Torras—and other are in course of establishment along the Frisco system.

New Roads, the parish seat, has two banks, and among its industries are several cotton gins, cotton oil mills, sugar mills, an ice plant, a brick-making plant, sawmills, and room for many more.

Nearly all religious denominations are represented in the parish. Among the churches are Catholic, Episcopalian, Methodist, Baptist and Presbyterian, and all show the liberal and progressive spirit which exists. In no section of the State is the cause of education more assiduously fostered than in Pointe Coupee. In New Roads is located the famous Poydras Academy, endowed by the great philanthropist, Julien Poydras, and which is open to every child in the parish, the tuition being absolutely free. The higher academic branches are taught in this institution. It is under the supervision of a Board of Trustees, appointed annually by the Police Jury.

Cattle raising can be made the source of a profitable income. Poultry of all kinds are raised in abundance and thrive to the fullest extent. Fresh eggs can be had every day of the year on any farm in the parish.

RAPIDES PARISH.

Rapides is the central parish of the State. and contains 975,440 acres of land. The formation is pine flats and alluvial land, with some bluff land and prairie. In the alluvial, bluff and prairie sections the soil is very fertile and productive, the chocolate formation being very rich.

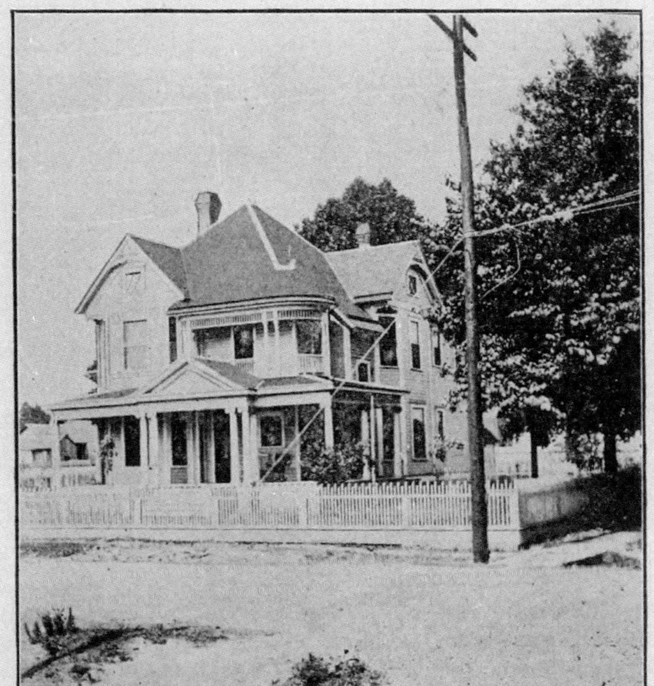

A PLANTATION HOME OF THE PRESENT DAY.

It is drained by Red and Calcasieu Rivers, the Bayous Saline, Rapides, Boeuf, Falcon and Cocoderie.

The Texas and Pacific, the Kansas City, Watkins and Gulf, the Louisiana Railway and Navigation Company, the Iron Mountain and the Southern Pacific Railroads pass through the parish, all centering at Alexandria, which is the parish seat.

Cotton and sugar are the chief crop productions for export; corn, oats, hay, peas, sweet and Irish potatoes, rice, tobacco, and garden truck are produced. The fruits and nuts are peaches, pears, plums, pecans, figs, pomegranates, grapes, apples, and the smaller varieties. The wild mayhaw grows abundantly throughout the parish; this fruit has no superior for jellying purposes. The timber is pine, oak, cypress, cottonwood, hickory, willow, locust, sycamore and gum; large areas of long-leaf pine.

Cattle, sheep, hogs and horses are raised. Game is found, consisting of squirrels, rabbits, coons, opossums, foxes, deer, wild turkeys, wild ducks, snipe, woodcock, partridges and rice birds. Fishing is good in the streams.

The hot wells at Boyce deserve particular mention. See analysis below:

ANALYSIS EXPRESSED IN PARTS.

	Per 1,000,000.
Condition	Cloudy and heavy sediment in bottom
Odor when heated to 100 Fahr.	None
Odor when heated to boiling	Brackish
Reaction	Alkaline
Nitrogen as free ammonia	0.022
Nitrogen as albuminoid ammonia	0.060
Nitrogen as nitrites	None
Nitrogen as nitrates	2.100
Phosphates	Trace
Oxygen consuming power	5.000
Total hardness	60.00
Temporary hardness	27.50
Permanent hardness	32.50

GASES.

Carbon dioxide (free)	3.50
Bicarbonates	32.20
Hydrogen sulphide	None

Remarks.—The chemico-sanitary analysis shows this water to be of excellent quality. Very respectfully,

(Signed) DR. A. L. METZ,

What has been done at Hot Springs, Arkansas, West Baden, Indiana, Mineral Wells, Texas, and Hot Springs, San Antonio, can and will be done at these wonderful hot wells at Boyce, Louisiana.

RED RIVER PARISH.

This parish is situated in the northwestern part of the State, and contains 256,000 acres of land. The formation is good upland and alluvial land, the soil being rich and productive. It is drained by Red River the Grand and Blacklake Bayous. Water is plentiful and generally good.

The Louisiana Railway and Navigation Company's line traverses the parish along the east bank of Red River. Coushatta, situated on the Red River, is the parish seat.

Cotton is the chief product; sugar cane and alfalfa, corn, oats, hay, peas, sweet and Irish potatoes, and the garden varieties all yield good returns. The fruits and nuts are peaches, pears, pecans, plums, apples, pomegranates, grapes, quinces and figs. The timber is oak, pine, cypress, gum, elm, beech, maple, holly, cottonwood, sycamore, poplar, hickory, willow and persimmon.

The live stock raised are cattle, hogs and sheep. Game is abundant, such as squirrels, coons, opossums, rabbits, deer, wild turkeys, partridges, robins, wild ducks and woodcock. Fish are found in the streams, among which are the trout, bass, pike and bar fish.

Great oil wells have been developed and the parish now boasts of an output of millions of barrels.

RICHLAND PARISH.

This parish is situated in the northeastern part of the State, and contains 369,920 acres of land. The formation is bluff land, alluvial land, and a little wooded swamp; soil fertile and productive. It is drained by Boeuf River and Bayous Macon, Lafourche and Big Creek. Water is abundant and generally good.

The Vicksburg, Shreveport and Pacific, and the New Orleans and Northwestern Railroads pass through the parish. Rayville, situated on these lines of railroad, is the parish seat.

Cotton is the chief crop produced for export; corn, oats, hay, sorghum, peas, sweet and Irish potatoes and garden varieties are grown. The fruits and nuts are peaches, apples, pears, pecans, plums, grapes, figs, pomegranates and quinces.

Live stock raised are mostly cattle and hogs. Game is found, consisting of deer, bear, coons, opossums, rabbits, squirrels, wild turkeys, wild ducks, partridges, rice birds, woodcock, and snipe. Fish of good quality are abundant in the streams and lakes.

The timber is oak, gum, cypress, cottonwood, willow, hickory, poplar and persimmon.

SABINE PARISH.

Sabine Parish includes 1029 square miles of territory, lying in the middle of the western border of the State; undulating hammock, hill and valley lands, watered by six creeks which rise near its eastern border on the divide between the Red and Sabine Rivers and flow swiftly in deep channels southwestwardly to the Sabine River, its western boundary.

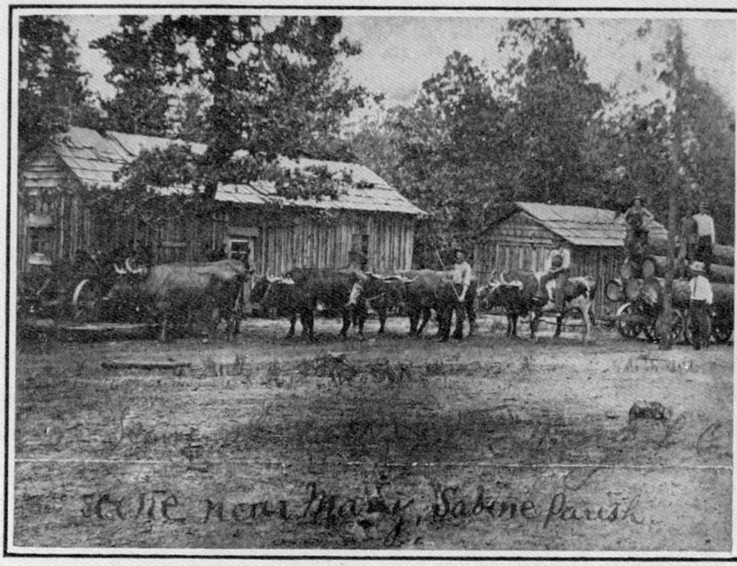

Soils.—In the highlands the surface is usually red clay, containing sand; in the hammocks and bottoms a rich sandy loam. Some spots are deep sand. Almost the whole is susceptible of cultivation, and is free and productive. Ninety thousand acres are cleared for farming, of which 171 acres are devoted to truck farming.

Climate and Water.—The climate is salubrious, owing to mild temperatures summer and winter, and the rarity of stagnant water. Good freestone water can be had generally by the sinking of wells.

Industries.—Probably three-fourths of the inhabitants are engaged in agriculture; others in sawmill work, in stave making, or tie making.

Farm Products.—Cotton, corn, sugar cane, sorghum, peanuts, peas and potatoes, both Irish and sweet, are the chief products. Cattle, hogs, sheep, horses and mules thrive and are cheaply raised on wild clover, Bermuda and other nutritious grasses on the open range. Figs, plums, dewberries and blackberries, beside garden vegetables usual to latitude 32, east of this, do well. Strawberries, grapes, peaches, pears and apricots are remunerative if given proper attention. Hickory nuts, walnuts, pecans and chinquepins grow spontaneously.

Population.—The population consists of natives, settlers from other parts of the Union and from foreign countries. Of the last, Belgians predominate. Of natives, 10 per cent are of Spanish extraction. About one-fifth of the whole are negroes.

Schools.—The public schools, numbering 104, are in a flourishing condition. The average term is six months, and the average salary of white teachers is $60. For school purposes during the past year $60,000 has been expended.

ST. BERNARD PARISH.

This parish is situated in the extreme southeastern part of the State, and contains 435,205 acres. The formation is coast marsh and alluvial land. It is drained by the Mississippi River, Lake Borgne, and Bayous Terre au Boeuf, Loutre and Biloxi, and also Lake Borgne Canal.

The Mississippi, Terre au Boeuf and Lake Railroad, having a line extending to Shell Beach, on Lake Borgne, passes through the parish. St. Bernard, situated on the Mississippi River, is the parish seat. The parish adjoins Orleans.

Sugar is the chief crop product; but rice, jute and the garden and truck varieties are extensively raised and shipped. Sea Island cotton also does well. The fruits and nuts are oranges, lemons, mandarins, figs, pecans, bananas, grapes, guavas, olives and prunes. Some few cattle and hogs are raised here. Game consists of becasine, snipe, rice birds, papabots, wild ducks, coons, opossums, squirrels, rabbits and deer. Fish of fine quality are plentiful; oysters, crabs and terrapin are also found. The timber is oak, cypress, willow, elm, pine and gum.

The settlement of this parish commenced with the hardy pioneers who came with De Bienville when he removed the seat of government from Mobile to New Orleans. Plantations of indigo and later on sugar cane were introduced, and to two citizens of the parish, Mendes and Solis, must be given the credit of having first planted sugar cane in the State, and to another, Mr. Coiron, the distinction of first cultivating ribbon cane. Judge Gayarre says that Mr. Etienne de Bore borrowed from Mendes and Solis the cane from which he succeeded in making sugar of satisfactory quality. The parish has still another claim to fame: it was on her plains of Chalmette that the Battle of New Orleans was fought and won; it was in the then "Palace of Versailles," a beautiful home in all its glory of fine Italian marble, that General Packenham had his headquarters. It was under four oaks of St. Bernard, back of the Mercier place, that the English General, from his horse, directed the batle, and thence, desperately wounded, was taken back to the "Palace" (from whose floors trees now spring) and then on down to the Villere home, near which, under a pecan tree, the heart and entrails of the General were buried. The lower part of this old house still stands in fair preservation, one hundred and seventy-five years old.

ST. CHARLES PARISH.

St. Charles Parish, incorporated March 31, 1807, is in the southeastern part of Louisiana, and has an area of 251,520 acres. It is bounded on the north by Lake Pontchartrain and the Parish of St. John the Baptist, south by Lafourche Parish and Lake Salvador, east by Lake Salvador and Jefferson Parish, west by the Parishes of Lafourche and St. John the Baptist and Lake Des Allemands. The population is approximately 15,000, of which 9,000 are negroes and 500 Italians.

The number of acres in cultivation and outlying is 28,000; about 23,000 in cultivation, and nearly 5,000 lying out and not in cultivation. The land consists of a rich alluvial soil, having much organic matter and being exceptionally fertile. The drainage takes place from natural causes, water running from the bluff on each side of the Mississippi

River to bayous and swamps in the rear. With the exception of these bluffs, the land is practically level, and the drainage is hastened by ditches.

The Mississippi River runs through the parish. There are numerous small bayous, the most important being Bayou Des Allemands and Bayou La Branche. Lake Pontchartrain, Lake Salvador and Lake Des Allemands all border on the parish.

There are six railroads running through the parish; The Texas and Pacific Railroad and the Morgan's Louisiana & Texas Railroad, on the west side of the river, and the Yazoo & Mississippi Valley Railroad, the Louisiana Railway & Navigation Company, the Frisco Lines and the Illinois Central Railroad on the east side of the river. The Yazoo and Mississippi Valley Railroad and the Texas & Pacific Railroad both run along the river.

In the parish are nine sugar-houses, and there is a large sawmill at Taft, which saws cypress timber.

The reclamation of swamp lands is beginning to be done on a large scale, and several thousand acres have already been reclaimed at La Branche and at Paradis.

The seining and shipping of fish at Des Allemands has grown into an important industry. The buffalo fish is caught and packed into barrels for shipment to northern packeries. Large quantities of minks, raccoons and muskrats are caught yearly during the trapping season, and large quantities of game are killed.

Sugar cane, rice, corn, all kinds of vegetables and some tropical fruits are produced. The principal crops are sugar and rice.

Large quantities of corn are also produced.

The raising of vegetables at St. Rose, where unusually large cabbages are produced and shipped to northern markets in refrigerator cars, is an important feature, and vegetables can be successfully raised during the entire year. Little attention is given to planting fruit trees, and cattle-raising is not given the attention it deserves. Farmers are beginning to raise hogs more abundantly. Cattle find good grazing nine months a year, and poultry raising can be carried on successfully throughout the year. Almost every kind of game is found in the woods, almost every species of fish in the river, lakes and bayous.

The rainfall is abundant. The dirt roads are as good as any other roads of a similar character.

ST. HELENA PARISH.

This parish is situated in the southeastern part of the State, and contains 264,320 acres of land. The formation is pine hills, flats and bluff land; soil fertile and productive. It is drained by the Amite and Tickfaw Rivers and their branches. Water is abundant and of good quality.

A logging steam tramroad connects Greensburg, the parish seat, with the main line of the Illinois Central Railroad.

Cotton is the chief crop production; corn, oats, hay, peas, sweet and Irish potatoes, sorghum, tobacco and sugar cane are raised. The fruits and nuts are pears, grapes, plums, pecans, apples, peaches, quinces and the smaller varieties. Live stock are cattle, sheep, hogs and horses.

The timber is pine, oak, beech, magnolia, holly, gum, hickory, poplar and persimmon. Long-leaf pine is extensive. Game is found, such as deer, coons, opossums, foxes, squirrels, rabbits, wild turkeys, wild ducks, partridges, woodcock and robins. Fish are found in the rivers and other streams, the Tickfaw being noted for its fine quality and quantity of trout.

ST. JAMES PARISH.

The parish is situated in the southeastern part of the State, and is divided by the Mississippi River. It contains 219,520 acres of land, the soil being very fertile and productive. The formation is alluvial land, wooded swamp, and a little coast marsh. It is drained by the Mississippi River, Bayou Des Acadians and several small bayous. Water is plentiful and good.

The Y. & M. V., L. R. & N., Frisco, and Texas and Pacific Railroads pass through the parish. Convent, situated on the east bank of the Mississippi River, is the parish seat. Sugar is the chief crop product; rice, corn, tobacco, hay, oats, beans and sweet and Irish potatoes are raised. The famous Perique tobacco is almost exclusively raised in this parish. Figs, oranges, lemons, mandarins, guavas, plums, peaches, pears, pecans, grapes and pomegranates are grown.

Game consists of becasine, snipe, rice birds, squirrels, coons, opossums, rabbits, and some few deer and bear. Fish are found in the bayous and lagoons, of good quality, among them bass and pike.

The timber is cypress, oak, gum, elm, willow and cottonwood.

ST. JOHN THE BAPTIST PARISH.

This parish is situated in the southeastern part of the State, and is divided by the Mississippi River. It contains 147,200 acres, and the formation is alluvial land, wooded swamp and coast marsh. The soil is rich and productive. It is drained by the Mississippi River and Lakes Pontchartrain, Maurepas and Des Allemands. Water is abundant and fairly good.

The Yazoo and Mississippi Valley, the Illinois Central, L. R. & N., Frisco and the Texas and Pacific Railroads extend through the parish. Edgard, situated on the west bank of the Mississippi River, is the parish seat.

Sugar is the chief product; rice, oats, corn, hay, sweet and Irish potatoes and peas are produced. Oranges, figs, grapes, plums, pecans, guavas and pomegranates are grown. Some cattle and hogs are raised.

Game consists of squirrels, coons, opossums, rabbits, wild ducks, becasine, snipe and rice birds. Some few deer and bear are found. Fish, of good quality, abound in the lakes and bayous.

The timber is cypress, oak, gum, elm, cottonwood, and willow.

ST. LANDRY PARISH.

St. Landry is situated in the south-central part of the State and contains 562,500 acres of land. The formation is prairie, alluvial land, pine flats, wooded swamp, and bluff land. The soil is very fertile and productive. It is drained by the Atchafalaya River, and Bayous Rouge,

Courtableu, Teche, Boeuf, Cocodrie, and Nezique. Water is plentiful and of good quality.

The Texas and Pacific Railroad passes through the northeastern portion, and the branch road of the Southern Pacific, extending from Lafayette to Cheneyville, runs through the parish. Opelousas, situated on Bellevue Bayou, is the parish seat.

Cotton, rice and sugar are the chief crops produced for export; and corn, oats, hay, sweet and Irish potatoes, beans, sorghum, and the garden varieties and truck are extensively raised. The fruits are peaches, pears, plums, apples, grapes, quinces, figs, pomegranates, persimmons and the smaller varieties.

Live stock is extensively raised; sheep, cattle, horses and hogs all do remarkably well here and are a very profitable investment. Game is found, consisting of squirrels, opossums, rabbits, beavers, deer, wild turkeys, wild ducks and geese, woodcocks, becasine, partridges, pheasants, snipe and rice birds. Fish abound in the streams, such as bass, trout and pike. The timber embraces pine, oak, beech, magnolia, holly, gum, elm, persimmon, hickory, pecan, walnut, willow and sycamore.

ST. MARTIN PARISH.

This parish is situated in the southern part of the State, and contains 395,520 acres. The formation is wooded, swamp, prairie, alluvial land, and a small area of bluff land; soil fertile and productive. It is

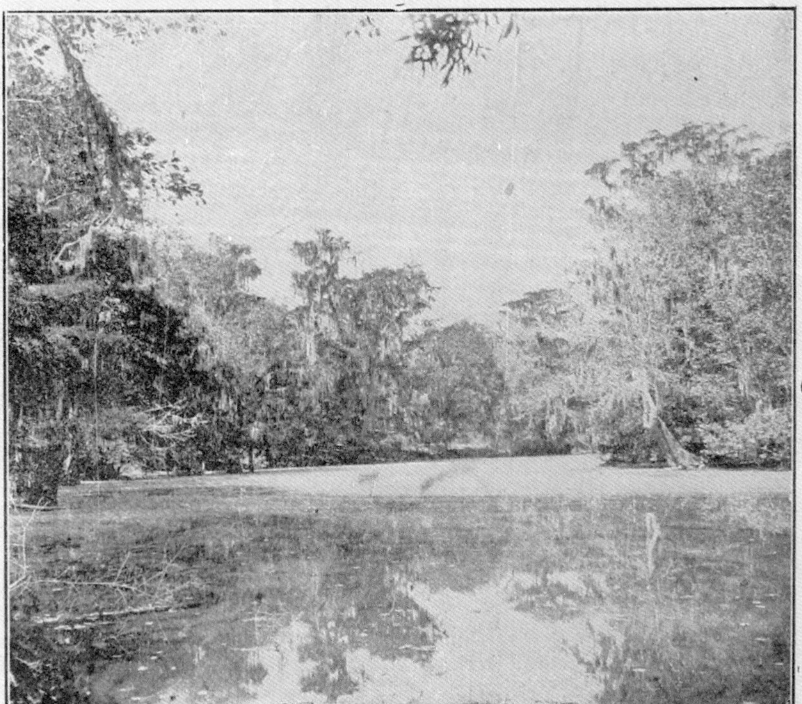

SCENE ON A BAYOU.

drained by the Atchafalaya River, Bayou Teche, Tortue, La Rose, L'Embarras and Catahoula Coulee.

St. Martinville, situated on the Teche, is the parish seat, and is connected with the Southern Pacific Railroad at Cade Station. Sugar is the chief crop production; rice, corn, oats, hay, sweet and Irish potatoes, tobacco, cotton and the garden varieties are also grown.

The fruits are oranges, lemons, mandarins, guavas, grapes, plums, prunes, pomegranates, peaches, pears, figs, apples, persimmons and quinces.

Cattle, sheep, hogs and horses are raised. Game, such as partridges, rice birds, pheasants, wild turkeys, squirrels, rabbits, coons, opossums, deer and bear are found. Fish are plentiful in the bayous, lakes and lagoons.

The Anse la Butte oil field lies just within the borders of this parish. Good results have already been obtained in this field, and much greater ones are expected when it is fully developed.

The timber embraces cypress, oak, gum, elm, willow, cottonwood, sugarwood and sycamore.

ST. MARY PARISH.

This parish is situated in the southern part of the State, and contains 414,720 acres. Its formation is coast marsh, alluvial land, prairie, wooded swamp, and a small amount of bluff land. The soil is exceedingly rich and productive. It is drained by the Atchafalaya River, Grand Lake and Bayous Teche, Sale and Cypremont. The Southern Pacific Railroad extends through the parish. Franklin, situated on the Teche, is the parish seat. Water is plentiful and good.

Sugar is the chief crop product; rice, corn, oats, hay, peas, sweet and Irish potatoes and garden varieties are extensively raised. The fruits and nuts are the orange, lemon, mandarin, fig, grape, persimmon, pomegranate, guava, plum, peach, pear, pecan, olive, banana and prune.

Cattle, hogs and some horses are raised. Game consists of snipe, becasine, pheasants, rice birds, partridges, squirrels, rabbits, coons, opossums and deer. Fish are plentiful in the bayous, lakes, lagoons and inlets, and oysters, crabs and terrapin are taken in the brackish waters. The timber is cypress, oak, cottonwood, gum, elm and willow.

ST. TAMMANY PARISH.

This parish is situated in the southeastern part of the State, and contains 590,720 acres of land. The formation is pine hills, pine flats, alluvial land and wooded swamp; soil, fertile and productive. It is drained by Pearl River, West Pearl, Chefuncta (or Tchefuncta) River, and Bogue Chitto, Bogue Falia and other streams. The New Orleans and Northeastern Railroad, belonging to the Queen and Crescent system, passes through the parish.

Covington, situated on the Bogue Falia, is the parish seat. It is connected with the New Orleans and Northeastern Railroad at West Pearl Station. Sugar, rice, cotton, corn, hay, oats, beans, sweet and Irish potatoes and truck garden varieties are extensively raised.

So famous has this parish become as a health resort, that it is known everywhere now as the "Ozone Belt." Thousands of cases of lung complaints have been successfully cured by this salubrious climate. Beautiful springs, whose waters are recognized as of great medicinal value, abound through the parish. The most famous of these is the Abita Spring, which has a capacity of 40,000 gallons daily.

The fruits and nuts are peaches, plums, pears, pecans, apples, figs, prunes, grapes, pomegranates, quinces and persimmons.

Cattle, hogs, sheep and a few horses are raised. Game consists of squirrels, rabbits, coons, opossums, deer, wild turkeys, wild ducks, papabots, bacasine, snipe, partridges and rice birds. Fish are plentiful in the streams and lakes; fine trout, bass and pike are taken. The timber is pine, oak, cypress, gum, elm and hickory.

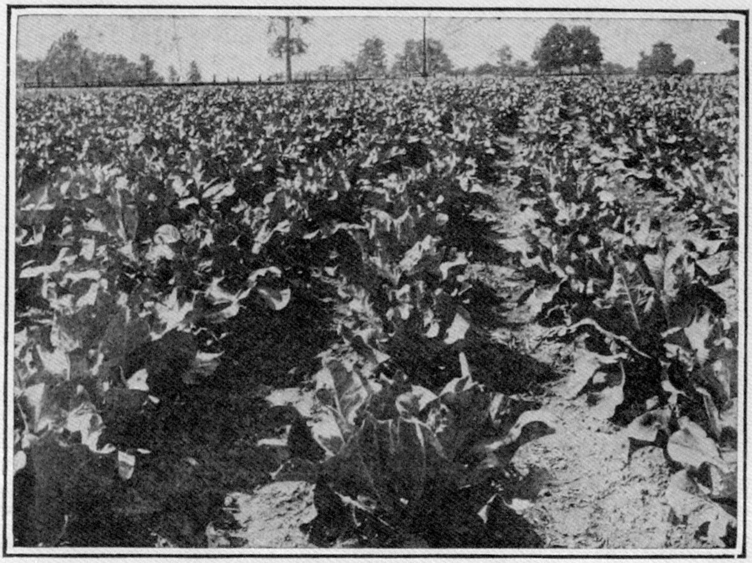

A CAULIFLOWER FIELD.

TANGIPAHOA PARISH.

This parish is situated in the southeastern part of the State, and contains 505,600 acres of land. The formation is pine hills, pine flats, wooded swamps, and a small amount of alluvial land. The soil is fertile and productive. It is drained by the Tangipahoa, Chefuncta, Natalbany and Ponchatoula Rivers, Chappapeela Creek and numerous smaller streams. Water is abundant and of good quality.

The Illinois Central Railroad extends through the parish, north and south. Amite City, situated on this line of road and near the Tangipahoa River, is the parish seat. Hammond has become very popular as a winter resort.

Cotton, corn, oats, hay, sugar cane, rice, tobacco, sorghum, sweet and Irish potatoes, peas and truck and garden varieties are grown. Along the line of the Illinois Central truck and strawberries are extensively grown and shipped. Fruits are peaches, pears, apples, plums, grapes, quinces, figs, pomegranates, persimmons and a variety of smaller kinds. Cattle, hogs, sheep and horses are raised. The timber is pine, oak, ash, gum, elm, hickory, poplar, cucumber, cottonwood, willow, beech and sycamore.

Game is found, such as squirrels, coons, opossums, foxes, rabbits, deer, wild turkeys, wild ducks, woodcock, snipe, becasine, rice birds, partridges and robins. Fish of excellent quality are taken from the streams; trout, bass, pike and blue cat are found.

TENSAS PARISH.

This parish is situated in the northeastern part of the State, and contains 410,240 acres of land. The formation is alluvial lands and wooded swamp; soil very rich and productive. It is drained by the Mississippi and Tensas Rivers, and Bayous Vidal, Durossett, Choctaw and Clark's. Water is plentiful and good. St. Joseph, situated on the Mississippi River, is the parish seat.

The new Gould line traverses the parish from north to south, furnishing direct communication with New Orleans and St. Louis.

Cotton is the chief crop product for export; corn, hay, oats, sweet and Irish potatoes, peas and garden varieties are grown. The fruits are peaches, plums, pears and apples. Cattle, hogs and some sheep and horses are raised.

The timber is oak, gum, cypress, cottonwood, pecan, persimmon, magnolia, elm, sycamore and willow.

Game is found, such as squirrels, rabbits, deer, bear, wild turkeys, wild ducks and geese, woodcock, snipe, partridges, plover, rice birds and robins.

Fish, in quantity, are taken from the lakes and bayous; bass, trout, white perch and pike are found.

TERREBONNE PARISH.

This parish is situated in the southern part of the State, and contains 1,265,280 acres. The formation is largely composed of coast marsh with a considerable area of alluvial lands and wooded swamp. The soil is exceedingly rich and productive. It is drained partially by Black, De Large, Grand and Petit Caillou Bayous, and Blue and Blue Hammock Bayous.

Houma, situated on Bayou Terrebonne, is the parish seat. It is connected with the Southern Pacific Railroad at Schriever Station. Sugar and rice are the chief crop productions; jute, peas, hay and Irish potatoes are grown. The fruits are oranges, lemons, mandarins, olives, bananas, prunes, figs, pomegranates, guavas and plums.

The timber is oak, cypress, gum, elm and willow.

Some cattle and hogs are raised. Game is found, such as wild ducks and geese, papabots, jack snipe, becasine, pheasants, rice birds, squirrels, deer and bear. Fish of fine quality are found; sheepshead, pompano, salt water trout, Spanish mackerel, pike and crabs. Oyster and shrimp canning is quite an important industry.

UNION PARISH.

This parish is situated in the northern part of the State, and contains 582,700 acres of lands. The formation is good upland, red, sandy clay, and some alluvial lands. The soil is very fertile and productive. It is drained by the Ouachita River, Bayou D'Arbonne, and affluents of these streams.

The Arkansas Southern and the Little Rock and Monroe Railroads run through the parish, north and south.

The Farmerville and Southern Railroad runs from the main line of the Little Rock and Monroe to Farmerville, which is the parish seat.

Water is abundant and of good quality, good springs and wells, and numerous branches and creeks.

Cotton is the chief crop product, and corn, oats, hay, wheat, sorghum, peas, sweet and Irish potatoes, tobacco and sugar cane are raised. Diversified farming is practiced.

The fruits are peaches, apples, pears, plums, grapes, pomegranates, figs and quinces. Excellent fruit is raised.

The timber is pine, oak, beech, hickory, maple, walnut, holly, gum, elm and poplar.

Live stock raised on the farms comprise cattle, sheep, hogs and horses. Game consists of squirrels, rabbits, coons, opossums, foxes, deer, wild turkeys, wild ducks, woodcock and partridges. Trout, bar fish and speckled and blue cat are found among the fish in the streams.

VERMILION PARISH.

Vermilion Parish is situated in the southwestern part of the State, and contains 800,000 acres of land. The formation is coast marsh, prairie, alluvial and bluff lands; soil rich and productive. It is drained by the Vermilion River and Bayous Queue de Tortue and Fresh Water. Abbeville, situated on the Vermilion River, is the parish seat.

A branch of the Southern Pacific Railroad runs through the parish.

Rice is the chief crop product; sugar, corn, oats, hay, peas, sweet and Irish potatoes, and truck varieties are raised. The fruits and nuts are oranges, lemons, mandarins, plums, pecans, guavas, figs, peaches, prunes, pomegranates and grapes. The timber varieties are oak, gum, elm, cypress, cottonwood and willow.

Live stock raised are cattle, hogs, sheep and horses. Game consists of rice birds, pheasants, becasine, snipe, partridges, papabots and wild ducks and deer. Fish are taken from the streams and inlets, and crabs, oysters, diamond-back terrapins and salt water varieties of fish are found.

VERNON PARISH.

This parish is situated in the western part of the State, and contains 986,600 acres of land. The formation is chiefly pine hills, with a little prairie and alluvial lands. The Kansas City Southern Railroad runs from north to south through this parish. It is drained by the Sabine and Calcasieu Rivers and Bayous, Comrade, Castor, Anacoco, and numerous small streams. Water is abundant and of good quality. The soil is fairly productive.

Leesville, on the Kansas City Southern Railroad, is the parish seat. Cotton is the chief crop product, and corn, hay, oats, peas, sweet and Irish potatoes, and sorghum are grown.

The fruits and nuts are peaches, pears, pecans, apples, figs, pomegranates, plums and grapes. Live stock comprises cattle, sheep, hogs and horses. Game consists of deer, squirrels, coons, opossums, rabbits, beaver, wild turkeys, wild ducks, partridges, woodcock, pheasant, becasine, snipe, plover and rice birds. There are fine varieties of fish found in the streams, among them trout, pike, bar fish and bass.

The timber is pine, oak, elm, gum, willow, hickory and cottonwood. Extensive areas of long-leaf pine exist.

WASHINGTON PARISH.

This parish is situated in the northeast corner of the southeast portion of the State, and contains 427,520 acres of land. The formation is pine hills and flats, with a little alluvial land along its eastern border. The soil is fairly good. It is drained by Pearl River, Bogue Chitto and Chefuncta Creek. Water is abundant and good.

The Kentwood and Eastern Railway runs through the northern part of the parish.

Franklinton, situated on the Bogue Chitto, is the parish seat. Cotton is the chief product; hay, oats, corn, sweet and Irish potatoes, tobacco, sorghum, peas and the truck varieties are grown. The fruits are peaches, pears, plums, apples, figs, quinces, pomegranates and grapes.

Live stock are cattle, horses, hogs and sheep. Game is found, such as deer, foxes, coons, opossums, squirrels, rabbits, beaver, wild turkeys, wild ducks, partridges, woodcock and rice birds. Fish abound in the creeks, and among the varieties are trout, bar fish, bass and pike.

The timber is pine, long-leaf, beech, holly, poplar, gum, elm, magnolia, oak and maple.

In this parish is the great little city of Bogalusa, which boasts of the largest sawmill in the United States, its capacity being one million feet per day.

WEBSTER PARISH.

This parish is situated in the northwestern part of the State, and contains 383,600 acres of land. The formation is good uplands and some alluvial lands. The soil is very good and fertile. It is drained by Dorchite, Crows and Black Lake Bayous and Lake Bisteneau. Minden is the parish seat. The water is plentiful and good; springs, wells and small streams abound.

The Vicksburg, Shreveport and Pacific Railroad extends east and West, and the Louisiana and Arkansas Railroad north and south through the parish. Cotton is the chief crop product, and corn, hay, oats, peas, sorghum, sugar cane, sweet and Irish potatoes and tobacco are grown.

The fruits are peaches, pears, apples, plums, figs, grapes, pomegranates and quinces. Salt deposits exist, and beds of potters' clay, fire clay, lignite and marl are found. Timber is pine, oak, gum, hickory, beech, holly, elm, poplar, walnut and maple.

Live stock raised are cattle, hogs, sheep, and a few horses. Game consists of squirrels, deer, foxes, rabbits, coons, opossums, wild turkeys, wild ducks, woodcock, robins and partridges. Fish of good quality are found in the streams.

WEST BATON ROUGE.

This parish is situated in the south-central part of the State, and lies west of the Mississippi River. In area it is the smallest parish, except Orleans, in the State, and contains 134,400 acres of land. The formation is alluvial land and wooded swamp, very fertile and productive. The Mississippi River drains the eastern borders, and Bayous Grosse Tete, Poydras and Stumpy the other sections. Drinking water is good.

The Texas and Pacific Railroad passes through the southern part of the parish, and has a branch road leading from Baton Rouge Junction to Ferriday. This branch line will form part of the main line of the new Gould line, St. Louis to New Orleans. Also the Frisco and Southern Pacific branch to Lafayette pass through the parish.

Port Allen, situated on the west bank of the Mississippi River, is the parish seat. The timber consists of oak, cypress, pecan, persimmon, gum, poplar, cottonwood, hackberry and willow. The general crop of the parish is sugar; rice, corn, hay, oats, sweet and Irish potatoes, peas, cotton and the garden varieties are produced. Fruits are pears, peaches, plums, apples, figs and grapes.

Some live stock are raised, such as cattle, hogs, sheep and horses. Game and fish abound; deer, bear, squirrels, coons, opossums, wild turkeys, wild geese and ducks, becasine, jack snipe, partridges, rice birds and robins are found.

WEST CARROLL PARISH.

This parish is situated in the northeastern part of the State, and contains 243,200 acres of land. It is of bluff formation chiefly, with some wooded swamp and alluvial land, the soil of which is rich and productive. It is drained by Bayou Macon on the eastern and Boeuf River on its western borders. Floyd, situated on Bayou Macon, is the parish seat. Water is abundant and of good quality.

Cotton is the chief crop product, and corn, hay, oats, sugar cane, sweet and Irish potatoes, sorghum, peas and the garden varieties are raised. The timber varieties are oak, cypress, ash, beech, elm, gum, cottonwood, pecan, locust, hickory, magnolia, holly, mulberry and persimmon.

Live stock, such as cattle, sheep, hogs and horses, are raised.

Game abounds, among which are deer, bear, squirrels, rabbits, coons, opossums, foxes, wild turkeys, wild ducks and geese, robins and woodcock. Fishing is good in the streams, and bass, bar fish, white perch and trout are found.

WEST FELICIANA PARISH.

This parish is situated in the southeastern part of the State, and contains 246,400 acres of land. The formation is bluff and alluvial land, with some wooded swamp. It is drained by the Mississippi River, Bayous Tunica and Sara, and Thompson's Creek. A branch line of the Mississippi Valley Railroad, from Slaughter Station to Woodville, Miss., extends through the parish. The Louisiana Railway and Navigation Company traverses the parish.

St. Francisville, situated on the Mississippi River, is the parish seat. The water throughout the parish is abundant and of good quality. The chief crop product is cotton; corn, hay, oats, peas, sweet and Irish potatoes, sorghum, sugar cane and tobacco are raised. The timber is cypress, cottonwood, willow, oak, pine, beech, gum, elm, magnolia, holly, hackberry, hickory, poplar, sycamore, walnut and persimmon. The fruits and nuts are peaches, pears, pecans, apples, prunes, pomegranates, figs, quinces and grapes. Live stock thrives remarkably well, and this parish has long been noted for its superior breeds of blooded cattle. Hogs, sheep and horses do well here. Game abounds, such as deer, coons, opossums, foxes, rabbits, squirrels, beavers, wild turkeys, wild ducks and geese, partridges, snipe, rice birds and woodcock. Excellent varieties of fish are taken from the lakes, bayous and creeks, among which are trout, bass, white perch and bar fish.

The Tunica hills are most suitable for grape culture and horticulture, the soil being a rich marl loam.

WINN PARISH.

Winn Parish is situated near the central part of the State, and contains 610,560 acres of land. The formation is pine hills, with a small amount of good uplands. The soil is fair, and the creek bottoms very good. It is drained by the Dugdemona River, Saline Bayou, Flat Creek, Bayou Jatt and other streams. The water is abundant and good.

The Louisiana Railway and Navigation Company and the Arkansas Southern Railroads run through the parish.

Winnfield, situated near the center, is the parish seat. Cotton is the chief product; corn, hay, oats, peas, sweet and Irish potatoes, sorghum, sugar cane and tobacco are grown. The fruits and nuts are peaches, pears, plums, apples, figs, pecans, English walnuts, quinces, grapes and pomegranates. The timber comprises pine, oak, elm, hickory and gum. There are extensive aeras of long-leaf pine. Live stock are cattle, sheep and hogs. Game consists of deer, coons, opossums, foxes, squirrels, rabbits, wild turkeys, robins, woodcock and partridges. Fish of good varieties are found in the streams. There are deposits of salt, marble, lignite, kaolin, gypsum, limestone, iron, fire clay and potters' clay.

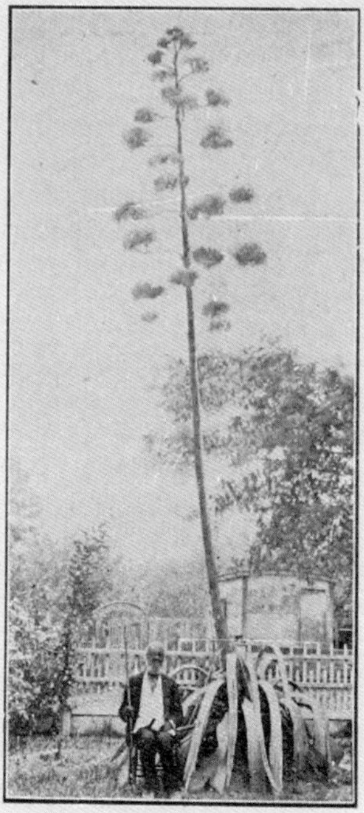

THE END OF TWO CENTURIES.

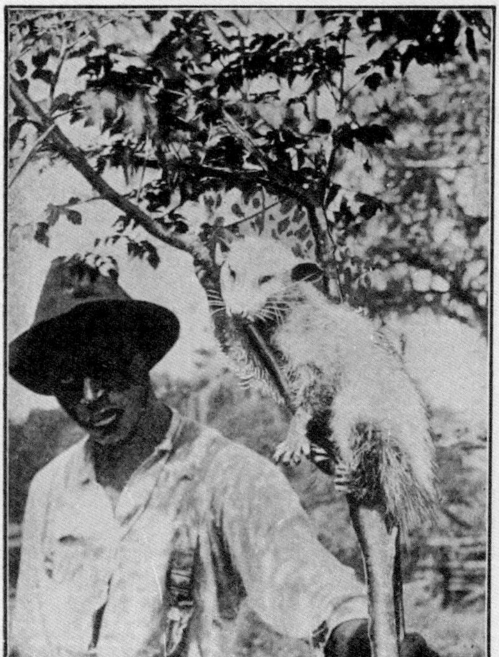

FORCES AT WORK IN BEHALF OF THE FARMER

BOARD OF AGRICULTURE AND IMMIGRATION.

THE DEPARTMENT endeavors to get as close to the farmers as possible. Periodically, crop reports, setting forth the prospects, conditions and variety of crops in Louisiana, accompanied with one or more papers relating to some particular question of importance in agriculture by some distinguished agriculturist, are distributed free to the farmers of the State. As a Bureau of Information, the Department invites, receives and answers thousands of letters annually, seeking agricultural information. It issues, from time to time, other agricultural literature for distribution, including the Market Report Bulletins every week.

THE LOUISIANA STATE UNIVERSITY AND AGRICULTURAL AND MECHANICAL COLLEGE

is doing a grand work in the education of young men of the State in Agriculture and its underlying sciences. Special courses are provided in Agriculture, the Mechanics, Chemistry, and the culture of sugar cane, Veterinary Science, Entomology, Horticulture, Geology and Biology, which fully equip many young men to engage in agricultural pursuits, where they become teachers and leaders in their respective communities throughout the State. The foundation is here being laid for an advanced and modern system of agriculture, which a great agricultural State like Louisiana stands in need of.

AGRICULTURAL EXPERIMENT STATIONS.

The Agricultural Experiment Stations of the Louisiana State University, created by an Act of Congress, known as the "Hatch Bill," passed in 1887, appropriates $15,000 annually for the establishment of Experiment Stations in connection with the State Agricultural Colleges. The Legislature of Louisiana appropriates annually a like amount for the maintenance of these Stations. The Board of Supervisors of the State University divided these funds equally between three Stations. One is located on the College grounds at Baton Rouge, Louisiana, known as the "State Experiment Station," and deals with general agriculture upon the bluff lands of the State. One is located at Audubon Park, New Orleans, Louisiana, known as "The Sugar Experiment Station," and deals especially with sugar cane and its manufacture and, incidentally, with oranges and semi-tropical crops. It is located upon alluvial lands. One located in north Louisiana, at Calhoun, known as "The North Louisiana Experiment Station," in the Parish of Ouachita, on the line of the Vicksburg, Shreveport and Pacific Railroad, deals with general diversified agriculture, dairying, live stock and poultry. It is situated on the oak, hickory, and short-leaf pine lands of the State, geologically known as "good uplands." Thus, it is seen, Louisiana has three Experiment Stations, located upon the different types of soils, each studying and solving the problems that concern education of the farmers of the State, and one at Crowley, which deals with the rice industry of the State.

PARISH AGRICULTURAL FAIRS.

are being organized and conducted in a great many of the parishes of Louisiana, the Department of Agriculture taking a leading part in this work. Quite a number of these fairs have already been organized, and a great many more are planned for organizing during the fall of 1917.

The Farmers' Institutes, Agricultural Clubs and Parish Fairs form a trinity of educational forces at work in the several parishes of the State that cannot be equaled.

FERTILIZER AND FEED STUFF LAWS.

The Department of Agriculture has the enforcement and control of the Fertilizer, Feed Stuff and Paris Green Laws, which secure to the farmer unadulterated fertilizers, cotton seed meal, feed stuff and Paris green, and protects him against fraud in their purchase. This is a most important work in behalf of agriculture.

THE MOVING PICTURE IN EXTENSION AND EDUCATIONAL WORK.

The most popular of all pleasures, the moving picture, has been brought forth as a great motive power in disseminating agricultural work and knowledge by Professor E. S. Richardson.

By using an automobile equipped with a small dynamo for producing current for lights, the Junior Extension Division of the Louisiana State University has been able to show educational moving pictures and lantern slides to more than 50,000 people during the past twenty-two months. During this time the Junior Extension staff have traveled 14,000 miles and visited 33 parishes. The remotest country districts were included in the itineraries. The pictures were shown usually at the schoolhouses and the programs attended by boys and girls belonging to the agricultural schools, by their parents, and farmers generally. Thousands of rural people, most of whom had never before seen moving pictures, have been entertained and instructed by this means. This machine is the only one of its kind in successful operation, and it is believed to have great possibilities in extension and educational work.

The auto-stereopticon and moving picture machine, as it has been termed, is the invention of Prof. E. S. Richardson, who is in charge of the boys' and girls' club work of Louisiana. For the past two months it has been operated by the Junior Extension Department of the State University, cooperating with the State Department of Agriculture. The State Department has furnished the services of an expert chauffeur. This cooperation has added much to the efficiency of the work of the picture machine.

Parish school superintendents and other rural school workers are very enthusiastic over the results of the visits that have been made to their parishes with this educational moving picture machine. In every instance there has been an increased interest in agricultural club and extension work. The parents, as well as the boys and girls, have been awakened to its practical value. All the parishes in which these educational pictures have been shown have requested return visits, and at the present time Professor Richardson has more requests for return engagements than he can comply with.

The following letter from Superintendent F. M. Hamilton of Calcasieu Parish is one of many received by President Thos. D. Boyd of the Louisiana State University in commendation of the work of the auto-stereopticon and moving picture machine:

"Mr. E. S. Richardson and his assistants, Mr. Balis and Mr. Guilbeau, have just completed a tour of Calcasieu Parish with the moving picture outfit. I wish to express to you and your department our appreciation for this work. I attended all the meetings held in this parish with one exception. At practically all points we had more people than anticipated, and a conservative estimate of the total number attending is twenty-three hundred. At no place did the machine fail to work, and at practically all places leading people of the community express themselves as highly gratified with the pictures and lectures. In my opinion, this work marks a new era in the extension movement."

Harry D. Wilson, State Commissioner of Agriculture, was highly impressed from the beginning with this machine, and believes it to be one of the most effective methods of reaching the rural people with educational and agricultural propaganda.

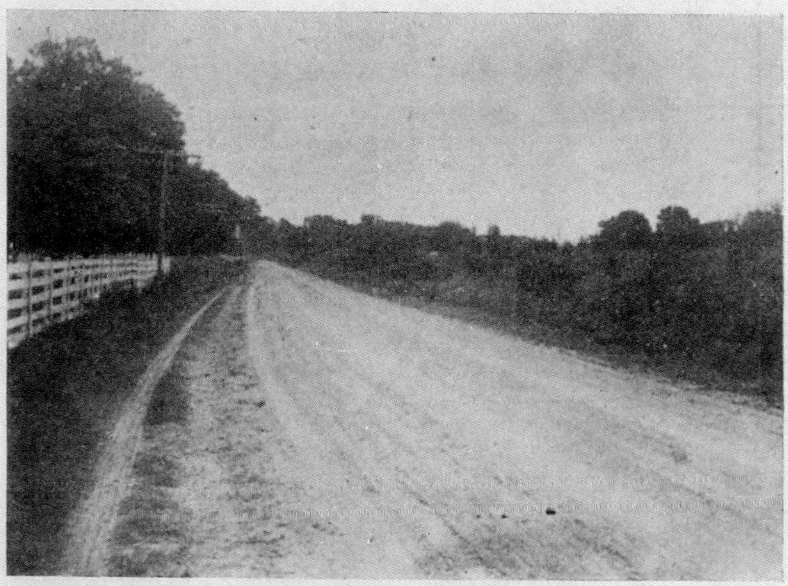

A GOOD ROAD BETWEEN ASCENSION AND ASSUMPTION

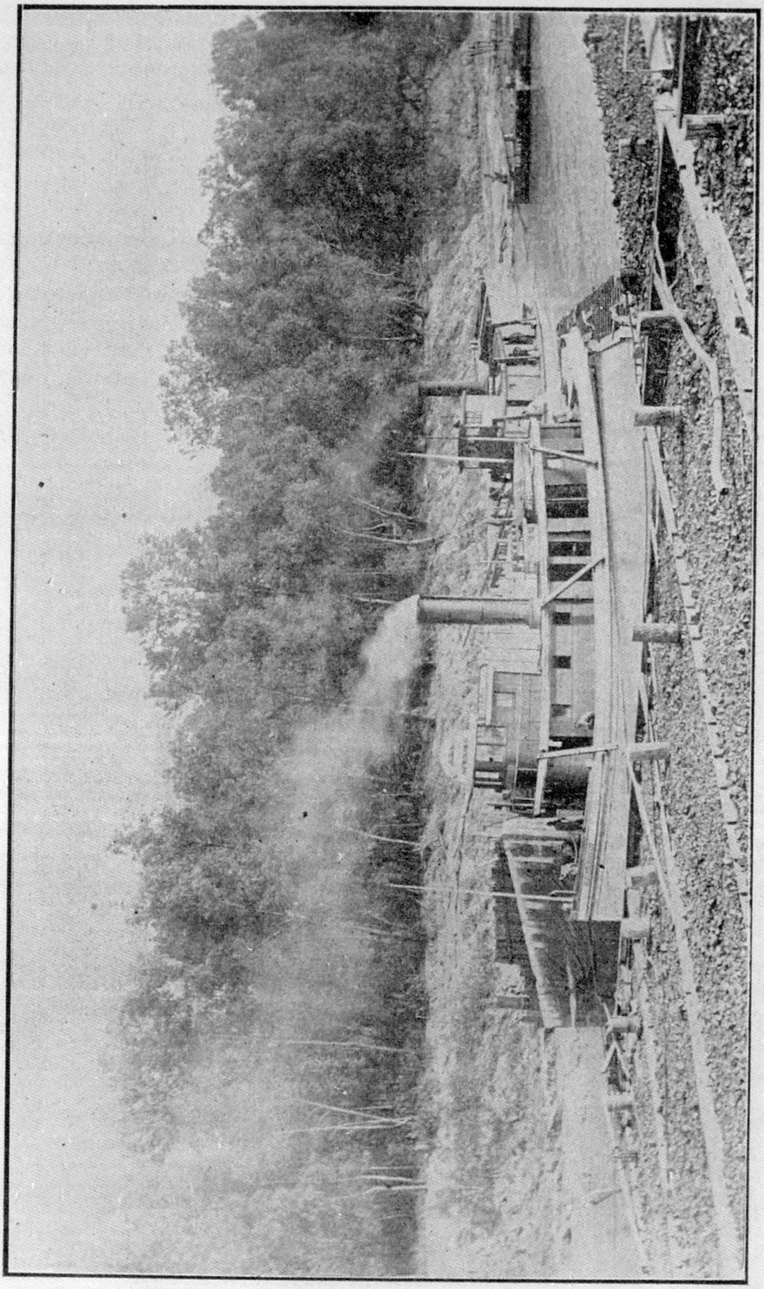

COAL BARGES FROM PITTSBURGH ON THE MISSISSIPPI RIVER.

GOOD ROADS

THE LEGISLATURE, at its session of 1910, enacted laws on this subject that can and will redound in great benefit to the entire people. In substance, they are as follows: The State employs a Highway Engineer, who will supervise the construction of all roads, the expenses for building the roads to be borne one-half by the State and one-half by the parish or town. The roads shall be built as far as practicable in the order of the date of receipt of the applications from Presidents of the Police Juries of the respective parishes. In order to further carry out the provisions of the act and provide sufficient labor to construct and maintain the public roads as provided for, the convicts of the State may be worked as authorized by the Constitution. The labor furnished by the convicts shall be secured by the State Highway Engineer making application to the Board of Control of the State Penitentiary, who shall furnish such convicts in case they are available, and free of charge; provided, however, that the cost of maintenance and operation shall be borne by the parish, municipality or road district having the work perforem.d The Board of Control of the State Penitentiary shall at all times retain control and supervision over said convicts

---

EDUCATION

MANY YEARS AGO the people of Louisiana, realizing the vast importance of education, determined to aim high in this grand work, and, step by step, as the years rolled 'round, the onward and upward march has continued. The Legislators have always shown a liberality in appropriations commensurate with a great State's great cause. The Police Juries and City or Town Councils have kept an even pace with the State, and a combination of all the various elements is a motive power so potent that no fears are now apprehended as to Louisiana's place among her sister States.

I.—SCHOOL SYSTEMS.

(1) A State system of public schools supported partly by State taxation, partly by police jury, and other local appropriations, and supervised by a State Superintendent of Public Instruction, a State Board of Education, and Parish School Boards.

(2) The city school systems separate in organization and supervision from the State system, but partially supported by the prorated school revenues of the State.

II.—HIGHER EDUCATION.

(1) High schools officially recognized by the State Board of Educations as pursuing an approved curriculum.

(2) The State University and Agricultural & Machanical College.

(3) Tulane University of Louisiana, which, although exacting tuition fees, may be considered a semi-public institution, owing to its scholarship system, and the fact that the State contributes indirectly largely to its support by exempting its investments from taxation.

III.—PROFESSIONAL EDUCATIONAL TRAINING

(1) The State Normal School at Natchitoches.

(2) The New Orleans Normal School.

Both of these institutions are preparing for the public school service of the State a corps of fully equipped and professionally trained teachers.

(3) State Teachers' Institutes and Summer Normal Schools. These give the opportunity of one month's training and professional study to teachers who are unable to take the more extended courses of the State Normal School, and are supported largely by annual appropriations from the Peabody fund.

(4) Parish Teachers' Institutes of one week's duration required by law to be held under the auspices of parish superintendents of education.

(5) Educational Associations, such as the annual convention of parish superintendents of education; the annual meeting of the State Teachers' Association; the monthly meetings of parish and city teachers' associations, all of which exert an influence in the direction of professionalizing the business of education.

IV.—INDUSTRIAL EDUCATION.

(1) The State Industrial Institute at Ruston, giving, free of charge, admirable instruction in English, science, mechanics, trades, occupations and industries to both sexes.

(2) The Southwestern Industrial Institute, at Lafayette, is an institution doing good work along the same lines.

V.—PRIVATE AND SECTARIAN SCHOOLS.

There are many of these for both sexes distributed through the State.

VI.—EDUCATION OF THE COLORED.

(1) Public schools in every town, city and parish.

(2) Southern University for the higher and industrial training of negro youth. Much of what the State might do for negro education is rendered unnecessary, owing to the large number of prosperous special institutions in our midst that are supported by endowment.

INDUSTRIAL.

The Southern Industrial University, located at Baton Rouge, under the management of Professor J. S. Clark, is doing splendid work. The president's courtesy under all circumstances has won for him and his institution universal esteem and kindly consideration. Besides the good work of this university, there are several colored farm demonstrators, who seem to be greatly aiding their people along agricultural and industrial lines.

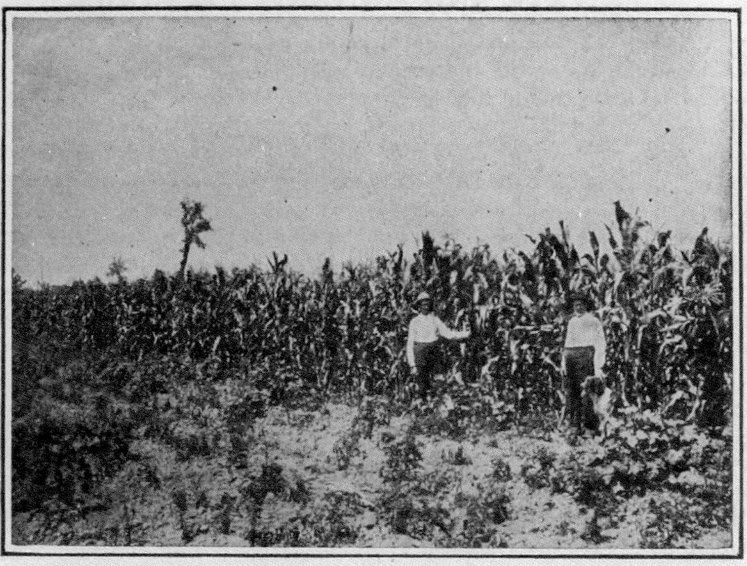

FIELD OF CORN IN CADDO PARISH

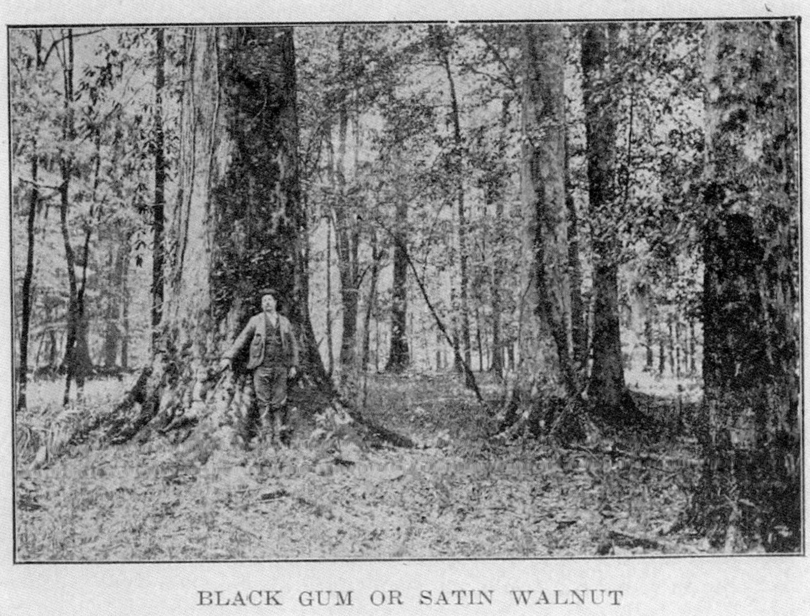

BLACK GUM OR SATIN WALNUT

PRIVATE AND SECTARIAN SCHOOLS

BESIDES the various school systems enumerated, the different denominations of the State have splendid schools and colleges. The Methodists have a male college, "Centenary," at Shreveport, and a female college at Mansfield. The Baptists have a male college at Mt. Lebanon and a female college at Keatchie. The Catholics have a university and several colleges in New Orleans, Jefferson College at Convent, and St. Charles College at Grand Coteau. They have numerous convents in New Orleans and convents in other cities and towns of the State. The Silliman Female College at Clinton has long been a famous girls' school. Private schools are successfully conducted in New Orleans, Shreveport, Baton Rouge and other cities and towns of the State.

TWO SPLENDID ADJUNCTS TO LOUISIANA'S EDUCATIONAL FORCES

ATTENTION is called to Memorial Hall and the State Museum.

The stranger, as he strolls up Camp street, New Orleans, is attracted by a peculiarly shaped building, whose inviting appearance bids him enter. He soon discovers that he is in the midst of historical reminders that tell him of the glories of Louisiana, that point out a chivalry so transcendantly brilliant that it has left a glow that sheds a brightness over the State's entire after-life, impressing upon the younger generations the sublime principles of virtue and manhood, a combination which practically is the bulwark of every country's safety and happiness.

From these relics or reminders of a superb inheritance housed by the generosity of a progressive citizen of New Orleans and cared for by State appropriations, he can cross Canal street, stroll among the quaint but interesting reminders of the French and Spanish domination and enter the historic Cabildo and Presbytere.

To Curator Robert Glenk we are indebted for the following:

"The Cabildo and the Presbytere both belong to the City of New Orleans, but have been transferred to the Board of Curators for all time by act of the City Council in 1908."

The following is a description of the museum and its workings, given by Mr. Glenk to the Shreveport Times:

One of the youngest of the State's institutions devoted to the advancement of Louisiana along educational and commercial lines is the Louisiana State Museum at New Orleans. The Museum owes its origin to the splendid collection of exhibits made at the World's Fair in St. Louis in 1904, which at the close of the Fair were brought back and temporarily housed in the Washington Artillery Hall. Since then the collections have grown prodigiously, numbering at the present day over 15,000 items and occupying 14,000 square feet of floor space. Within the past year, the City Council of New Orleans has transferred to the Board of Curators of the State Museum the historic Cabildo and the Civil District Court buildings, facing Jackson Square, to permanently house the rapidly growing and valuable collections of the museum. The Cabildo will contain the precious historical matter relating to Louisiana. In this building the transfer ceremonies took place when Louisiana was ceded to the United States in 1803 and during the visit of General Lafayette to New Orleans it was the home of the distinguished soldier. Being itself the most historical in the Mississippi Valley, it is eminently fitted to be the repository of the State's rich historical treasures. The Antommarchie bronze of Napoleon, presented to New Orleans in 1834 by the physician of the distinguished Corsican, is one of the valuable relics.

Recently the museum has acquired extremely valuable documents, letters, commissions, edicts and imprints of French and Spanish colonial Louisiana belonging to the Gaspar Cusacks, Major Robinson, T. P. Thompson, H. Gibbs Morgan, Jr., collections and to the Louisiana Historical Society, U. S. Daughters of 1776-1812, and Dr. Joseph Jones. The museum also contains many maps of Louisiana, relics from the battlefield of Chalmette and Eugene Lami's famous picture of the Battle of New Orleans.

The Art Department contains numerous paintings in oil and water color, engravings, sculpture and ceramics by some of the best of Louisiana's artists. One of the most noteworthy of the museum's exhibits is the large and comprehensive collection of relics of the mound-builders of Louisiana, embracing arrow points, axes, celts, ceremonial and game implements and pottery collected and loaned by Professor George Williamson of Natchitoches.

The Natural History Department contains specimens of the common and many rare varieties of the animals, birds, fishes, reptiles, insects, shells, fossils and minerals, and of the plants, trees and cultivated crops.

The Commercial Department contains manufactured articles made in Louisiana, together with numerous working models, statistics and literature and a complete model of a cane sugar factory, rice mill and pumping plant and a cotton oil mill.

The museum contains one of the best libraries in the South on science, technology, commercial and trade statistics, and the Bureau of Information is at all times at the service of the public.

During the winter months a series of free lectures are given by prominent lecturers at the museum on subjects dealing with the various activities of the several departments.

A series of publications based upon a natural history survey of the State is contemplated by the Museum Board. The first number, by Professor R. S. Cocks, has been issued and will be mailed to applicants in the State free.

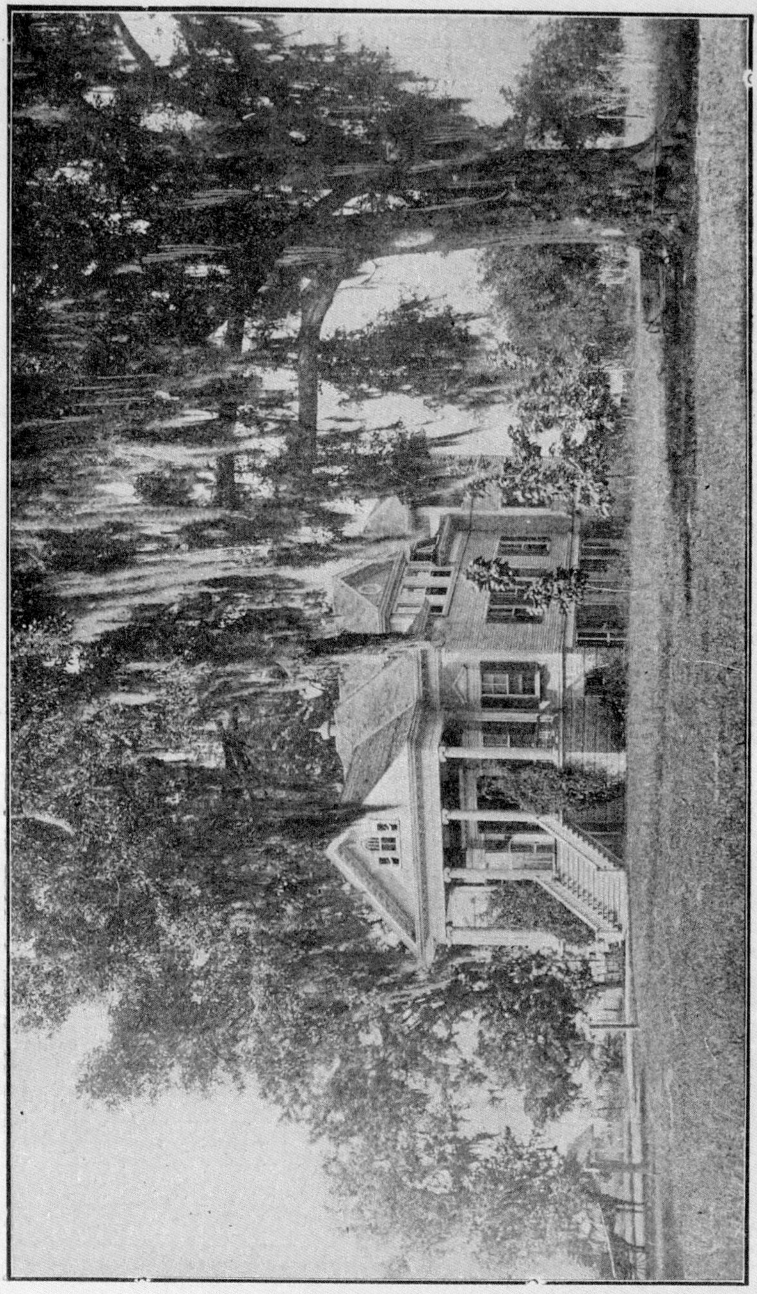

RESIDENE IN TERREBONNE PARISH

STATE INSTITUTIONS

INSTITUTE FOR THE DEAF AND DUMB.

THIS INSTITUTION is located at Baton Rouge. The grounds and buildings are in excellent condition. Its financial showing, and everything pertaining to its management are all that could be desired. Its class departments, oral teaching and industrial instructions are conducted on both scientific and practical methods, and it has already sent out a number of expert and highly intelligent instructors and teachers from among its pupils. Its chief aim is to prepare its pupils for the affairs of life, and make them industrious and self-supporting citizens. Several industrial trades, such as furniture-making and wood-working, shoe-making and printing and typesetting, are taught with marked success, and it is hoped to further enlarge and extend these departments.

INSTITUTE FOR THE BLIND.

Situated at Baton Rouge, this institution does a great work in educating and fitting for various walks in life the unfortunate ones whose sight is gone.

Like the other institution referred to above, one of the chief aims of the Institute for the Blind is, and should be, not only to educate but to fit pupils for the ordinary affairs of life, and make them self-sustaining. When there is any aptitude whatever, music is taught, and many of the pupils have attained great proficiency upon several musical instruments Wicker and cane work are taught; also sewing, embroidery, etc., and the manufacture of brooms has become quite a factor in the industrial department.

SOLDIERS' HOME.

This institution is situated in New Orleans, and provides a home for the disabled veterans of the Civil War who fought on the Confederate side, and whose homes were in Louisiana. A commodious two-story building has been erected, which has added much to the comfort of the inmates.

As time moves on, the lines of those who followed Lee, Johnston and Jackson are growing thinner, and from the active walks of life the number of those disabled and infirm, and without the means of support, is gradually increasing. These veterans of the Lost Cause appeal not only to our charity, love and benevolence, but also to our sense of justice, and the State should always liberally provide for them, as care and want overtake them in their declining years.

Article 302 of the present Constitution recognizes this Home as a State institution, and provides that it shall be maintained by the State by an annual appropriation which is to be based upon the number of inmates in the Home on the first day of April of the year in which the appropriation is made, of $130 per capita, for the maintenance and clothing of such inmates.

INSANE ASYLUM.

This institution, located at Jackson, La., stands preeminently as a monument to the true charity and benevolence and exalted humanity of our people. Its 1400 or more inmates are provided with a home, furnished with every modern convenience, presided over and directed by a superintendent and corps of assistants and attendants, who exercise kindly and even paternal supervision over them. They are supplied with abundant pure water for all purposes, ample baths, electric lights, artificial heat, ice manufactured by the asylum, wholesome and abundant food, and healthful grounds and surroundings. Each individual inmate is made the object of investigation and study by the resident physician and his assistants, and as a result of skillful and painstaking treatment and attention, a very large percentage of the inmates are, from time to time, discharged as completely restored. If our people throughout the State could become more intimately acquainted with the details and management of this institution, the usual prejudice against it as a gloomy madhouse would be dispelled, and it would be seen to be what it is—a sanitarium and home for those suffering from disordered and diseased minds. It would be a revelation to those who have never visited it, to observe the extent of its grounds, and the style and number of its handsome buildings, the completeness of its equipment, its scrupulous cleanliness, and its picturesque and beautiful situation and surroundings.

The Legislature, at its session in 1902, passed an act providing for the building and establishing of another Hospital for the Insane, near Alexandria, funds were appropriated and the work begun at once. At the extra session of the Legislature in 1903, another appropriation was made to complete the buildings, and, like the Hospital for the Insane at Jackson, it is doing thorough work and is an institution that all Louisianians are proud of.

CHARITY HOSPITAL, NEW ORLEANS.

This hospital was situated in the City of New Orleans, and was established in 1832, being among the first free hospitals ever established in the United States.

How well its obligation to humanity is performed is attested by the records of this institution. The hospital grounds embrace two squares, with ambulance house situated in a third square. The Richard Milliken Memorial Annex for Children has been recently built, and is thorough and modern in every appointment. The Pasteur Department, which is also free, was added in 1903.

Year by year, through the State's bounty, and with the assistance of donations from her philanthropic citizens, modern new buildings and equipments have been added, until our hospital stands among those at the head of the list of such institutions upon this continent.

Its able board of administrators and officers, and skilled and experienced surgeons and physicians have for years past maintained its well-established reputation, and more deeply rooted this institution in the hearts of all our people.

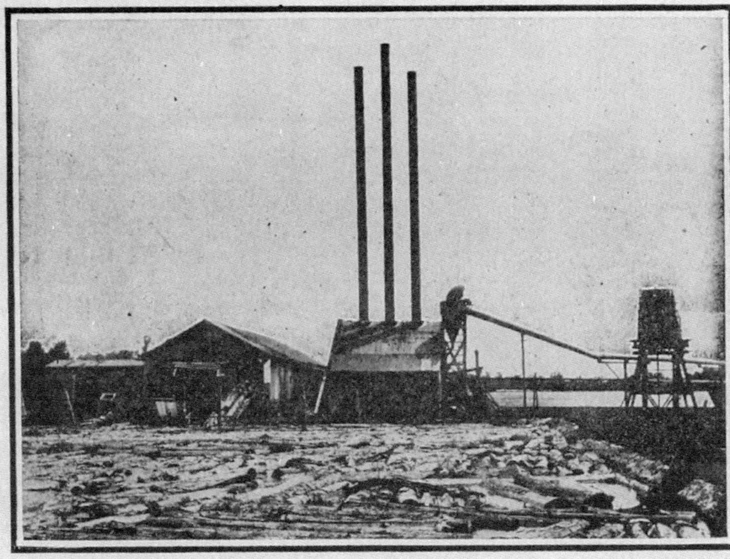

SAWMILL AT TAFT, ST. CHARLES PARISH

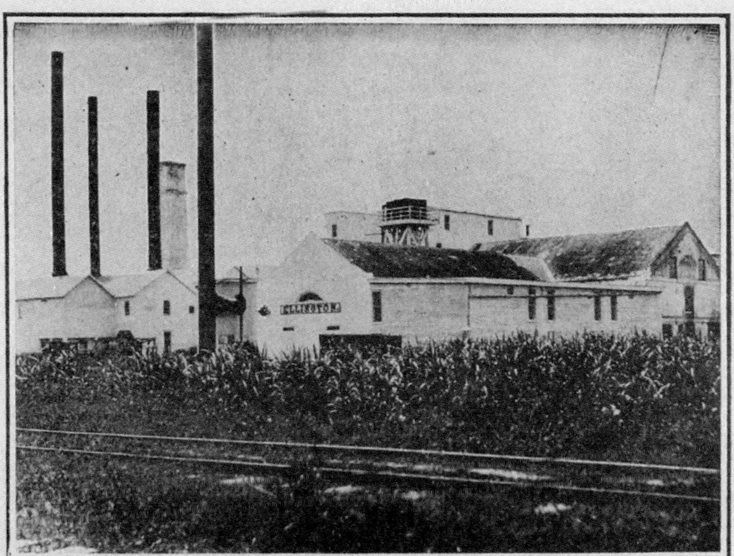

A SUGAR MILL IN ST. CHARLES PARISH

SHREVEPORT CHARITY HOSPITAL.

Situated at Shreveport, Louisiana, is another hospital, whose charitable and benevolent work has spread wide all over Louisiana. A very modern four-room brick aseptic operating building has been erected and furnished with the latest and most approved paraphernalia and appurtenances. This has grown to be one of the fixed State institutions of north Louisiana, and its successful conduct, and the humane, skillful and scientific treatment of the indigent sick, and those requiring surgical attention, have grounded it deep in the affections of our people. It also affords the opportunity of splendid training and practical expereience to young men pursuing the study of medicine and surgery.

STATE PENITENTIARY AND CONVICT FARMS.

The Legislature, at its session of 1890, passed an act carrying into effect the provision of the new Constitution, which prohibited any form of leasing State prisoners and directed that they be employed under absolute State control. It was determined to continue the work of State building only in so far as it could be furnished for such work, first-class men, graded physically, and employ the rest in agriculture. For this latter purpose, Angola plantation, embracing 8,000 acres of splendid alluvial land, on the Mississippi River, in West Feliciana Parish, and Hope plantation, a sugar estate of some 2,800 acres, on Bayou Teche, Iberia Parish, were purchased. These farms have now been in operation for several years, and the results are most gratifying. Cotton is the money crop raised on Angola and sugar on Hope. Another farm, Oakley, has been purchased in Iberville Parish, and is now equipped as a penal farm.

The crops sold and proceeds of levee work have brought in good revenues, besides the agricultural product such as corn, potatoes, onions, etc., preserved for prison use, which aggregate a large value. The system now pays its own expenses of operation, and affords a surplus to complete payments on property purchased.

The small factory at the Baton Rouge Penitentiary supplies the force with shoes and clothing.

There have been constructed on these farms permanent quarters on the most approved sanitary lines. The prisoners are compelled to work, according to their strength, but they are provided with the best quality of food, all they can eat, including an abundance of vegetables, and are well clothed and humanely treated.

The late lamented Hon. S. M. Jones, at that time Mayor of Toledo, Ohio, known over the United States as "Golden Rule" Jones, after a recent visit to Hope convict farm, wrote an article for one of the leading journals of the East, and among other things said:

"I have felt, because a great mass of the convicts of the South have been worked at outdoor employment, that if they were badly treated they were not in the long run as badly off as our convicts in the North, who are contracted out to work in dingy, ill-ventilated and disease-breeding shops, where they are doomed to breathe poisoned air and almost entirely shut out from eyer seeing a ray of sunshine. I was, however, quite unprepared to find that the State of Louisiana has taken a step in the matter of dealing with convicted human beings that easily places her a century ahead of the methods in common practice in the [illegible] North and South."

AS OTHERS SEE US

PROFESSOR HILGARD, in his preliminary report of a Geological Survey of Western Louisiana, remarks: "Few sections of the United States, indeed, can offer such inducements to settlers as the prairie region between the Mississippi Bottoms, the Nez Pique and Mermentau. Healthier by far than the prairies of the Northwest, fanned by the sea breeze, well watered—the scarcity of wood rendered of less moment by the blandness of the climate, and the extraordinary rapidity with which natural hedges can be grown for fences, while the exuberantly fertile soil produces both sugar cane and cotton in profusion, continuing to do so in many cases after seventy years' exhaustive cultivation. Well may the Teche country be styled, by its enthusiastic inhabitants, the 'Garden of Louisiana.'"

One of the largest and most intelligent farmers in central Illinois, after a careful examination of the Teche and Attakapas country, said:

"I have heretofore thought that central Illinois was the finest farming country in the world. I own a large farm there, with improvements equal to any in the country. I cultivate about two thousand acres in small grain, besides other crops; but since I have seen the Teche and Attakapas country, I do not see how any man who has seen this country can be satisfied to live in Illinois.

"I find that I can raise everything in Louisiana that can be raised in Illinois, and that I can raise a hundred things there which cannot be raised in Illinois. I find the lands easier worked in Louisiana, infinitely richer and yielding far more, and with the fairest climate on earth, and no trouble to get to market. I shall return to Illinois, sell out, and persuade my neighbors to do the same, and return to Louisiana to spend the remainder of my days."

The editor of the Chicago Tribune, after visiting the Teche country, said to his 50,000 subscribers: "If, by some supreme effort of Nature, Western Louisiana, with its soil, climate and production, could be taken up and transported north to the latitude of Illinois and Indiana, and be there set down in the pathway of Eastern travel, it would create a commotion that would throw the discovery of gold in California in the shade at the time of the greatest excitement. The people would rush to it in countless thousands. Every man would be intent on securing a few acres of these wonderfully productive and profitable sugar plains. These Teche lands, if in Illinois, would bring from three to five hundred dollars per acre."

Robert Ridgeway, formerly of Indiana, now of Louisiana, said: "Too much cannot be said in praise of Louisiana. I find, at least, from personal observation, that Louisiana possesses to a most wonderful degree, great opportunities for making money, and a young man with any get-up about him, with only a little money, or even nothing but his energy, can, in a few years, make a fortune as an agriculturist alone. There is no country on earth that has any greater advantage than Louisiana.

"We have twelve months working season, and products for the year round. In the North and West we can labor only part of the year, and during the other three months they have to consume or eat up what they have laid by—not so here—Louisiana offers most wonderful advantages for the enterprising man to come and take hold of. There has been

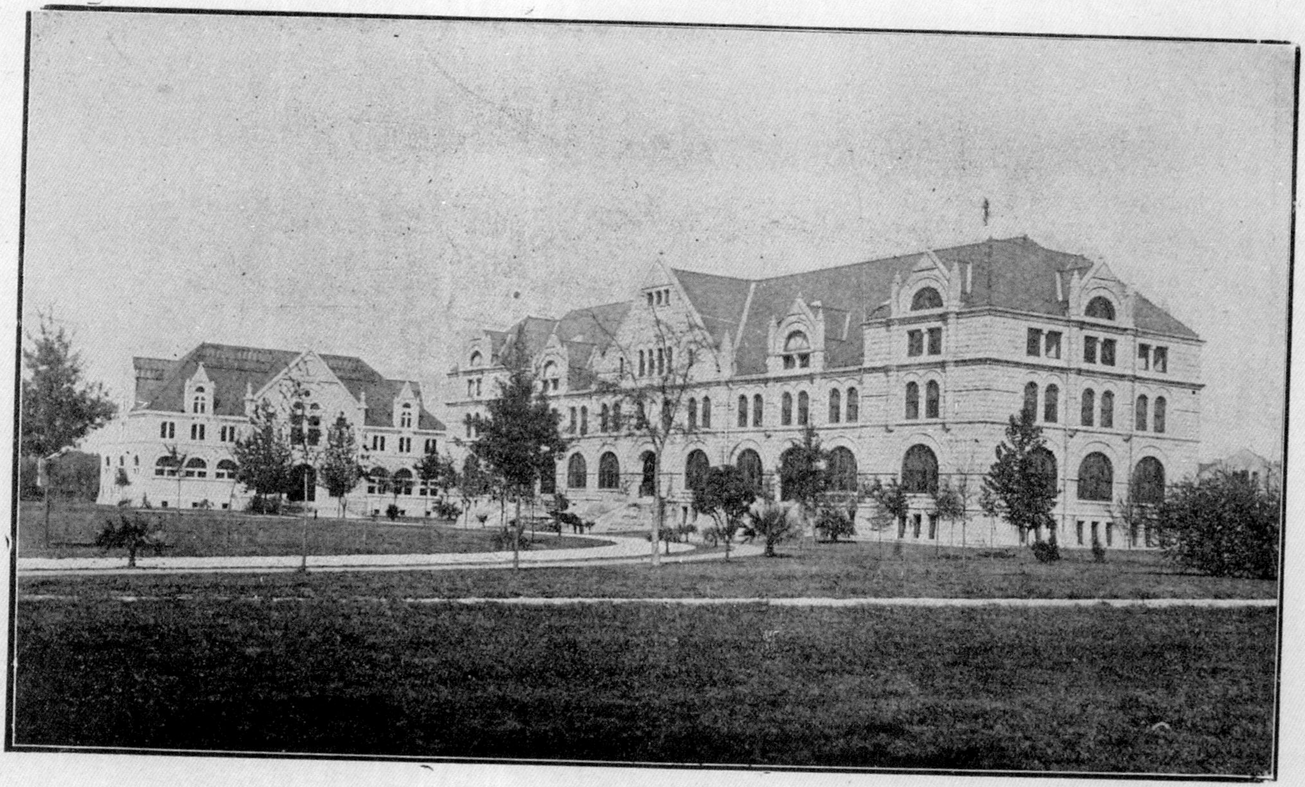

TULANE UNIVERSITY, NEW ORLEANS

much said of Louisiana, of her benefits and advantages, by tongues more flowery than mine, but I will say that the whole has not been told."

J. H. Keyser, of Bellevue, Bossier, Parish, La., formerly of Pennsylvania, said: "I traveled, years ago, portions of Ohio, Indiana, Illinois, Iowa and Michigan, and spent my early life in Pennsylvania, and have been living since 1870 in Bossier Parish, La., and, taking everything into consideration, I believe a man can live with as much comfort and enjoyment in Louisiana as in any other State of the Union. The people are kind, generous and hospitable, and rarely intermeddle with the political or religious opinions of any one. The great need of the State is immigrants to fill up her waste places, that only need proper culture to produce in abundance.

"And the State and its capabilities only need to be made known generally to attract immigration, and the time is not far distant when Louisiana will be recognized as among the first States of the Union."

J. M. Howell, of Lafourche, La., formerly of Mississippi, says: "During my residence in Louisiana of twenty-five years, from personal observation, I find that the laws are as fairly and impartially administered here as in any other State in the Union. My observations lead me to believe that, without regard to race, sex or former conditions, that nowhere in the United States are the laws more impartially administered than here in this State."

W. J. Ornett, formerly of Michigan, said: "I left Michigan on March 18, 1888, for the South, and landed in the city of Natchitoches one week later. When I left Michigan there was plenty of snow and ice, and when I arrived in Natchitoches I found things altogether different. There was plenty of grass for stock, the fruit trees had bloomed, and garden vegetables of all kinds were growing, and flowers all ready to bloom, and, if I remember right, some had bloomed.

"Ladies, why stay at the North and burn fifty dollars' worth of wood to keep a few flowers from freezing, when you can come South and have them bloom nine months in the year, and have them outdoors, and then you can have your early vegetables all through April. Just think of it! And, let me tell you, I ate some as fine dewberries as I ever ate in my life in the last week in April, and you people that were in the North were shivering around the fire. I think fruit of most any kind will grow here in abundance. There is soil to be found adapted to most everything, and excellent soil, too; and the climate, so far as I have experienced it, is very nice. It did not affect me disagreeably so far. I think, if anything, it has benefited me, as I have gained several pounds in weight; and in regard to the reception I received from the people, I must say that it was better than I expected. I find them pleasant and hospitable in every way. There is a variety of openings, plenty for all classes; plenty of fine farming lands, both improved and unimproved, to be had cheap, and plenty of timber of all kinds; fine chance for stock raising, as you need to feed for so short a time during the year that the expense is small compared to where you feed six months in the year. There is opening for a cotton factory, oil mill, furniture factory, grist mill, banks, hotels, photographers, and other too numerous to mention."

Professor S. A. Knapp, says: "It would be necessary to take the prairies of Iowa, the rugged timber lands of Maine, and the entire delta of the Nile, twist them together, and thrust through them the Amazon to produce another Louisiana."

Started Without a Dollar.

"I came to the United States from Germany, landing in the City of New Orleans, State of Louisiana, in the month of September, 1869. I came to Clinton, East Feliciana Parish, La., from there same year; remained here one year and worked on the farm; then left and went to Illinois, traveling over three Northern States. I was gone from here about ten months. I soon came to the conclusion that this country offered better opportunity for men in the financial condition I was in than the North or Northwest. I returned here and commenced railroading, following that for five or six years. I then purchased me a home, where I now live; first bought 75 acres. I now own 378 acres, for which I would not accept $6,000 cash. I live on what I make on my place, except flour and rice This I could grow. I have made one bale of cotton per acre, and from 40 to 50 bushels of corn per acre. This land will grow as fine grapes as can be grown anywhere. All kinds of garden stuff grows here, and some of them can be grown two crops in a year. I can grow two fine crops of sweet potatoes. Any person can come and locate here and make a living at home and pay for the house at the same time. I commenced here without a dollar, and I have raised a large family and have plenty around me, such as horses, mules, cattle and hogs, and such other things as belong to a farm.

I can recommend these lands to any person wanting to gain for himself a home. I know of many other Germans who have come here in the same condition I was in and today own good houses. The same things any person can do here who will come and try.

THOMAS AULL.

Raises All His Supplies.

This is to certify that I came to the Parish of East Feliciana in the year 1866 and have lived here and have been engaged in farming since that time. I have raised all of my work stock and everything needed to supply my farm. During this entire time I have never had to incur any debt, as there was always a demand for my surplus of corn, molasses, hay, chickens and eggs, to settle in cash for what my family needed, leaving my cotton crop each year as a surplus. One year my family made and gathered 30 bales of cotton, 750 bushels of corn, 200 gallons of molasses, 75 bushels of potatoes, and house all the hay needed for my stock, and sold $75.00 worth of hay. Besides making all of my lard, bacon and hams, I sold $75.00 worth of fresh meat, and my boys made, after my crop was harvested, $250.00 on the sugar farm, which they now have on hand. This is a healthy country and offers fine inducement to any man willing to work and who has any idea of management.

GEORGE ANDERSON.

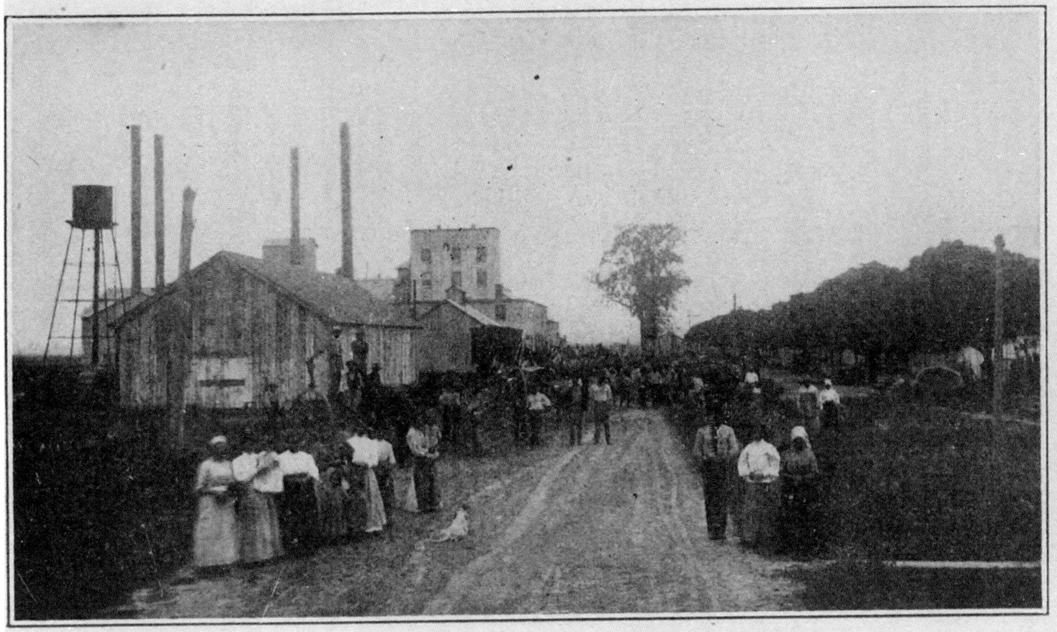

A 12 O'CLOCK SCENE AT A LOUISIANA SUGAR HOUSE

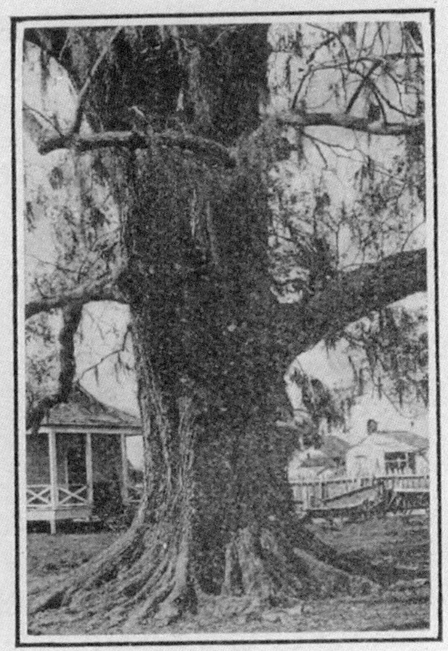

GIANT PECAN TREE,
ASCENSION PARISH

THE UNTOLD TREASURES OF LOUISIANA

(From the National Magazine)

BY GARNAULT AGASSIZ.

BEFORE THE WAR, Louisiana, from an agricultural standpoint, was in many respects the banner state of the Union. Her great plantations were the pride of the nation. Rich beyond her needs in her resources of cotton and sugar, secure in her feudal system of labor, prosperous to a degree, she neither invited nor needed to invite capital or labor to her shores.

Some idea of her prosperity can be gained from the fact that many of her alluvial lands, valued today at from twenty-five to fifty dollars an acre, were then held in reserve for from a hundred to two hundred; indeed, it is estimated that sixty per cent more lands in the alluvial parishes were under cultivation then than now.

NO YELLOW FEVER NOW.

Fifteen years ago yellow fever might have been a legitimate factor in keeping people from Louisiana, for it is an incontrovertible fact that New Orleans, as a port of entry for tropical Central America, was subject to intermittent epidemics of this disease, just as New York or Boston, without rigid quarantine measures, would be subject to outbreaks of cholera or the bubonic plague. Sanitary conditions in New Orleans, however, have changed radically in the past ten years; the old open sewers have been superseded by a modern drainage system, adequate quarantine laws have been introduced, and general health conditions have been materially improved. New Orleans has not had a single case of yellow fever for more than seven years—and scientists say she will never have another, for in the past decade, from an unknown dreaded disease, this ailment has become a treatable and preventable malady, easily confined to certain limits. The medical conquest of the tropics constitutes one of the most remarkable .scientific accomplishments of all time.

THE FACTOR SYSTEM.

But the one factor more than any other that was responsible for Louisiana's slow growth was the pernicious factor system, with its attendant negro-tenant and one-crop features. The war freed the Louisiana bondsman, it is true, but it made a veritable slave of many of the free men, slaves to a system of monetary servitude that prevented Louisiana from occupying her merited position in the vanguard of the world's agriculture for nearly half a century.

Under the obnoxious factor system, the factor agreed to advance a planter enough money to make his crop on condition that he would devote so many acres of his farm to the cultivation of cotton, sugar or rice, as the case might be, and designate him as his broker in the marketing of the crop. This sounded all very well. The money was turned over, the crop was made, the harvest was abundant—for a time the factor seemed to be a philanthropist indeed. Then came the day of reckoning. The New York bank said to the New Orleans bank, "Pay"; the New Orleans bank said to the country bank, "Pay"; the country bank said to the factor, "Pay"; the factor said to the planter, "Pay." And all he could do was to sell his crop, irrespective of market conditions or his hopes of the future.

A good crop and a bad year, a strange anomaly. But the planter has grown only one crop, perhaps on the negro tenant basis. He has purchased his mules in Missouri or Texas, his corn in Illinois or Indiana, his oats in Kansas or Iowa, his own provisions in almost every state of the Union. The day of settlement finds him literally a bankrupt—the only hope of the tomorrow, the factor and another year.

That hope of the tomorrow, the factor and another year, held good for more than forty years, and it might have held good for forty more had not Nature herself intervened—Nature in the shape of the intrepid boll weevil who, in his forced march from Mexico, camped with his legions on the snow-white cotton fields of Louisiana, and, in a single night, as it were, undermined the whole industrial fabric of the state.

For a time things looked desperate indeed to the Louisiana cotton planter, but just as water finds its own level, so man, failing in one direction, inevitably courts success in another—and the direction taken by the Louisiana planter was one that spelt not only salvation to him, but pointed him to a greater success than he had ever dared to dream. That road was diversified farming.

DIVERSIFICATION.

What diversified farming has done for the Louisiana planter needs no recital. It is what it has done for the planter everywhere who depended for his success on one staple crop. When the boll weevil made its appearance in Louisiana, the state's corn crop was less than a quarter of a million bushels; last year it was fifty-eight million, and next year it promises to reach seventy-five million bushels. And what is true of corn is true also of oats, wheat, rye and every other staple crop.

Two or more crops can be grown anywhere in Louisiana, and in some sections, under favorable conditions, three and four. The two most widely grown crops are potatoes and peanuts; oats and sweet potatoes, oats and June corn, sweet and Irish potatoes, and in every case cowpeas, velvet beans, or some other self-nitrogenous crop can be sown in the corn. Throughout North and Middle Louisiana there are many large farms that would do credit to Illinois or Indiana, farms that are conducted on the most improved scientific lines, that employ the very latest machinery, and that return a dividend on the investment that to the average Northern farmer would seem incredible. In a majority of instances, these farms are absolutely self-sustaining, raising everything that is required for their maintenance, and breeding their own horses and mules. These large farms raise chiefly oats, corn, cotton, wheat, Irish and sweet potatoes, lespedeza, Bermuda and other hays, truck live stock and poultry.

AN ILLUSTRATION OF WHAT ONE FARM CAN DO WITH DIVERSIFIED CROPS.

As an illustration of what a Louisiana farm is capable of under intelligent management and scientific crop rotation might be mentioned the splendid plantation of J. H. and R. W. Boisseau, of Shreveport. This farm has 1100 acres under cultivation. Up to a few years ago it

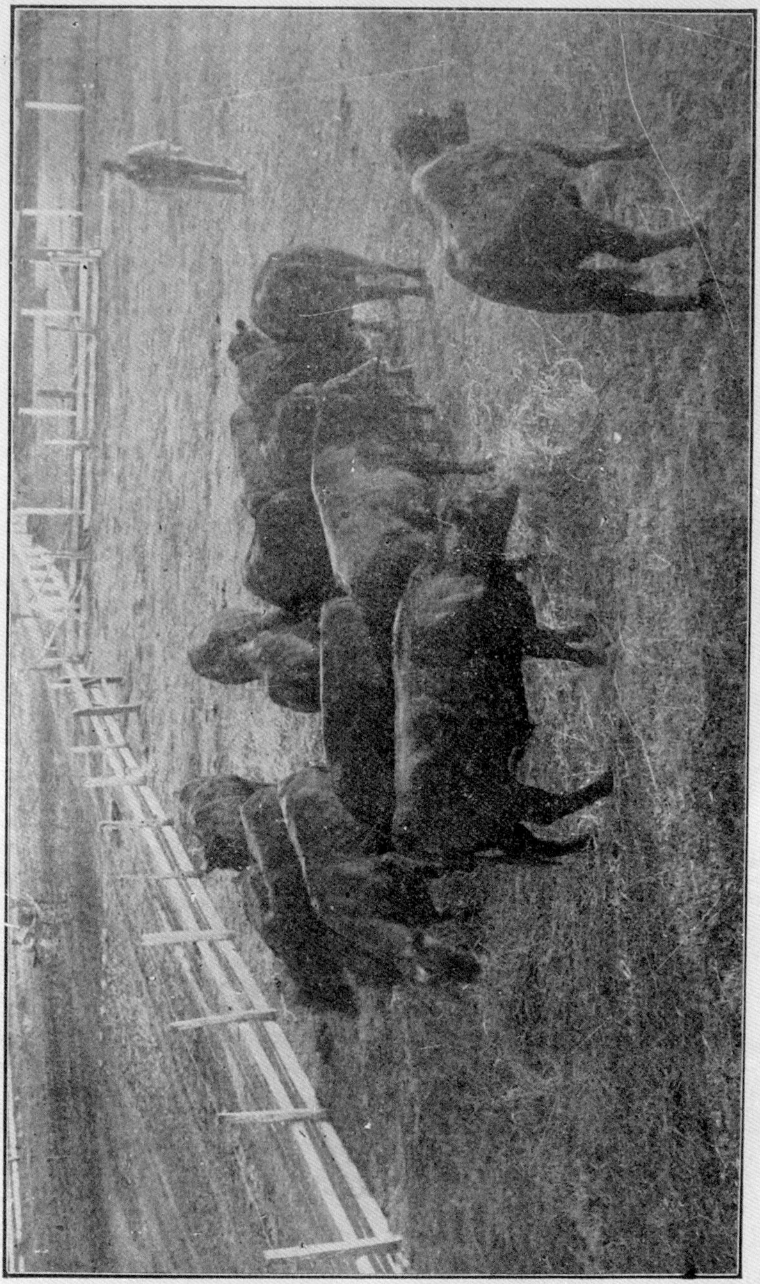

A HERD OF POLLED ANGUS CATTLE

was essentially a cotton plantation, over 1100 acres being under cultivation to the cotton plant and 100 acres in corn constituting the factotum of everything else raised. Then came the boll weevil, with its demand for changed conditions. Unlike many other Louisiana planters at the time, the Boisseau brothers were not so discouraged with the future as to neglect their farm entirely or lease it out on a profit-sharing basis to negro tenants. They foresaw that new conditions called for new methods, and with this resolve in view prepared to enter the field of diversified farming on an elaborate scale. And the results have been all that could have been desired. Last year this plantation cultivated: 300 acres of alfalfa, yielding four to six tons an acre, valued at $13 to $25 a ton, conditioned on the season and market; 200 acres of oats, yielding without fertilizer, from 40 to 85 bushels an acre, the yield being conditioned on the time of planting; 25 acres of wheat, yielding 25 bushels to the acre; 300 acres of cotton, averaging nearly a bale to the acre; twenty acres of peanuts, and a large acreage of pasturage and truck.

This farm maintained, in addition to its 200 work animals, nearly all home raised, some 300 head of cattle, 500 graded hogs, a large number of sheep, some poultry, and shipped something every working day in the year. Its gross income was $78,000, of which $25,000 was clear profit. Not a bad return on the investment!

WHAT IS CLAIMED BY A TOWN.

The little town of Mansura, in Avoyelles Parish, is another concrete example of the success of diversified farming in Louisiana. In 1908, when this town depended on the one-crop system for its upbuilding, marketing about 4000 bales of cotton a year, its only bank had total deposits of $52,000. In the fall of 1910 only a thousand bales of cotton were sold in the town, but diversified farming had so enriched the surrounding country that the deposits of that bank had increased to $102,000, in spite of the fact that five other banks had been established in the parish in the interim.

* * * *

CORN RAISING.

With the farmer beginning to appreciate more and more the great possibilities of intelligent corn culture, Louisiana is fast taking a ranking position among the leading corn states of the country. And this is as it should be, for in the general scheme of diversified farming, corn is unquestionably the most important unit. The yield is being steadily increased, not by fertilization alone, but by deep plowing, adequate cultivation and a systematic rotation of crops.

Nothing is more important to the corn grower than the question of deep plowing. Under the old three-inch method of plowing, the yield for the whole state was less than 12 bushels to the acre, while 25 bushels was a splendid average for even the most productive soil. Deep plowing has increased the yield, irrespective of conditions, wherever tried. This has been remarkably demonstrated by a Louisiana farmer, who this year, by plowing to a uniform depth of six inches, raised 70 bushels of corn to the acre on two acres of ground that under the old method of plowing had never been known to yield more than 25 bushels to the acre. And he used no fertilizer whatsoever. Next year this farmer intends to plow up ten acres to a depth of one foot, accomplishing this with a 6-inch disc plow and a 6-inch subsoiler.

In speaking of corn-raising in Louisiana, one cannot lose sight of the splendid work being accomplished by the Boys' Corn Clubs, an important branch of the United States Department of Agriculture's Farm Demonstration Bureau, which is doing such a noble work in uplifting Southern agriculture. There are now 42 individual corn clubs in the state, with a total enrollment of 3,875 members, Louisiana laying claim, by the way, to the boy, in Stephen Henry, of Melrose, near Natchitoches, who, by "making" 139.45 bushels of corn to the acre, at a cost of 13.6 cents a bushel, not only won the Department of Agriculture's grand prize, but established beyond dispute the peculiar advantages of Louisiana soil for corn culture.

* * * *

WHEAT AND OATS.

Wheat and oats are two other staple crops that are finding each year more favor with the modern Louisiana farmer as integral urits in the scheme of diversification, this being true especially in the northern and middle sections of the state. And with good reason. Either of these grains can be planted from the first of September to the first of November and provide a splendid pasturage for cattle from late autumn until the first of April without any deterioration to the growing grain. Wheat will produce 20 to 30 bushels and oats from 30 to 90 bushels to the acre, and be followed by peas, peanuts, soy or other beans, sweet potatoes, sorghum, kaffir corn, milo maize, or June corn. An Arcadia, Bienville Parish, farmer this year harvested 85 bushels to the acre on fifty contiguous acres. He followed his oats by peanuts, which as a second crop practically represent a clear profit.

Louisiana's 50,000 acres of oats yield approximately a million bushels a year. The yield of wheat is inconsiderable at present, hardly computable, but the acreage is being increased yearly, due chiefly to the success attained by the Department of Agriculture in the acclimation of a seed well suited to the particular needs of the state.

* * * *

IRISH POTATOES.

Irish potatoes constitute another important unit in the general scheme of modern farming, it being quite possible in Louisiana to raise two good crops on the same ground annually, the second at little expense, as additional fertilizer is rarely necessary, and the small potatoes from the first crop serve as seed for the second.

The first crop is planted in January and February and harvested in May; the second in the latter part of July and the beginning of August and harvested in late autumn.

Irish potatoes bring from $60 to $175 a car for the spring crop, while the fall crop sells as a rule at from $75 to $200, the higher price being conditioned to some extent on the larger home demand.

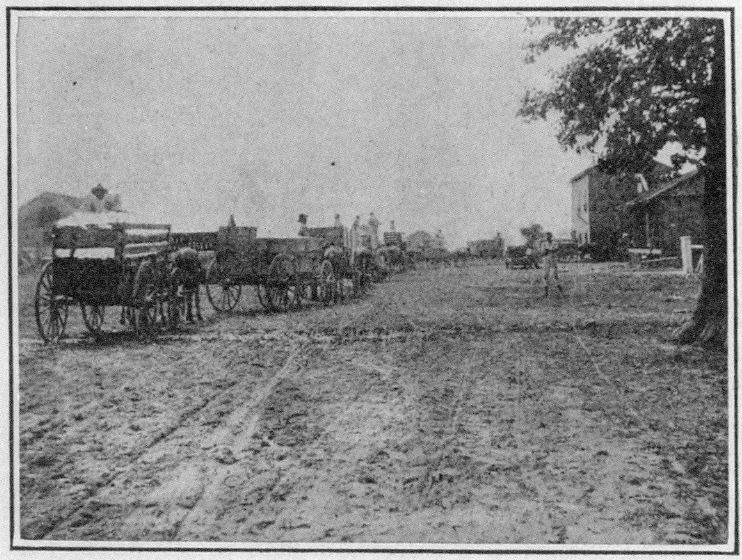

HAULING SEED COTTON TO KILLODEN GIN

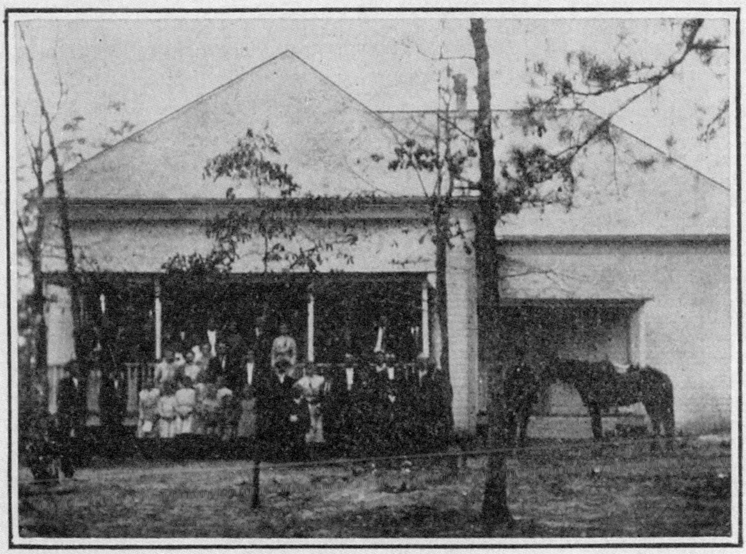

LA NANA SCHOOLHOUSE, IN SABINE PARISH

The profit in Irish potatoes in conjunction with some other crop is well illustrated by the experience of Benjamin Gray, an up-to-date farmer in the famous Red River Valley, who last year made more than a hundred dollars an acre on ten acres of land from this source. This was accomplished as follows: He harvested 868 bushels of Irish potatoes, for which he received $1.10 to $1.15 a bushel, or about 77 cents net when freight and commissions had been deducted. On the same 10 acres he later harvested 610 bushels of peanuts, for which he received $140 net, and 23 tons of peanut hay, which returned him $12 to $14 a ton.

And the potato crop, owing to climatic conditions, was an unusually short one.

At the present time Louisiana imports no small proportion of her potato supply, which means that the Louisiana farmer has the local market to fall back upon when conditions in the higher-priced Northern and Western markets are not favorable.

* * * *

PEANUTS.

In this scheme of diversification, peanuts also occupy an important role, for no state in the Union, not excepting the greatest of all peanut states, Virginia, combines in a happier manner the peculiar requisite to peanut growth. And as peanuts in Louisiana, as in all the far Southern states, can be grown as a second crop to potatoes, oats or wheat, peanut culture would seem to be a more profitable venture in the Pelican than in the Old Dominion State.

And it is a crop that requires no great investment of capital. A man and two mules can cultivate with ease from fifty to sixty acres of peanuts, which should yield from forty to sixty bushels an acre, with an average price of about $1.00 a bushel, not to mention the high-grade hay, which in itself is said to pay for the seed, cultivation and harvesting of the crop. The present state average, it is true, is only 15 bushels to the acre, but this is due to poor cultivation, inadequate fertilization, and a lack of diversification, for crop rotation is one of the chief essentials in successful paying culture.

Peanut hay will yield from a ton to a ton and a half an acre, worth according to the conditions of market from $15 to $18 a ton. Most farmers think it more advisable to make the hay with the pea still on the vine, feeling that the increase in the value of hay will more than counterbalance the attendant loss, just as many of the more up-to-date consider it wiser if the peanut itself is harvested, to plough the vines under for the enrichment of the soil.

The Louisiana peanut, which at present is the Spanish variety exclusively, although all varieties, with the exception of the Virginia, will do well, finds its chief uses today in the peculiarly high-grade oil which is extracted from it, in the manufacture of peanut butter and salted peanuts, and as a staple article of diet for the stock farm. Peanut factories, controlled for the most part by Virginia corporations, are now located at Ruston, the seat of Lincoln Parish, the largest peanut-raising parish in the state, Shreveport and other points in north Louisiana, so that the farmer who wants to grow peanuts on a commercial scale has a good market at his very door. There is no peanut oil factory in the state at the present time, but as the Spanish peanut will average more than a gallon of high-grade oil to the bushel, there would seem to be no reason why an oil factory would not be a paying investment.

But it will be more for a food for live stock, especially hogs, that the progressive Louisiana farmer will cultivate the peanut. In this connection it may be said that there is no better or more economical diet for hogs, for not only does the peanut produce a meat of a peculiarly distinctive flavor, as witness the famous Smithfield ham, but the expense of feeding the hogs in the regular way is almost done away with, as they are allowed to root for their own living. In a recent experiment, indeed, the State Department of Agriculture cleared $50 an acre from hogs raised in this way. As a rule, however, the farmer finds it better to give a ten-day diet of corn before slaughtering, as the corn imparts a tenacity to the flesh that it would not otherwise have.

* * * *

SWEET POTATOES.

In the hill country of middle north Louisiana, that portion of the state which is embraced by the Red and Ouachita Rivers, an area approximately of ten thousand square miles, sweet potatoes can be grown to better advantage, perhaps, than in any other portion of the United States, for not only are these sweet potatoes of an especially good variety, but they will yield from $200 to $500 an acre, depending on the methods of cultivation and crop conditions. And as with peanuts, sweet potatoes are a second crop.

STOCK RAISING.

Still another industry that is rapidly becoming an important unit in this new era of diversified farming is the raising of live stock. Louisiana has been a great cattle-raising country since the day of her settlement, her vast prairies, which until the coming of the white man, were black with buffalo, having been the home of as picturesque and as unique a cattle industry as can be found in the United States.

But it is to the stock farm more than the range that Louisiana will have to look for the future upbuilding of this industry. In this connection it can be said that no state in the Union is better adapted to the raising of high-grade stock. The natural pasturage to be found anywhere in the state alone will provide for the yearly sustenance of from one to five head of stock to the acre, while on cultivated pasturages, such as oats, wheat, velvet beans, cow peas and other legumes, from five to ten head can be fed.

Nothing is more important to the stockgrower than good pasturage. In this respect Louisiana is especially well endowed. Her native grasses embrace white and red clover, timothy, beggarweed, Bermuda and other of the chief domestic varieties, while such exotics as alfalfa and lespedeza grow to splendid advantage in every section of the state. Cowpeas and velvet beans also grow luxuriously, and, both being nitrogenous plants, assist materially in enriching the soil. Cowpeas are planted principally for hay, although every farmer retains enough seed for the following year's planting, as they are an annual crop and grow only from the seed.

Lespedeza, a member of the legume family, and a native of Japan, is finding greater favor in Louisiana than alfalfa, and alfalfa will grow in Louisiana as well as anywhere, and it will not only yield from two to three cuttings a year with an average of a ton to an acre, but one planting will last from three to four years. It might last very much longer were it not for the fact that after the fourth year volunteer grasses and weeds as a rule spring up to such an extent as to preclude its sale as a high-grade hay. Lespedeza, too, is a nitrogenous self-fertilizer, and is said to bring the land in the three or four years of its life up to a high state of fertility for the cultivation of staple crops.

Lespedeza is sown broadcast in oats or wheat when they are 12 to 14 inches high, this time being selected as all danger of a killing frost has passed, young lespedeza being very susceptible to cold. Oats are harvested May 25, and the first cutting of lespedeza occurs a month later. Lespedeza, like cowpeas and velvet beans, is also a nitrogenous self-fertilizer.

Another branch of the live stock industry that is annually receiving more attention from the progressive Louisiana planter is the raising of mules. This is almost a departure for Louisiana, but it is a departure of tremendous importance not only to the planter himself, but to the state at large. A 3-year-old mule is worth anywhere from $200 to $300; it can be raised for $25. This means a saving to the farmer and to the state of at least $200 on every home-bred mule employed on the farm, and some of the larger planters utilize from 300 to 500 head. The mare that is used for raising mules on the larger Louisiana plantations is a common working mare. This represents a great saving, also, as she can be worked within a few days of foaling time and ten days after and raise a colt every year.

Sheep, too, can be raised very profitably throughout Louisiana, particularly in the cutover pine lands, which afford splendid ranges—ranges that on account of Louisiana's equable climate are available all the year round. While all breeds do well, the native sheep thrive better than any other kind, for being acclimated they require less attention, and consequently are more profitable to raise.

At Lake Providence, in East Carroll Parish, a beautiful old trading post on the Mississippi, sheep-raising is a very important and profitable industry, as it is also in Calcasieu, Cameron, Winn, Ouachita, and a number of other parishes.

* * * *

SUGAR CANE: ITS PLANTING AND VARIOUS PROCESSES THROUGH WHICH ITS MANUFACTURE IN SUGAR IS ACCOMPLIHED.

Sugar was first made in Louisiana in 1795, though sugar cane had been grown in various parts of the state before the Revolution for the manufacture of syrup and rum, the sugar cane having been introduced into Louisiana in 1751 by the Jesuit Fathers from San Domingo, where their confreres had built up quite a considerable industry.

The cane grew well, but all attempts to manufacture sugar from it were abortive, and it was not until 1791 that Don Antonio Mendez

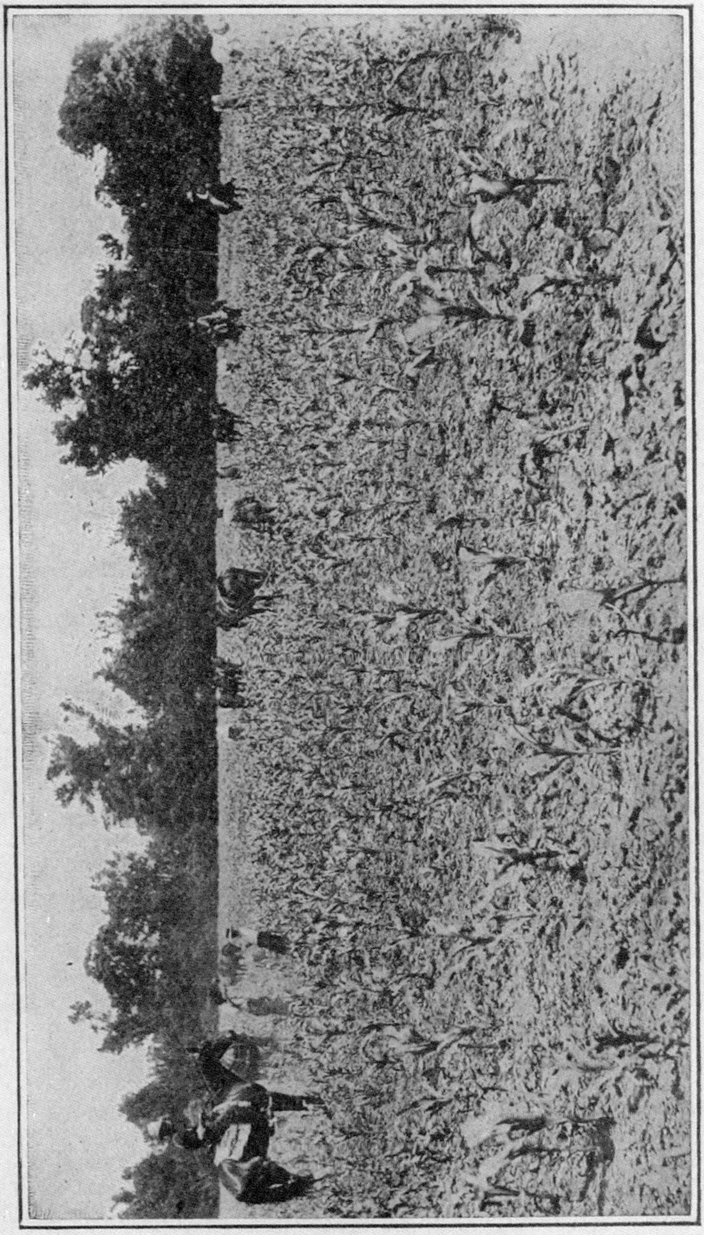

CULTIVATING CORN ON TRAVELERS' REST STOCK FARM

succeeded in extracting sugar from cane. Three years later Etienne de Bore made such a large crop of sugar that many were induced to go into the industry, and it is to him that the real credit of being the father of the industry belongs.

In common with all industries in the experimental stage, the sugar cane industry of Louisiana was at its inception a very crude and unimportant one, both as to its cultural and manufacturing methods and the insignificance of its annual output, but as the progressive planter, realizing its future possibilities, abandoned indigo entirely and to some extent cotton to sugar cane, it commenced to enjoy a period of steady growth, until in 1820 the crop approximated some 20,000,000 pounds of sugar.

From 1820 the industry developed rapidly, due entirely to the foresight and intelligence of the planter, who by the application of improved cultural and manufacturing methods placed himself in a position to compete successfully with his great tropical rivals, Barbados and Cuba.

The Louisiana planter has always been a potent factor in the development of the state, distinctive in his type and representative of her best class of citizenship, and he has been ever ready to introduce any innovation, no matter how expensive, that would promote the welfare of the industry and the welfare of the state. This is well illustrated by the fact that while the steam mill was a rarity in the United States up to 1840, steam began to supersede the horse in the larger Louisiana sugar plants nearly twenty years before, in 1830 no less than half the mills in the state being operated by it.

From the first year or two of its adoption, steam was used only as the source of power in the grinding of the cane, but about 1824 the planters commenced to use it in the actual boiling of the syrup. This marked the invention of the vacuum pan, which is the technical term for boiling the syrup in vacuo, i. e., below the normal pressure of the air. This new method of boiling the syrup was a great improvement over the old open kettle method, as the heat could be regulated, thus causing a great deal of loss from inversion, inversion being the chemical change from sucrose to glucose.

Under the old method, a large proportion of the saccharine content of the juice was inverted into glucose, and although a superior molasses was obtained—known as open kettle molasses, and commanding a great premium over the molasses obtained under the now method of boiling—the increase of sugar, calculated at 156 pounds for the vacuum pan as against 92 pounds for the open kettle, more than counterbalanced the difference.

The revolutionizing discovery of Isaac Watts having been applied with success to the industry, the enterprising planter, not content to derive only the one-eighth power value from his steam that comes from a single effect, now turned his attention to the problem of how to secure a larger proportion of the theoretical value of his fuel—a problem which the engineers of the world were lending their best efforts to solve. Various solutions, such as heating the water with the exhaust steam, heating rooms with it, and utilizing it in devious directions, were suggested, but it remained for a Louisiana cane operative to find, in what is known the world over as the multiple effect, the real solution to this all-important problem. This Louisianian was an octoroon by the name of Robert Rilleux, a free man of color, who had been educated by his sponsor as an engineer in one of the greatest educational institutions of France, and who had ability far beyond his day and race. Rilleux's invention was introduced in 1830. The multiple effect consists of the utilization of the vapor of the same steam in concurrent effects, the vacuum and temperature being lower on each effect, the latter falling from 200 to as low as 120 degrees Fahrenheit.

From 1830 to 1844, when the annual output was more than double that of the year previous, the industry enjoyed a regular growth, and from then until the Civil War, when in common with other Southern industries it was entirely obliterated, an era of prosperity that even in these days would have been considered remarkable, in 1854, nearly 500,000,000 pounds of sugar being produced, an output that was not surpassed until 1906.

The war dealt a stunning blow to the sugar industry, and it was many years before economic conditions had so adjusted themselves as to warrant a comprehensive rehabilitation.

The real dawn of the present industry may be said to date from 1882, the year that gave birth to the centralized plant. Up to this time the industry had been prosecuted in a crude way, both as to its agricultural and manufacturing methods, the planter seldom knowing the actual cost of his operations.

The centralized plant changed all this. Its operator was as a rule a big planter of the old school, who recognized that sugar could be manufactured successfully only by the most improved methods, and the practice of the most rigid economy. Thus he not only improved his lands by an intelligent rotation of crops, but he cultivated and fertilized them more thoroughly than had been the custom, and eliminated every possible source of waste. He began, too, to compute the amount of sugar that could be manufactured from a ton of cane, something never before attempted in the sugar industry, the effect of this being that in the last thirty years he has increased the yield of sugar to the ton by over 50 per cent.

Very few people have even the remotest idea of the great investment that a sugar plantation represents. The average large sugar planter pays out in wages alone from $100,000 to $250,000 annually, and labor is not by any means the only factor of expense in the operation of a sugar plantation. There is the machinery bill, fertilizer bill, the maintenance of the railroad—a cardinal requisite to every up-to-date plantation—and last but not least the sugar factory. A good sugar factory will cost anywhere from $150,000 to $600,000, and will have to be almost entirely renewed every ten to fifteen years.

More than three-quarters of the year idle, the depreciation of the machinery and the plant is greater when idle than when in active operation. Then there is the repairing of the machinery—$8,000 to $15,000 a year is no uncommon figure for this.

One ten thousand acre plantation in Lafourche Parish might be cited. This plantation, which has 3,400 acres in cultivation to sugar, has an annual payroll of $150,000. Its immense sugar house is valued at over

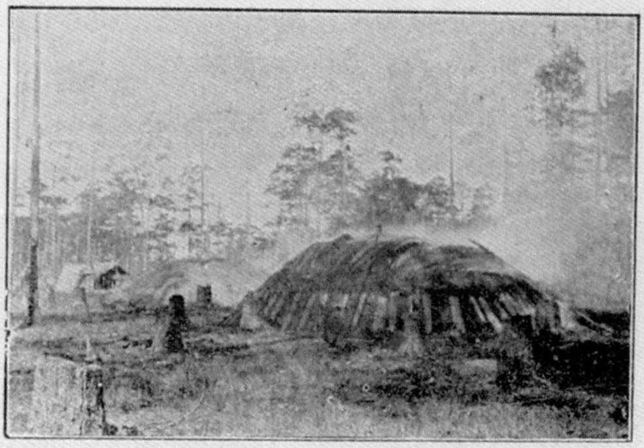

CHARCOAL BURNING

$300,000. It has 35 miles of 36-inch gauge railroad, with three 17-ton engines and 262 cars of from 5 to 10 tons capacity. Its mill will grind, on the average, 1200 tons of cane a day. Over 15 miles from end to end, this great farm employs from 800 to 1000 people all the year and 30 per cent more during the planting and harvesting seasons, and maintains a population of nearly 2000 souls. It has its own public school, with an eleven months term, as against six months for the ordinary parish institution.

And this is not by any means the largest single sugar interest in the state.

One great holding corporation, for instance, operates four great plants under such a unique and comprehensive system as to make the four integral units constitute to all intents and purposes one single plantation, with no less than 18,000 acres under cultivation to sugar cane, and employing 3000 people throughout the year—8000 during the harvesting season— maintaining a stable population of 5000 people, and paying out a million and a half dollars in wages. The original investment in these properties represents no less than $7,000,000, which, considering the extraordinary increase in their efficiency, due to improvements in agricultural methods, centralization of manufacture, and scientific disposal of the crop, is worth today at least $15,000,000.

These large plantations are conducted in much the same way as are the great railroad systems of the country. Records of all kinds are kept showing the daily cost of plowing, hoeing, ditching, and cultivating an acre to each unit as compared with the same undertaking on each of the other units, effecting an economy in the cost of annual maintenance that would be impossible under ordinary conditions.

The advantages of the centralization of effort can be realized very readily when it is said that the four great factories of this corporation are today manufacturing more sugar and at cheaper rate than the figures represented by the output of the twenty-odd factories, before this centralization was effected.

This great plantation uses 1200 mules, 75 miles of railroad, 650 cars of 6 to 10 tons capacity each, and produces 80,000,000 pounds of sugar—a figure that twenty years ago would have been the aggregate product of over seventy sugar houses—and has an annual gross income of three to three and a half million dollars.

The first operation in the growing of sugar, as in the growing of any staple crop, is the proper preparation of the land. A sugar plantation is divided into and operated as three integral units in order to permit the regular and systematic rotation. Each year finds one of these units growing plant cane, one growing second and third year cane, and the third corn and peas. The peas are planted after the corn and are plowed under to bring the land into condition for the planting of the new cane crop. This system of rotation is followed with little deviation year after year.

The ground that is to be planted in sugar cane is plowed twice, once in the fall and once just before planting time, which for two-thirds of the crop is in the latter part of February or the beginning of March, the vicissitudes of season sometimes prolonging it until the middle of April. The fall planting season ranges from the middle of October until the middle of November. Plowing over, the land is tilled up in 6-foot rows which are opened up and the cane placed in them by hand; three stalks side by side ensure a stand, as very frequently cane is defective, the ulterior appearance of the stock not being indicative of its ability to germinate. The cane is then covered with 3 to 5 inches of soil. this operation being performed by a light plow. A heavy roller is then passed over the field, and the cane left to grow. After the cane sprouts, or shortly before, the season of active cultivation commenced. A plow is first passed on either side of each row and all surplus soil removed from the cane by hoe, an operation which, requiring manual labor, is very tedious and expensive. As the cane grows, the dirt is continually stirred around it with standard riding cultivators; is continually fertilized with tankage, cotton seed meal, and various commercial fertilizers, and every weed is religiously kept down. From then on until the cane has attained a height and density as to make it impracticable, the growing cane is regularly cultivated with plows and discs, the soil being completely hilled up around it. The last period of cultivation commences as a rule about July 1, at which time the middle of the rows is plowed to a depth of 15 inches, and the drainage perfected by the cutting of quarter drains, which run perpendicular to the rows and empty into the regular drainage ditches. The cane is then left until harvest time, the yield depending on the bounty of nature and the extent of the ravages of the cane-borer.

The cane-borer, a worm three-quarters of an inch in length, is to the sugar cane what the boll weevil is to cotton—a vital, unrelenting, ever-active destructionist. It is estimated by those in authority to know that its relative damage to the growing crop is from ten to twelve per cent, sometimes more.

In the past few years strenuous efforts have been made to eradicate it by both federal and state governments, as well as by the larger planters, and although the annual loss occasioned by it has been somewhat reduced, no effective measure of relief has been devised. Fall planting, the burning of the corn stalks where the borer propagates to especial advantage, the destruction of all other waste, and the cutting out and burning of the cane killed by the borer, are some of the

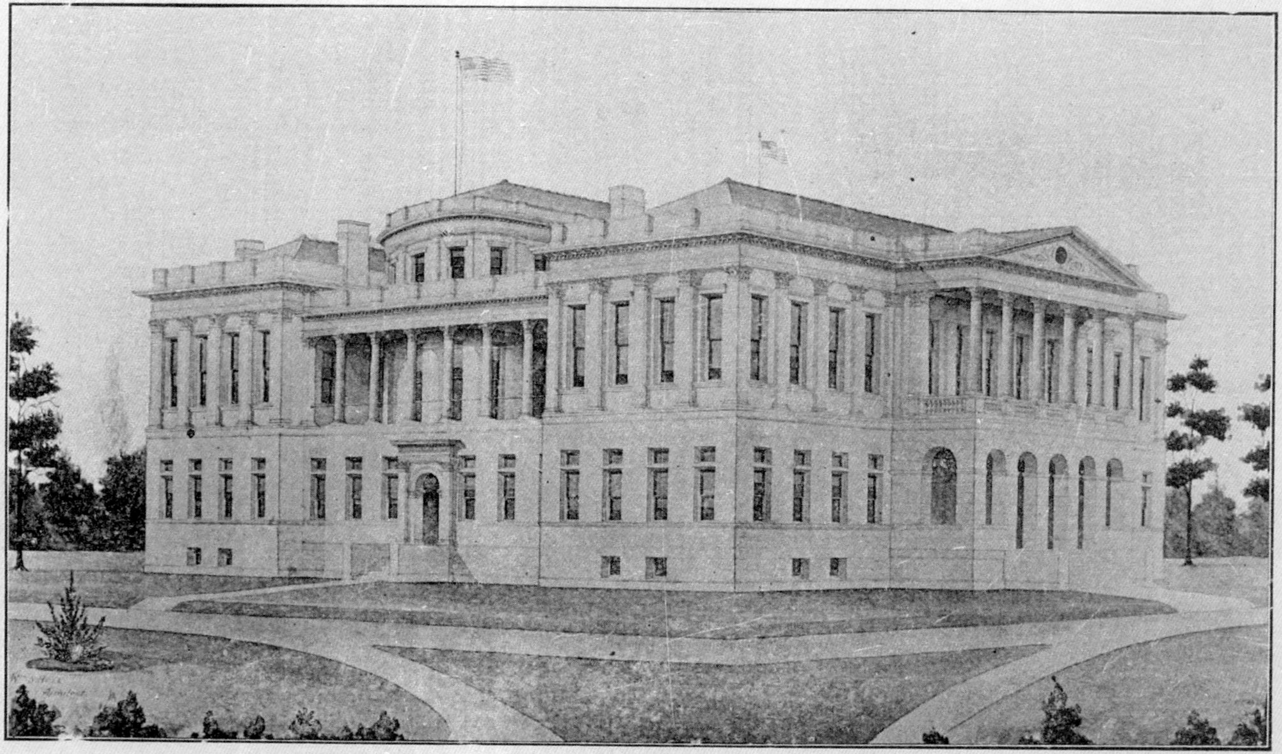

RAPIDES COURTHOUSE AT ALEXANDRIA

measures in its eradication that are meeting with a certain measure of success.

The Georgia plantation, one of the largest sugar plantations in the state, has devised a very unique method of cane-borer destruction. Lamps of 3,000 candle-power are placed on flatcars at defined distances along the plantation railroad, while wood and coal oil fires are burned at convenient points throughout the fields themselves, and the cane-borers, in moth form, are said to fly by thousands into the flames, it being estimated that in the last few months many billions have been destroyed.

The harvesting and grinding of the cane is a most strenuous period to the cane grower, who has little time at this season for even his meals.

At the present time the cane is stripped and cut by hand, man having not yet devised a machine commercially adapted to the work. Experiments, however, are being made, and it is expected that before long a suitable machine will be on the market. Many machines have been introduced to date, but none has embraced the requirements of the successful harvester.

As the cane is cut, it is loaded by mechanical loaders, operated by gas engine, into wagons of from one and a half to two tons capacity each. These are driven to the hoisting derricks, placed at convenient distances throughout the plantation, ominous looking contrivances that bear a striking resemblance to the gibbet. These derricks load the cane on to the cars, which as loaded are run to the sugar house, where the cane is automatically discharged into a patented carrier which conveys it to the corrugated steel crushers. After being crushed the cane is run under six to nine heavy rollers, each exerting a hydraulic pressure of 300 to 400 tons. The consequent juice is then run into what are known as the liming tanks to correct acidity and cause coagulation and the precipitation of all foreign matter. The juice is then pumped into a cylindrical heater through numberless copper tubes where it is heated to 180 to 230 degrees Fahrenheit, conditioned on the results desired, after which it is run into settlers, or clarifiers, and its impurities allowed to settle. The juice is then subjected to the double, triple, and quadruple effects, where it is concentrated into syrup, the residuum in the bottom of the settlers being caried to the filters. The syrup is then conveyed by pump to the charge tanks, where it is concentrated into sugar by a system of vacuum boiling. It is then passed through the centrifugal machines, where the coherent grain sugar is separated from the masquitte, this being the technical term for the syrup in a highly concentrated form. The masquitte is then reboiled, and second sugars are extracted from it in the same way. The syrup is then boiled again, and generally allowed several months to concentrate, or grain up, when it is once more run through the centrifugals and a small-grained, low-grade sugar obtained from it. The residuum is sold as common molasses or black strap.

According to the successful planter it costs $2.75 to $3.00 a ton to make and harvest a crop of cane. The average yield per acre amounts to 20 tons, although 30 are frequently, and 45 have been made. About one-fifth of the yield, however, is used to make the next crop.

As a rule the cane is sold on the sugar basis, the price being conditioned on the market value of sugar, the grower being paid 90 cents a ton, for each cent that yellow clarified sugar commands in the open market, which means that if sugar is selling for 4 cents a pound, the grower realizes $3.60 a ton for his cane.

At the present time about two-thirds of the annual crop is sold to the refiners, the remainder, comprising the higher-grade sugars, being consigned direct to the trade.

* * * *

COTTON.

Nor must it be supposed for a moment that "King" Cotton has been forced to relinquish entirely his inherent right to a throne in the agricultural domain of Louisiana. Agriculturally, Louisiana may be defined as a triumvirate, with "King" Cotton, "King" Sugar, and "King" Rice, the triple monarchs.

"King" Cotton, it is true, never again will be the absolute monarch of Louisiana; her arrogant dictator, the usurper of her every prerogative, but he will be a limited monarch, contributing more effectively to the wealth of the Commonwealth than when, in the zenith of his power, he enjoyed undisputed homage, secure in the knowledge that no pretender threatened his supremacy.

When in 1903 the boll weevil camped with his legions on the cotton fields of Louisiana—beyond question the most prolific cotton fields in the world—there were few indeed who did not believe that "King" Cotton had met his final Waterloo. And there seemed to be justification for the belief, for from over a million bales the annual production fell to two hundred thousand.

Less than a decade has passed since the dawn broke on what was then thought to be the blackest day in all Louisiana's history, but mem-

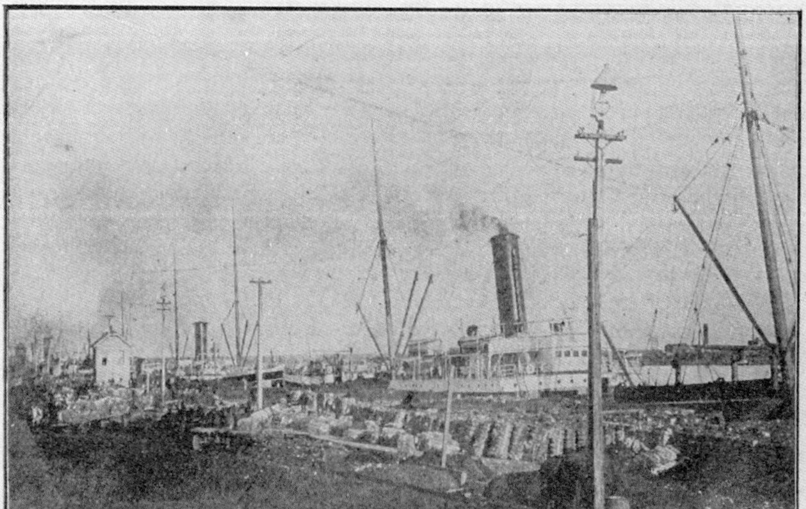

LOADING WITH COTTON AT NEW ORLEANS

ory alone stands monument to that giant struggle in which "King" Cotton went down in defeat to the myriad-legions of the invader from Mexico.

True, Louisiana may never regain her proud position as the third largest cotton-producing state in the Union, but there is every reason to believe that cotton will forever remain one of her most potent sources of agricultural wealth. For cotton is the great money crop, the one crop which has a staple value in every market place of the world, its bill of lading a universally negotiable instrument.

"King" Cotton's restoration is already evident. This year Louisiana raised over four hundred thousand bales of cotton, and next year, with an increased acreage and an improved agriculture, she looks forward with confidence to a yield of a half million bales.

Where formerly a planter consumed a whole year in making a bale of cotton, he is now, by fall plowing, the planting of an early variety of seed, by more scientific methods of cultivation, by adequate fertilization, by systematic picking off and burning of the affected bolls, by the destruction of the cotton stalks, and by an intelligent scheme of diversification, making it in from eight to nine months.

Ten years ago, when it was the custom to hold Farmer's Independence Day picnics in various parts of the state, a farmer was indeed proud who could exhibit a cotton bloom as evidence of his skill on these occasions; on July the Fourth of this year not only was cotton generally in bloom, but fully matured bolls were not uncommon, something that the most progressive planter would not have considered within the region of the possible even five years ago.

For this happy condition, great credit must be given to the Farm Demonstration Bureau of the Department of Agriculture, which is doing such a colossal work in advancing the welfare of Southern agriculture.

The Bureau has forty-six experiment stations in the State, which, by constantly advocating fall and winter plowing, the rehabilitation of the soil, diversification, the use of more and better machinery, and proper seed selection, are doing a splendid work in assisting the Louisiana planter in his efforts to repulse the invader.

The Louisiana planter, perhaps, has not yet seen the day when he will acknowledge that the boll weevil was the saviour of the state, but he has begun to discount its power for evil, and work intelligently for its subjugation.

The reign of the boll weevil will be short-lived. Even now, in the height of its power its dominion is threatened. And day and night, scientist and expert are endeavoring to find an effective parasite for the destruction of the little pest that has cost the Southern farmer so many millions of dollars.

Cotton can be grown in every parish in Louisiana; last year, indeed, there were only two parishes in which cotton was not raised. In some of these parishes, of course, the output was inappreciable, this being due to the fact that other crops such as sugar and rice could be grown to greater profit.

COTTON SEED OIL INDUSTRY.

Another source of great wealth to the Louisiana cotton planter is the cotton seed oil industry.

While not so great as a few years ago, when the yield of cotton was appreciably larger, the cotton seed oil industry, returning this year over six million dollars to those engaged in it, still occupies an important role in the industrial life of the State.

More than forty cotton-seed oil mills with an average capacity of 125 tons each are in operation at various strategic points throughout the cotton belt.

The cotton seed oil industry is so co-dependent on the cotton industry as to prevent any forecast as to its future other than that which would be reflected from a forecast of the cotton industry itself, for the cotton seed oil industry of every state is governed by the rise and fall of that state's annual production of cotton.

The use of cotton seed is entering into the economic life of the people and is utilized more and more for domestic use. The use of cotton seed oil meal in fattening stock, and hundreds of by-products now manufactured from cotton seed is one of the astonishing economic evolutions that has added millions to the productive value of the cotton lands of the South.

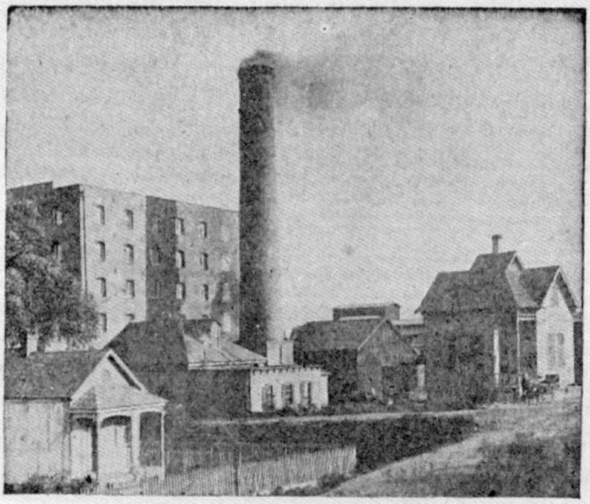

CAPITAL CITY OIL MILL, BATON ROUGE.

RICE.

With nearly 400,000 acres under active cultivation at the present time, with an estimated yield this year of some ten million bushels, with a rapidly increasing acreage and a regular and sustained improvement in its agricultural and marketing methods, the rice industry of Louisiana, returning over ten million dollars annually to those engaged in it, and constituting in itself over one-half of the rice industry of the nation, is one of the Pelican State's most important, profitable and growing branches of agriculture.

Perhaps no industry in the South has enjoyed a more remarkable or a more romantic growth. First raised in Louisiana on a commercial scale during the Civil War in an attempt to offset the ill effects experienced by the South in the wanton destruction of the Carolina industry, and found to be so peculiarly responsive to its fertile soil and genial climate, rice soon became a recognized staple in the state, its culture gradually being extended, until in 1880 the harvest aggregated over a hundred thousand bushels.

But the real birth of the industry may be said to date from 1884, when a colony of sturdy farmers from the Middle West, disheartened by successive crop failures and tired of the interminable, rigorous winters of the North, migrated to the prairies of Southwest Louisiana, where rice-growing had just been commenced in a small way, the industry up to this time having been confined to the alluvial and delta lands of the state.

Until the arrival of the newcomers, rice culture in the United States had differed only in detail from rice culture in the Orient—the same methods of cultivation and harvesting as had obtained throughout the centuries being in vogue. But the Western farmer, fresh from his wheat farm, could not be expected to tolerate a continuation of these conditions—the hand method of sowing must be superseded by the modern drill; the primitive sickle by the binder; ancient methods of threshing—such as pounding the grain with a club and whipping it over a barrel, by the modern steam thresher, and such old-time methods of milling as tramping the rice out by horse, by the steam mill.

This, indeed, was a revolution, and the native population, strong in its inherent prejudice against conditions that were foreign to it—a common prejudice throughout the world, viewed with pessimism the dawn of the new era in the industry—the drill was a myth; the binder, on such wet soil, an impracticability; the steam thresher as a substitute to the window, a dream; the steam mill, an innovation of a tomorrow far distant. But Western enterprise and Western courage could not be daunted, and they find their vindication today in such prosperous and picturesque communities as Crowley, Jennings and Rayne, which, rising from the surrounding lateral plain, veritable oases in the desert, stand as lasting monuments to those intrepid pioneers from the far-away West, who, by hewing out a new trail in the wilderness, made possible the present wonderful development of the rice industry of Louisiana.

The next great era—beyond question the most important in the history of the rice industry—dates from 1896, the year in which the irrigation canal was introduced. The canal was built by the Abbott brothers and the Duson brothers, who have been potent factors in the development of Western Louisiana.

Up to this time the farmer had had to depend entirely upon the rain supply for the irrigation of his crop, the canal, except as it applied to the primitive waterway in which the planter stored his rainfall against a later day, being unknown.

What the irrigation canal spelt to the rice grower of Louisiana needs no emphasis. How many growers had experienced total crop failures through their inability to afford adequate nurture to the growing grain

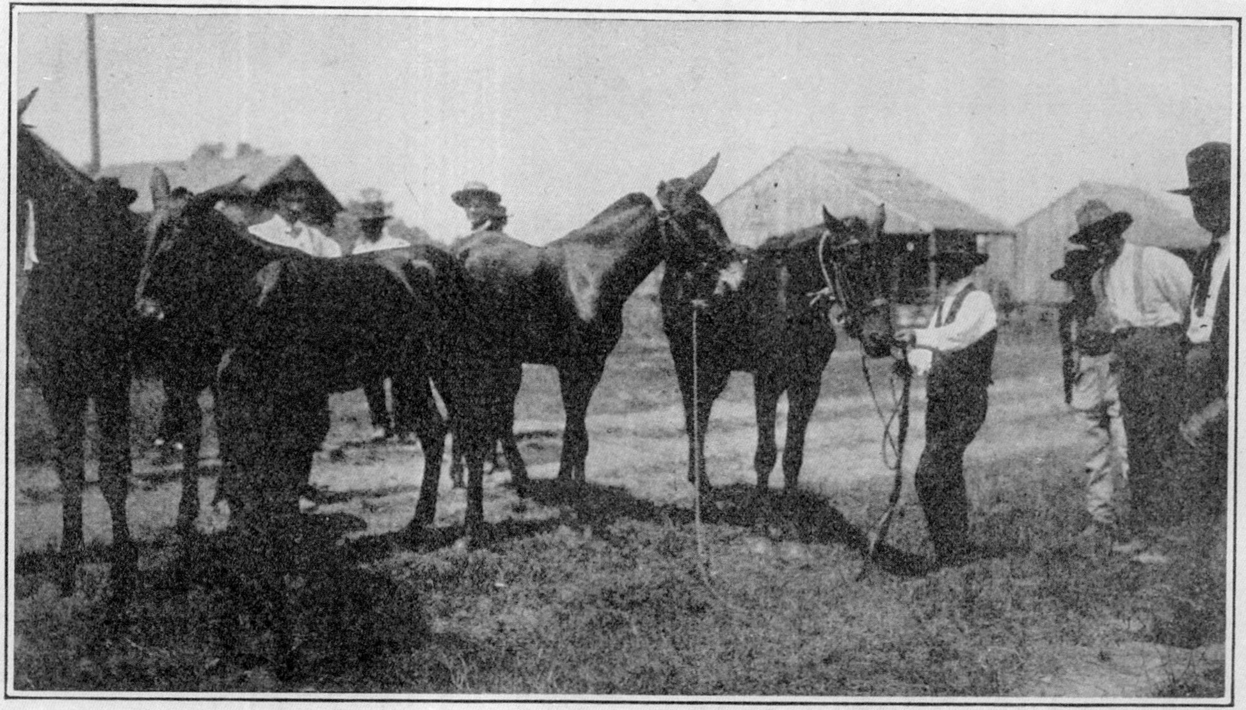

HOME-RAISED HORSES AND MULES IN BOSSIER

can never be calculated. But their number is legion. The irrigation canal changed all this. It made the grower entirely independent of the elements. Jupiter Pluvius was no longer the patron saint of the industry—his dethronement had been absolute. A new star has arisen in the firmament.

* * * *

IRRIGATION.

The canal method of irrigation was a tremendous success from the day of its inception, and it completely revolutionized the industry, extending the growing area to sections that up to that time had been regarded as waste lands, wholly unfitted for the growing of any commercial crops.

Unromantic figures can best relate, perhaps, the story of the marvelous growth of the industry since the introduction into it of this great new factor. In 1897, the year after the irrigation canal was introduced, there was only one plant with less than ten miles of canal; seven years later there were no less than eighty distinct plants in operation, each capable of irrigating from 160 to 20,000 acres, while today 150 individual companies control 2,500 miles of canal and irrigate in the aggregate over 300,000 acres of land. In the same time the number of binders has been increased from 3,000 to 10,000, while the annual crop has grown from 3,000,000 to 10,000,000 bushels, with a value to those engaged in it of over $10,000,000.

Most of the big canal companies have for their primary object the irrigation of their own lands or the lands of some other big rice-growing corporation, although every company is willing to sell water to the smaller growers. This is generally arranged on a basis of one-fifth of the crop, which, in case of a poor crop or an unsatisfactory market, materially reduces the obligation of the small grower.

In commencing operations the canal company first makes a thorough topographical survey, which makes possible the construction of the main canals and laterals in such manner as to allow the water to go on at the higher levels and inundate the lower by gravitation.

Some of these canals are enormous propositions, costing anywhere from $50,000 to $300,000 and sometimes more; and all of them represent the investment of a great deal of capital, as not only the work of cutting and maintaining the main canal and the lateral ditches must be provided for, but also the erection and operation of power plants adequate to the needs of the particular undertaking, for practically all of the rice in Louisiana is irrigated by pump, the exceptions being the alluvial sections, where the water is syphoned from the river—which, too, have to maintain auxiliary power plants for emergency purposes—and the flowing well, of which there are now about 600 in the state.

Rice culture, the irrigation feature eliminated, differs very little from the cultivation of wheat or any other of the great staples. The ground is broken in the late fall and again in February or January, being harrowed and planted from the first of March to the first of June, according to climatic conditions and the condition of the soil. As a rule the seed is planted by drill, although in the alluvial districts a great many growers cling to the old method of broadcasting. Unless the ground is sufficiently wet, the water is turned on immediately after seeding, being turned off again until the grain has not only germinated but attained a growth of four or five inches, when it is reflooded to about the same depth until a week or so before harvesting time, which commences from the latter part of July, according to locality, and extends to about the 15th of November.

A crop of rice will yield anywhere from 20 to 80 bushels an acre, this remarkable divergency in the figures being attributable to some extent to local weather conditions, but more largely to careless planting and cultivation and the failure of the grower to restore the fertility of his lands by crop diversification. Some farmers have raised only 16 to 20 bushels to the acre, as against a common average for the state of 32 bushels, while more progressive farmers realize an average yield of from 72 to 80 bushels.

In the past the average Louisiana rice grower has been extremely improvident. In the early history of the industry, the pioneers coined money. Not infrequently, indeed, a farmer would purchase from 200 to 300 acres of land on time payments, and pay for it out of the net proceeds of his initial crop. Fortunes were made on every hand, and it was only natural that the planter should plant rice to the exclusion of every other crop.

This led to a decided deterioration not only in the productivity of the land, but in the quality of the rice, which soon became impregnated with a very inferior variety, now known as "red" rice, a seed absolutely untrue to its parent Honduran type. The appearance of this "red" rice was the signal of a fall in the yield per acre and the market value of the grain, and sounded the death knell of the one-crop idea.

With the dawn of diversification the rice industry of Louisiana is beginning to assume a stability that would not have been possible under the old order of things. Many rice farms are now absolutely self-sustaining, raising their own corn, food-stuffs, cattle, mules and poultry, and leaving rice as the money crop. Crop rotation is fast restoring the fertility of the soil, and seed selection, the quality of the grain.

After being threshed the rice is either sold in the field to the agent of one or other of the big mills, shipped to the mill direct, or consigned to one of the central rice milling points, such as New Orleans, Beaumont, or Houston. about one-third of the total crop being disposed of through the factor on the floor of the New Orleans Board of Trade, which organization is a ruling factor in controlling the prices of this commodity for the entire country. About three-quarters of the annual crop goes direct to the mills, of which there are some fifty in the state, thirteen of which are located in New Orleans, and the balance distributed at convenient points throughout the rice belt.

A visit to a rice mill is a unique experience. The rice is received at the mill warehouse in sacks weighing about 180 pounds each, which are unloaded from the cars by belt-conveying machinery of a somewhat similar character to that employed in the grain elevators of the West, being elevated into bins by regular grain elevator machinery. From the bins the rice is run through separators, which remove all foreign substances from it. It is then fed into the center of the hulling stones, where it is revolved at the rate of 250 revolutions a minute, and through centrifugal action forced through the perforated ends of the upper and lower stones, a process which removes the hull from the grain. From these the rice is passed through what are known as the fanning machines, which remove the hulls by suction. A very ingenious German separator then turns back the unhulled grains to another set of stones, for about 25 per cent of the rice that goes through the initial set of stones comes out unhulled. The rice is then passed through what are technically known as hullers, this really being a misnomer as the hulls have been removed already. The huller is a cylinder within a metal case, the rice going in at one end and out at the other. This removes the oily cuticle that covers the grain, this by-product being known as rice bran, and commanding a high value as a cattle food. From here the rice goes to what are known as the brushes. The brushes are upright cylinders covered with leather, which polish the rice against a wire screen, leaving behind a white powder known as rice polish. From the brushes the rice goes to the polishing drum, where, through friction, the highly polished appearance, which is found in nearly all finished rice, is obtained. From there the rice goes to the clean rice separator, where the broken grains are separated from the whole grains and the various commercial grades are separately packed.

Rice finds its chief uses today as a staple article of human food and in the manufacture of beer, about 10 per cent of all the Louisiana crop being used for the latter purpose. Approximately one-sixth of the entire American crop is shipped at present to Porto Rico, the balance, with the exception of occasional shipments to Cuba and European ports, being consumed at home.

More than a million bags of rice are sold annually on the New Orleans Board of Trade. Not all of this, however, is Louisiana rice, about one-tenth of it coming from Texas and approximately the same amount from Arkansas. All of this is sold through the medium of the factor, the rice factor being to the rice grower what the cotton factor is to the planter, advancing him the money necessary to grow and harvest his crop at a regular rate of interest, and selling it for him afterward on a commission basis. Most of the rice disposed of on the New Orleans Board of Trade is sold to the local mills, the balance being shipped to the South Atlantic market, such as Savannah, Charleston and Morehead City.

The future of the rice industry would appear to be very great.

The late Dr. S. A. Knapp of the Bureau of Plant Industry of the Department of Agriculture, who played a more important role than any other man in the upbuilding of this industry, in speaking of rice, once said:

"Rice forms the principal food for one-half the population of the earth. It is more widely and generally used as a food material than any other cereal. Where dense populations are dependent for food on an annual crop, and the climate permits its cultivation, rice has been selected as the staple food. A combination of rice and legumes is a much cheaper complete food ration than wheat and meat, and can be produced on a much smaller area. As a food material rice is nutritious and easily digested. Even rice polish, or flour, which is now sold at the mills at about a cent a pound for cattle feed, or exported to

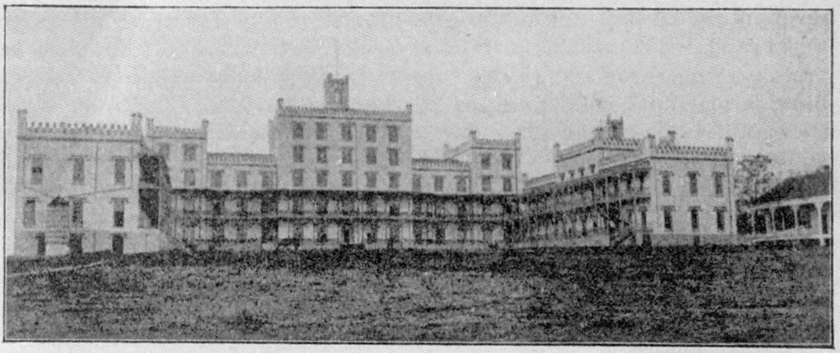

SCHOOL FOR THE DEAF AND DUMB, AT BATON ROUGE.

Germany, will, when appreciated, be in demand for human food, as it contains 10.95 per cent of protein, in comparison with 7.4 for the clean rice."

The consumption of rice in the United States is ridiculously low. As the American people are educated, however, to its real food value and to the many ways it can be prepared, this consumption will no doubt be greatly increased. A per capita increase of five pounds alone would represent a most enormous increase in the domestic consumption. Nor is the United States the only market that the Louisiana rice grower has to look for his future. With higher paid labor, more modern agricultural machinery, a more comprehensive system of irrigation, the American rice grower should be in a position one day to compete successfully with the rice growers of the world.

To the good farmer, the growing of rice would seem to offer a more profitable return than the growing of wheat. The cost of labor is practically the same. Rice, however, under intelligent cultivation, should yield at least sixty bushels to the acre, worth from 65 cents to $1.00 a bushel in the field, according to market conditions.

A story of a grocery clerk, who three years ago was working for $50 a month at Crowley, the rice center, well illustrates the profits to be derived from a rice farm by intelligent management. This grocery clerk rented a rice farm in the northern part of Acadia Parish, on what is known as the crop percentage basis. He made no money investment whatsoever. This year, after paying all his family and farm expenses, he netted nearly $5,000. The farm was 235 acres in extent.

Any Western farmer who really wants to engage in rice cultivation can buy land in the rice belt on very reasonable terms.

* * * *

PERIQUE TOBACCO.

Forty-odd miles from New Orleans, in the Parish of St. James, is being carried on an historic and picturesque industry, infinitesimal in comparison with many of the other great agricultural industries of the State, but so peculiarly Louisianian as to make a story of her industrial life incomplete without its incorporation.

First grown long before the Civil War by an Acadian whose name the tobacco now bears, the cultivation of Perique tobacco has been kept up continuously ever since, the direct lineal descendants of Perique being still engaged in the industry.

Perique tobacco culture is confined to a very small area on the banks of the Mississippi, where soil and climatic conditions are peculiarly adapted to its growth, and is marketed from Lutcher, a great cypress manufacturing center, Convent and Grand Pointe. Altogether there are but 500 acres in cultivation, although about 2,000 acres are available.

Perique tobacco is cultivated in much the same manner as any other sun tobacco, the land being plowed over and planted in rows five feet apart. The tobacco is sown in the early part of January and replanted in March or April, the crop being harvested in the latter part of June or the beginning of July.

After harvesting, the tobacco is hung in sheds to dry, after which it is stripped and placed in presses until the following March or April, when it is ready for market, although frequently it is not sold until three or four years old, Perique tobacco, like wine, improving with age.

Perique tobacco yields about 500 to 600 pounds to the acre, and commands a price of from 25 to 50 cents a pound. The present yield is about 275,000 pounds a year.

Perique tobacco finds its chief use as a seasoner for mixtures, it being an exceedingly strong tobacco, with a distinct flavor and aroma. It is shipped to all American tobacco markets, to Canada, England and elsewhere.

* * * *

TRUCKING.

Louisiana has been so frequently alluded to as the Holland of America as to need no introduction as a trucking state. From the day of her settlement, indeed, trucking has been one of her most important native industries, New Orleans for more than a century having been the center of an intensive agriculture that has served as a model for truckers in every quarter of the land. Today this industry is valued at more than $10,000,000 annually, and is growing in importance each year. The State of Louisiana could have no better all-the-year-round exhibit than this living monument to the tremendous advantages that the Pelican State offers to the tiller of the soil.

Louisiana's trucking industry is not confined to the environs of New Orleans by any means, however. Louisiana, like Florida, has built up in the past few years commercial trucking interests of varying character in different parts of the state. There is the famous strawberry industry of Tangipahoa Parish, the general truck industry of Rapides, the tomato industry of Ouachita, the cabbage industry of Calcasieu, and the potato and cantaloupe industries of Caddo and Bossier.

The trucking industry of Tangipahoa Parish has a world-wide fame—especially the strawberry part of it. Six million dollars' worth of strawberries were shipped from Hammond, Independence, and Amite, the chief shipping points of the parish, in 1911—and all from a district that 25 years ago was an indefinable part of the great pine forest.

In 1885, the year of the Cotton Exposition at New Orleans, Hammond, then known as Hammond's Crossing, had only half a dozen families. Not a single family had been added to its population in 20 years. Its lands had only a nominal value; in fact, two years before a wise investor had purchased 5,000 acres of land at a tax sale for the munificent sum of $117. These same lands, by the way, are now held at $30 an acre, or $149,883 more than the investor paid out. But conditions changed materially in 1885, for in that year the Illinois Central Railroad acquired control of the old New Orleans, Jackson & Great Northern, and inaugurated a real policy of progression. The direction of this policy was in able hands—in the hands of a man who has done a noble work in the upbuilding of the South—Captain J. F. Merry, of Manchester, Iowa, now retired, but for a quarter of a century general immigration agent of the Illinois Central System, and a living potent factor in the economic life of the South.

Starting its work by bringing in a few families, the Illinois Central gradually extended its policy to include desirable foreign immigration. The wisdom of this movement was seriously questioned by the people of Louisiana at the time. But it has seen its justification already. The great Tangipahoa strawberry industry is almost wholly in the hands of Italians. But these Italians have nothing in common with their city brothers. They are agrarians, pure and simple. Crime is practically unknown to them. They are orderly in the extreme, industrious, provident. And best of all, their children are growing up to be real Americans, just as good Americans as the Germans and Scandinavians have become in the West.

* * * *

HOW FOREIGNERS ARE PROSPERING.

This is true also of every foreign colony in Louisiana. Take the Belgian colony at Alexandria, for instance. When the Rock Island Railroad brought out these immigrants from the Province of Bragant, Belgium, some ten years ago, none of them had aught but the clothes he wore; most were ill-clad. For a time they sought employment in the sawmills. But they were farmers by nature and calling, and after a while, with their meagre savings, they bought on time payments some of the rich bottom lands that are to be found anywhere around Alexandria, which lies in the famous Red River Valley. Their success belongs really to the category of the marvelous. There are approximately a hundred farmers in the colony, and they are rated on an average at over $10,000 each—some, indeed, are said to be worth nearly $100,000. And all in the space of a decade.

Some of the younger members of this colony, too, are beginning to sell their valuable bottom lands and locate on the lower-priced upland, or cut-over pine land, as they are more usually called. They find them just as good as the bottom lands for most purposes, and for strawberries and some vegetables, better. A farmer and son are making between two and three thousand dollars net every year on less than 25 acres of cut-over land, while a northern settler this year made $1,400 clear profit on nine acres of strawberries.

The Rock Island has recently established a new French colony on the cut-over pine land region of Alexandria. The members of this colony do not come direct from their native soil, but from Saskatchewan, Canada, where for the past two or three years they have found an indifferent success. This colony will devote itself to the growing of truck for the present, but ultimately it hopes to establish a wine industry in Louisiana, such as the Italian Colony established with such success in California. And their efforts should not be in vain, for the wine grape grows luxuriantly in Louisiana, and Louisiana is much closer to the great consuming centers of the country.

Tomatoes, cabbage, cauliflower, celery, lettuce, radishes, onions, eggplants, parsley and all the other chief vegetables of the temperate zone will grow as well in Louisiana as anywhere in the United States.

* * * *

WHAT AN ACRE CAN PRODUCE.

Three hundred and fifty-three dollars net to the acre on 46 acres of tomatoes sounds large, but that is what one enterprising farmer, Mr. L. P. Alexander, of Monroe, did this year. And that did not represent the sum total of his year's work, either. On the same land he raised 40 bushels of potatoes to the acre as a second crop, for which he received $1.40 a bushel. And this was an exceptionally poor year for potatoes, for he has made 225 bushels to the acre as a second crop. Mr. Alexander raises peas, various varieties of beans, carrots and other vegetables, following them by cowpeas, potatoes, or peanuts as he deems best. This year he cultivated 175 acres and cleared $17,000. Next year he expects to do even better.

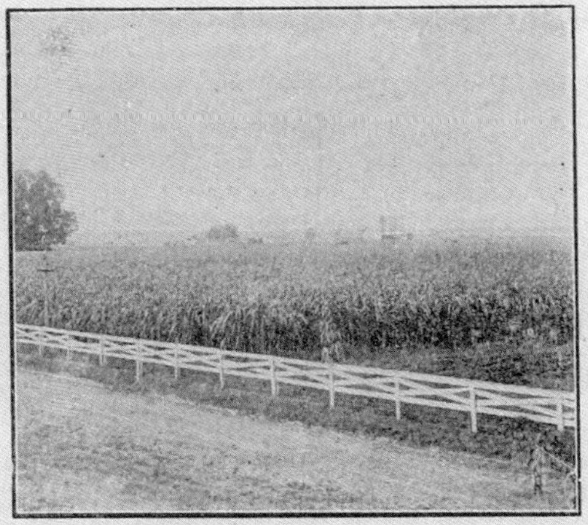

FIELD OF SUGAR CANE IN EAST BATON ROUGE PARISH.

CANTELOUPES.

Louisiana also is coming to the front in the raising of canteloupes. Louisiana raises the famous Rocky Ford exclusively, and it is said to produce a fruit that is absolutely true to the parent seed. The Louisiana melon is marketed about the same time as that of South Georgia, so reaches the market at a time when conditions are, as a rule, very favorable, and the price is a great deal higher than the most successful Colorado growers can realize. At least $75 to $100 net can be made from canteloupes, subject, of course, to climatic and market conditions.

Canteloupes can be followed by peanuts or by California peas, which command $3.00 a bushel in local markets and yield 12 to 15 bushels an acre. Canteloupes are sold for the most part in Cincinnati, Cleveland, Pittsburg, Detroit, Erie and Wheeling, but next year it is intended to invade the West, where the Louisiana grower will not have to compete with Georgia and Florida.

* * * *

CITRUS FRUITS.

In the growing of citrus fruits Louisiana is becoming yearly more prominent, this year raising 400,000 boxes of her famous "sweets," or native seedlings, said to be the highest priced oranges on the market. The chief orange groves in the state are situated along the Mississippi River, south of New Orleans, although there are many fine groves throughout the Gulf Coast country, especially in the Parish of Calcasieu. In the latter parish at Lake Charles, there has been evolved a system of grove protection from frost by inundation that promises to give the citrus industry of that section a wonderful impetus. The grapefruit also does well in Louisiana, as do Satsuma oranges, and figs. The fig industry around Jennings, built up through the efforts of "Father" Cary, the town's founder, and one of the chief factors in the development of southwest Louisiana, has become one of the most important fruit industries of the state.

* * * *

PECANS.

One of Louisiana's indigenous trees, the pecan, grows to especial advantage in the Pelican State. Louisiana has a larger native pecan area than any state but Texas. The grafted pecan industry is also becoming an important one, especially in Ouachita, Rapides, Jefferson and West Baton Rouge parishes. Properly cultivated, a pecan grove is a safe and conservative investment.

* * * *

MINERAL WEALTH—SULPHUR, ETC.

Nature has endowed Louisiana with many wonderful natural resources. Within her borders can be found in inexhaustible quantities vast deposits of sulphur, oil, natural gas, salt, lignite and many fine kaolins and clays; while throughout her tertiary strata there occur in varying quantities, marble, limestone, sandstone, iron, gypsum, Fuller's earth, green sand, and other less important minerals.

Of these, sulphur, oil, natural gas, salt, and, to a limited extent, marble, are the only ones that have been commercially developed, and even they have not seen the dawn break on the horizon of the future, for almost every day witnesses an extension of Louisiana's mineralogical area; almost every day sees the necessity for a revision of her geological textbooks; in fact, no other state in the entire Union seems to be experiencing a more remarkable or more striking development in this respect.

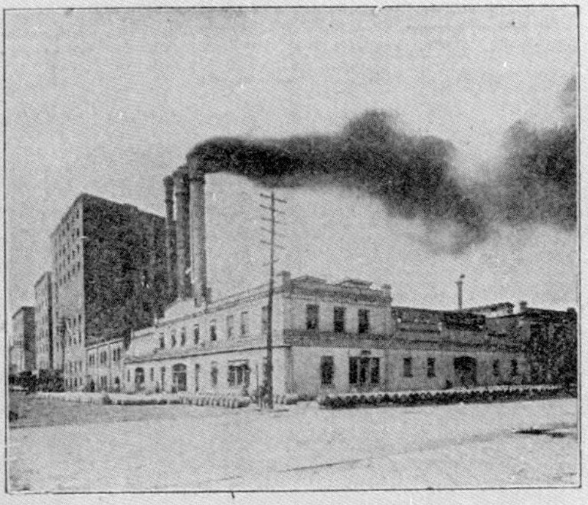

A SUGAR FACTORY

Four hundred men and American ingenuity to produce the same results in the United States as 21,000 men in Italy—that is the wonderful story of the sulphur industry in Louisiana.

The history of this industry is typically American in its vicissitudes. Discovered as long ago as 1858, it is only within the past few years that the deposit has been commercially worked.

It must not be supposed, however, that this was due in any measure to a lack of knowledge as to its value. How many millions of dollars were lost, how many hundreds of people financially ruined, how many lives were sacrified in the many vain attempts that were intermittently made to utilize this magnificent gift of Nature before success at last came, no man can tell.

From the close of the War until 1870, however, when a great French syndicate acquired an option on the property, numerous attempts were made to mine it, all, for one reason or another, unsuccessful, and from that time until the present interests gained control, almost as many more.

The operations of the French syndicate, being undertaken on the usual elaborate scale of all things French, deserve special mention. How to get at the sulphur no one knew, but the engineers in charge determined to sink an 11-foot shaft to the deposit. This was a gigantic enterprise in itself, for at that time there was no foundry in the United States that could pretend to manufacture the casting required for such a great engineering enterprise. These, therefore, had to be imported from France, an arduous and an expensive task, for each casting was eleven feet in diameter and five feet long and weighed seven and a half tons. At that time there, too, was no railroad to the mines, and the machinery had to be coneveyed thereto by wagon from a point on the Calcasieu River, nine miles away. The cost of transportation on machinery and castings alone amounted, according to the company, to over $300,000.

This enormous expenditure of money and time was, however, all to no purpose, for before the engineers in charge had sunk their shaft to a depth necessary to insert even the first ring of the caisson, the company abandoned the project, feeling that, having expended over a million and a half dollars with no tangible results, to invest more money in what appeared, from their long range, a fruitless undertaking, would be an absurdity.

The great castings and the magnificent machinery, left to rust in the wilderness, are today the only reminders of France's interest in the sulphur resources of Louisiana!

The next big attempt to develop the mines was made in 1889 by a New York syndicate, which, in the face of expert advice, proceeded to sink an elaborate shaft to the mines, the only result from this attempt being the loss of a million dollars and a number of lives and the reversion of the property to its original owners.

But every problem in Nature is bound at last to yield to the ingenuity of man—that has been the law and order of things in the evolution of the ages. Man and the hour must eventually meet—and in the meeting Nature must succumb.

Thus it was with the sulphur industry of Louisiana. In 1902 a scientist, with the scientist's faculty of delving into the region of the unknown, directed his efforts toward the solution of the one great problem that for so long had thwarted the energies of science and engineering, namely, how to mine the sulphur in some other way than by the shaft method, which could never be successful, owing to the inconsistency of tho overlying strata.

It took Herman Frasch, the inventor of the process for desulphurizing Lima oil, some time to find a practical solution to the problem, but that solution not only gave birth to the Louisiana sulphur industry, but it completely revolutionized the sulphur industry of the world.

Mr. Frasch's invention consists roughly in melting the sulphur from the sulphur-bearing rock by the application of hot water and steam, and the pumping by compressed air of the consequent liquid sulphur to the surface. Here it is run into vats and allowed to congeal, the vat being formed on an eight-inch plank enclosure. As each layer of sulphur congeals, the operation is repeated, until the sulphur pile has attained a height of 60 or 70 feet and becomes to all intents and purposes a solid mountain of sulphur.

Scintillating in the sunshine, these huge masses of sulphur, over 99 per cent pure, constitute one of the most remarkable sights to be found anywhere on this continent. It is said, indeed, that there is over two years' supply of sulphur above ground at the present time.

A unique thing about the Frasch method of sulphur mining is that not a single workman ever goes beneath the surface, every operation being carried on above ground; in the Italian government mines in Sicily, on the contrary, the sulphur is all produced on the shaft and tunnel principle, the consequent loss of life being very great.

The annual output of the Louisiana sulphur mines is about 200,000 tons, the value of the product being estimated at over $4,000,000.

Most of this sulphur is shipped in the company's own steamers from Port Sabine, Texas, to North Atlantic seaports for distribution throughout the United States and Canada, about ten per cent of it going to the Eastern refineries, the largest of which are in New York, the National

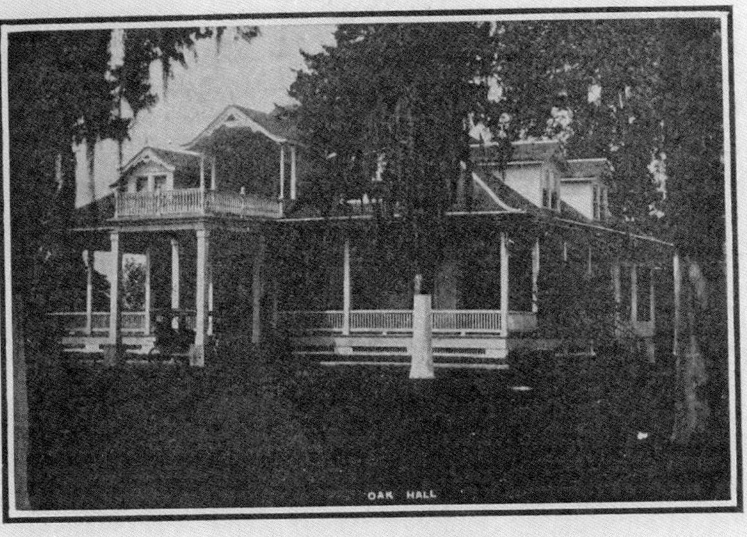

A RESIDENCE IN AVOYELLES

Sulphur Company's plan in that city being the largest sulphur refinery in the world.

About 70 per cent of the domestic supply of sulphur is now used in the manufacture of paper. The sulphur is burned into gas and passed through a tank containing milk of lime, and then finely chopped-up wood, usually spruce, is mixed with the resultant fluid, which induces a process of decomposition in the wood, and converts it into what is technically known as wood pulp.

* * * *

OIL PRODUCTION.

With the production in 1910 of 6,841,395 barrels of crude oil, valued at $3,574,069, Louisiana now stands eighth among the great oil-producing states of the Union, and as almost every week witnesses the bringing in of new wells, or the finding of oil indications in various parts of the state, there would seem to be every reason to believe that she will have outranked at least four of these states in the next two or three years. Louisiana increased her output in 1910 123 per cent. The year 1911 should record a production of at least 10,000,000 barrels.

And the oil industry of Louisiana is yet in its infancy. Oil, it is true, has been prospected for in Louisiana from long before the War, the magnificent sulphur deposits of the state having been uncovered in one of the many unsuccessful attempts to tap the oil deposits of southwest Louisiana. But it is only since 1901, when the famous Spindletop gusher of the Beaumont district turned the attention of the great oil operators to the Gulf Coast country, and the Jennings field, which in point of production has been one of the most remarkable confined oil fields in the world, was discovered, that the petroleum industry has been a factor in the industrial life of Louisiana.

The Jennings oil field is said to be the largest single oil pool in the world, having produced 60,000,000 barrels of oil since 1902. This field reached the height of its production in 1906, when it produced 9,025,174 barrels. Since that time it has dropped off appreciably, in 1909 making less than 2,000,000 barrels and in 1910 even a smaller record.

The Jennings field has had a number of large gushers, the Wilkins No. — having been, when it came, the greatest oil well in the world. Since that time many great gushers have been brought in, especially in California and Mexico, that have been far greater producers than this pioneer well of the Jennings field, but it is doubtful if many wells can claim a better record, this well having produced over 3,000,000 barrels of oil, or, in other words, over one-twentieth of the total amount of oil taken from the field. Unlike the Jennings field, the Caddo field is supposed to be a series of pools, with the first wells in the proven territory getting the bulk of the oil.

When oil was discovered in the Caddo district in 1905, it was not thought that the field was an important one, but the production has increased at a tremendous rate, until now, with nearly 500 producing wells, many of them gushers, the production averages over 25,000 barrels a day, and the Caddo field has become by far the most important oil-producing section of the southwest.

In the Harrel Number 7, the Caddo field has one of the largest single oil wells in the United States; indeed, it is estimated that when this well was first brought in it made nearly 50,000 barrels of oil a day, a production that was reduced materially only because the pipe line facilities in the Caddo field were inadequate. This is the oil well that furnished the sensational fire that for so many months defied every engineering effort, and was brought under control only after the engineers had tunneled below the point of combustion and piped out a large portion of the oil and gas that fed the flames.

There are three pipe lines from the Caddo field, namely to Beaumont, Texas, Baton Rouge, where is located the great three-million-dollar refinery of the Standard Oil Company, and to Port Arthur, Texas, the seaport through which most of the oil produced in Texas and Louisiana is shipped to the markets of the world.

The Vinton oil field has not lived up to expectations. In its early days it made 22,000 barrels a day, while it now averages less than 5,000. For a new field, however, the Vinton district has a remarkable record, having produced approximately 3,000,000 barrels of oil in less than ten months. When this field first came in, two to ten thousand gushers were quite common, but the gushers appear to have given out entirely, all of the oil now being produced entirely by the pump method.

What the future holds forth for the oil industry of Louisiana, no one can foretell. All of Louisiana's oil is at present said to be produced from the pockets, no regular stratum of oil having been found to date. Some geologists hold, however, that oil underlies a great portion of the surface of Louisiana, and that the Louisiana oil field is a continuation of the Texas and Mid-continent oil fields, and that one day Louisiana will be second only to California as an oil-producing state. Out in the Gulf of Mexico, too, there is said to be a veritable oil pool in which ships ride regardless of the storm, and which is said to mark the outlet for this great subterranean stream.

Oil is being prospected for in various parts of Louisiana, and as the prospecting is not of the "wildcat" variety, but is being carried on by close corporations along intelligent lines, there seems to be good reason for conceding a real future to this romantic industry.

* * * *

NATURAL GAS.

Another of Louisiana's great natural resources are her wonderful deposits of natural gas.

Although she cannot pretend to rank at present with West Virginia and Pennsylvania in point of natural gas production, Louisiana is in possession, in the Caddo gas field, of the largest single natural gas field in the United States.

Some idea of the vastness of this field can be gained from the fact that it has no less than 47 huge producing wells in active operation at the present time, although the entire field, as at present defined, is embraced in an area of 10 to 12 square miles. It is believed, however, that this field is a continuation of the Mid-continent field, and that it will one day extend, with interruptions, to the Gulf of Mexico.

Gas at Caddo is found at depths of 800, 1,800, and 2,200 feet, varying slightly with the topography. Some wells have made as high as eighty to a hundred million cubic feet every 24 hours from a 6-inch open pipe, while others, again, have greatly exceeded that figure.

Only a small portion of the available gas in the Caddo field is consumed at present, hundreds and hundreds of millions of feet being lost daily from the larger oil wells. This, however, is unavoidable, as there is no way of utilizing gas and oil simultaneously. The gas from the Caddo field is of a very superior grade, having very little fume, and being absolutely non-noxious. In theoretical fuel value it is also very high, 60 per cent of this gas being equal to a hundred per cent of gas manufactured from coal.

The natural gas flows from the wells at a pressure of from 35 to 300 pounds to the square inch, depending on the amount of gas required. From the well to the pipe or field line, a pressure, regulated to conditions, of 150 to 400 pounds is maintained. The natural pressure answers all present purposes, but unless this field differs materially from the older gas fields of the country, compresses eventually will be necessary for long-distance transmission.

Caddo natural gas is piped at present to Texarkana, Little Rock and Shreveport, there being a 10-inch main to Texarkana, and three pipe lines, of 4, 6 and 8-inch capacity, respectively, to Shreveport.

The Little Rock line is 180 miles long, has two compressor stations, and, besides Little Rock, supplies Arkadelphia, Hope, Garden, Hot Springs, Poplar Bluff, and other towns.

Ultimately it is hoped that pipe lines will be laid to New Orleans, Memphis and St. Louis.

The natural gas field should offer great opportunities to the manufacturer of all classes of articles in whose manufacture fuel is a consid-

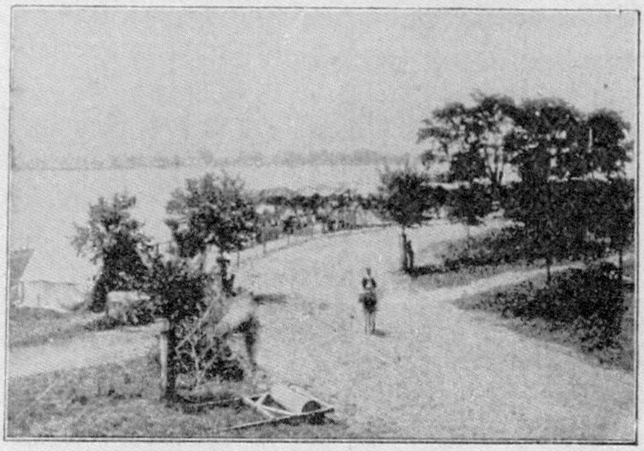

OLD RACE TRACK, 1858. CLUMP OF TREES IS WHERE ZACHARY TAYLOR'S RESIDENCE ONCE STOOD.

eration. When natural gas was first utilized in 1900, gas was sold in Shreveport at $3.00 a thousand feet for lighting purposes and $1.75 for fuel, the gas being generated from Oklahoma coal; today gas for domestic purposes sells at 18 to 22 cents net and power gas from 4 to 11 cents. The citizens of Chicago, just celebrating their 80-cent gas victory, should regard Shreveport with envy. In Pittsburg, too, where the producers of natural gas have to compete with the very best class of Pittsburg-mined coal, the rates for natural gas are 12½ cents for power and 27 cents for domestic uses. The highest rate for electricity generated from natural gas, is eight cents per kilowatt hour for domestic purposes and for from 3 to 8 cents for manufactories, large consumers getting an even lower rate.

* * * *

ROCK SALT.

Five hundred feet beneath the surface, veritable mammoth caves, cut from the solid transparent rock, seemingly by a master hand, glittering with a thousand crystals, reflecting strange colors and weird phantom shapes, converting men and mules into diminutive denizens of a strange world—awful in their magnitude, awe-inspiring in their unknown depths, forever veiled in mystic shades, the great rock salt mines of Louisiana well might be the prototypes of those mystic caverns that inspired the facile pens of such visionary romanticists as Jules Verne and Robert Louis Stevenson.

With a visible supply of some twenty billion tons of rock salt, sufficient salt to supply the demands of the world for centuries to come, the great rock salt deposits of Louisiana are larger than any yet uncovered on this continent, eminent scientists the world over comparing them to the famous Strassfurt and Sperenberg deposits of Prussia, the Gallicia deposits of Austria, and the world-renowned Trans-Indus salt beds of Hindoostani, most of them admitting that they are at least third, perhaps second, among the great salt deposits of the earth.

The only two salt deposits that have reached a greated depth than those of Louisiana are the Gallicia and Sperenberg workings. The former has reached a depth of 4,600 feet, but this does not represent by any means 4,600 feet of solid salt, for there are a number of geological interruptions, various strata of foreign matter occurring at irregular intervals. The Sperenberg deposit, however, is 3,769 feet in depth, the salt occurring in a conglomerate mass. The famous Strassfurt deposits are only 685 feet deep, while those of India average from 300 to 700 feet, and at no point show a greater depth than 1,200 feet. The deepest boring made in Louisiana to date is 2,090 feet, and as at this depth there seemed to be absolutely no change in the character of the salt or the consistency of the stratum, there is every reason to believe that the Louisiana deposits are equally as deep as any to be found anywhere.

From whence these great deposits spring is a mystery—a mystery that geologists from almost the first settlement of this country have attempted in vain to solve. Some scientists, such as Thomassy, have claimed them to be of volcanic origin; others, like Dr. Richard Owen, non-volcanic, but due to the action of wind and waves; some claim that they are due to alluvion, that is, the imprisoning of an arm of the sea through alluvial deposit, and the consequent evaporation of the salt water so enclosed; while others claim that salt water springs, and not the sea, have figured in their formation.

Louisiana's rock salt mines have been confined up to the present to certain islands on the Gulf Coast, but it is the opinion of scientists that rock salt underlies not only the great salt springs at Natchitoches, Bienville, Monroe, and other parts of North Louisiana, but a considerable proportion of the entire tertiary strata. At Pine Prairie, a few miles southwest of Alexandria, indeed, a rock salt bed has been uncovered that is thought to be larger than any heretofore unearthed.

Hardly islands, in the accepted sense of the term, being separated from the mainland only by a low salt marsh, these remarkable promonitories, rising to a height of from 125 to 200 feet above the surrounding country, differ so radically in character and formation from the mainland itself, as to be geographically distinct, and fully entitled to the appellation, island.

The names of these islands are: Grand Cote, commonly known as Weeks Island; Petite Anse, better known as Avery Island; Cote Carline, known to all Louisiana as Jefferson Island, because it was for many years the beloved home of America's great actor; Belle Isle, the chief rendezvous of the intrepid Lafitte and his piratical band, and Cote Blanche, the last named being the only one of the five on which rock salt has not been found, due probably to the fact that few borings have been made there.

The production of salt is Louisiana's oldest industry, for not only has it been produced more or less extensively since the day the House of Bourbon unfurled its flag upon her shores, but long, long before the tread of the white man's foot resounded through the noble forests of Louisiana, it had been used as a valuable trading commodity among the Indian aborigines, the very first white settlers of Louisiana having reported meeting with Indian salt traders at various points, one of these being no other than the great Bienville.

The salt produced by the aboriginees was all evaporated, a fact that has been borne out by the finding at the salt springs of north Louisiana and at least three of the five Gulf Islands of large accumulations of potsherds, the crude clay vessels fashioned by the Indians for this purpose.

The extensiveness of Louisiana's rock salt deposits does not appear to have been known to the Indians, but certain discoveries have been made that would seem to indicate that prehistoric man both knew of and worked them—either that, or the scientific theory that man and mastadon did not exist on the earth at one and the same time has been successfully refuted, for in the sinking of the shafts mastadon bones have been found intermingled in the same stratum with human bones, pottery and other relics, while at Avery Island a fragment of cane basket work was picked up on the face of the salt itself.

The evaporated salt industry was quite an important one from the first settlement of Louisiana until after the war, not only in north Louisiana, where were located Price's salt works, King's salt works, and Rayburn's salt works, all known to fame, but also at Petite Anse, where salt had been manufactured from the year 1795, three years from the first attempt to evaporate salt from the great brine springs of New York State. During the war salt sold as high as $15 a barrel, and both Confederates and Federals depended upon Louisiana for a large portion of their supply.

With the march of progress, however, with its incident economy of manufacture, its increased transportation facilities, its freight rate differentials—all speaking active competition, the industry, carried on intermittently until 1894, died out altogether in that year, and has never been revived.

The great rock salt deposits of Louisiana were discovered by accident in May, 1862. Salt was very scarce at that time, and the proprietor of the Island's salt works, John Marsh Avery, determined to profit by it. With this end in view he commenced to deepen his wells. One negro workman, after going down 16 feet, came to Mr. Avery with the news that he had struck a sunken log, and could proceed no further. Mr. Avery investigated, and found, not a log, but the great rock salt deposit that has made Louisiana famous throughout the country. The discovery did not come altogether as a surprise, as Thomassy had predicted that a great rock salt deposit would be one day uncovered in each of the five Gulf Islands, and perhaps in other portions of the state.

Since the close of the war, rock salt has been an important contributing factor in the mineral wealth of the state. Until 1903, when mining operations were commenced by the Myles Salt Company at the great Weeks' Island deposit, Avery Island had the only active salt mine in the state. The deposit at Belle Isle was worked for some time, but the shaft was destroyed by water, with a loss estimated at over a million and a half dollars.

Weeks' Island is situated a hundred miles west of New Orleans, and about twenty-five miles from Franklin, on an arm of beautiful Vermilion Bay, being connected to the mainland by a branch of the Southern Pacific Railway. It is a beautiful island, with a topography and an outlook as charming as can be found anywhere on the Gulf

Coast. Archaelogically, also, it is interesting, for it is the possessor of one of the largest Indian shell mounds known. This mound is 600 feet long, 3,260 feet broad and 10 feet high, and from it numerous skeletons, arrow heads and other Indian relics have been taken. It is supposed to have been the burial ground of an important Indian tribe.

Although salt was not discovered at Weeks' Island until 1897, it had been prospected for at intervals from 1862, in the excitement following the discovery of the Avery deposit.

The discoverer of the Weeks' Island deposit was General F. F. Myles, who with his brother, Mr. Beverly B. Myles, present president of the Myles Salt Company, has done more, perhaps, than any living man to develop the salt resources of the state.

A visit to the Myles salt mine is of peculiar interest. Arriving at Weeks' Island, on the company's own train, we ascend the sloping hill to the plant, which stands sentinel above the Gulf. A few minutes later we enter the shaft, and are being carried down to the mine itself, 600 feet below the surface, a unique sensation, especially when we look upward, and watch that ball of light, the last vestige of the outside world, gradually grow smaller and smaller, and ultimately disappear. Arriving at the bottom, we step out on to a floor of solid salt—salt everywhere—no artificial scaffolding as in most mines, just pillars and columns, columns and pillars, of solid salt—six billion tons of it altogether, so the scientists say. The depth of this deposit is unknown, as no shaft has been sunk lower than 650 feet, this not having been necessary, as the amount of salt available at this depth is more than sufficient to meet the demand for many years to come.

Having found our bearings, we start out for an inspection of the mine itself, each carrying a tallow candle to light him on his way, and warn the mule trains, which seem to wind like grim octopuses in every conceivable direction.

Passing through the first great chamber, which has the appearance and the grim grandeur of some ancient cathedral, we arrive at a point where active operations are being carried on.

Rock salt is mined in very much the same manner as are all the baser minerals. The first operation is the drilling of the holes for the insertion of the dynamic charges, rock salt having a resisting power

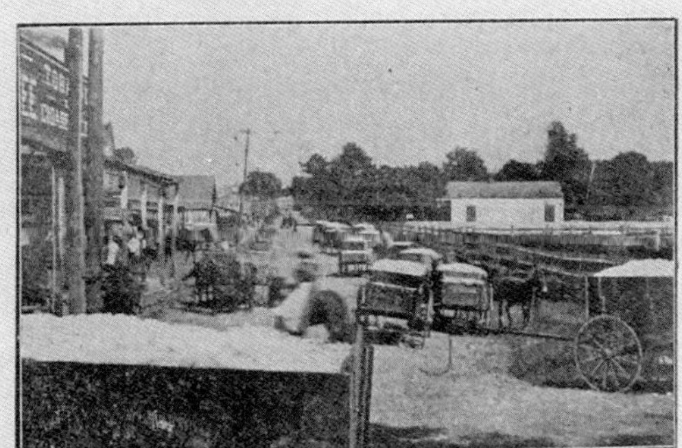

AWAITING TURN AT THE GIN

of 5,000 pounds to the square inch. This is accomplished by 11-foot drills. The salt is cut out in tunnel form, arched columns being left to prevent a collapse. These tunnels are 750 to 1,000 feet long and 80 to 100 feet wide, and of about the same height. The blasting is generally done at night, as well to prevent accident as to allow the atmosphere to clear in time for the following day's work. As blasted, the salt is loaded on regular narrow gauge mule trains, which carry it to the foot of the shaft. The negroes who do this work are all swarthy-looking fellows, with skins as smooth and as shiny as the finest porpoise leather, due to the action of the salt, for salt is unquestionably the greatest skin remedy known.

As we stand and look around us, we are indeed inspired and awed—the dusky shovelers clothed only from the waist, the mule trains, some empty, some loaded, flitting here, there and everywhere, the huge piles of salt, 99.84 per cent pure chloride of sodium, the glittering lights, the lurking shadows, and above all the grandeur of the mines themselves, they constitute indeed a scene that will focus itself forever upon our memories.

Retracing our steps to the foot of the shaft, we pause for a moment to watch the salt pass through the great 40 horse-power electric-motor-driven crusher, an operation that is accomplished so speedily that we cannot detect even a single detail.

After being crushed, the salt is fed by gravitation into the cage and carried to the mill, where it is fed automatically into screens and separated into the various commercial grades, and, if shipped in bulk, deposited by gravity into the cars; if the contrary, automatically fed into sacks.

Again we are headed for terra firma, glad to be once more in God's own outdoors, but sorry to leave behind us what is undoubtedly one of the most remarkable sights in this state of many wonders.

* * * *

TIMBER RESOURCES.

Second only to the much larger state of Washington in the vastness of her timber resources and the value of her annual cut, Louisiana, possessing, in untold quantities, such soft and hard woods as long and short leaf pine, cypress, almost every known variety of oak; hickory, gum, pecan, cottonwood, ash, magnolia, maple, and the largest known varieties of elm is, by a very large margin, the greatest lumbering state in the South.

With a timber area of over four million acres, with more than five hundred sawmills in constant operation, with an army of at least 25,000 men in active employment, with an annual cut of two and a half billion feet, or one-sixth of the total yellow pine cut of the country, the manufacture of yellow pine is at present the most important branch of Louisiana's great lumber industry.

Yellow pine occurs in 31 of Louisiana's 60 parishes, and is said to cut more to the acre than the pine of any other state. In the southern and middle part of the state there are to be found immense forests of

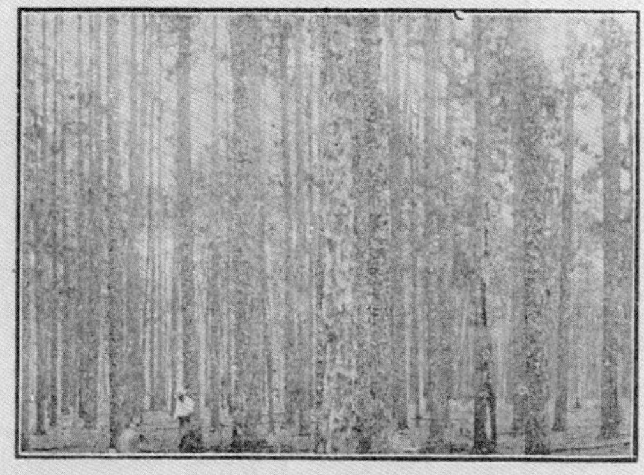

SECOND GROWTH PINE

the long-leafed pine that has built up the famous lumber industries of Georgia and Florida, while throughout the northern sections of the state short-leafed pine of a superior character is very plentiful. Scattered throughout the state, too, there are hundreds of sawmills that in construction and capacity are the equal of any to be found in the world; in fact it can be said with truth that the Louisiana lumberman has set a new standard in sawmill construction.

In Bogalusa, Louisiana boasts the largest lumber town in the United States, if not in the world—and one of the most unique. Not one of those lumber towns that is established today to be abandoned tomorrow, Bogalusa has been built up on the broad and comprehensive lines of permanency that should assure her a continuation of prosperity long after the timber to which she owes her present well-being has become a memory of yesterday.

The City of Bogalusa, owned and controlled by the Great Southern Lumber Company—every building in the corporate limits being either leased or rented from it, is a pleasing example of the prosperous American city. Modern in every detail, it has two hotels—one of which, the Great Southern, would be a monument to any town of 50,000 inhabitants or more—a splendid high and two good common schools, churches of all denominations, a modern hospital, a fine library, one of the most substantial Y. M. C. A.'s in the state, a modern sewerage system, an elaborate electric light plant, a good water system, cement sidewalks, a fire protection service and all the other conveniences of the city of today.

The help is entirely segregated, the white, Italian and colored elements all being established in different sections of the town. The houses, of which there are about 700, are rented by the company to the help at a nominal figure, those for the white hands being lighted by electricity and equipped with bath, running water, model washstand, and all other modern conveniences; those for the colored differing very materially from the class of residence that is usually found in a mill town, being fitted with glass windows and running water.

Six hundred and fifty thousand to seven hundred and fifty thousand feet a day—that is the capacity of the great Bogalusa sawmill. In other words, this great mill is devastating the pine forests of its territory at the rate of 40 to 50 acres a day. How this is accomplished is an interesting story. The company's own 45-mile standard railroad extends its tentacles into the surrounding woods, where some four hundred and fifty men are constantly employed in felling the trees, cutting them to the desired length and operating the great steam jiggers which load the finished log on to the train.

When loaded, the train is run to the mill pond, which is encircled by a track elevated to an angle of 30 degrees, which permits the logs to roll off into the water immediately the supports have been removed. This pond is over 27 acres in extent and has a storage capacity of about 7,000,000 cubic feet of timber. The logs are diverted to the slip by the slip feeders, men who are especially trained to maintain their balance on floating logs. The slip, a chain contrivance, grips the log and automatically carries it up to the saw. There are two slips in this mill, each having a capacity of 150 logs an hour. The saw's automatic machinery, controlled by two doggers, men who work the levers of the dogs, the technical name for the vise that grapples the log, grips the log with lightning swiftness; the setter does his work, the sawyer his; the log is sized and cut into the length required in a moment of time that to the uninitiated seems both infinitesimal and marvelous.

There are four band saws in the Bogalusa mill, each 44 feet in length and each capable of cutting simultaneously two logs in as many as 32 1-inch boards. As the log is cut, the resultant lumber is carried off automatically to either the shipping platforms or to the drying kilns, of which there are 22. These kilns are heated by 65 miles of steam pipes, and have an aggregate capacity of about two million feet of lumber. From the kiln the lumber goes to the cooling shed and from there to either the plant's own magnificent planing mill or to the shipping platform. Over 45 per cent of all Bogalusa's lumber output is dressed on the grounds.

An idea of the power required to operate this mill can be gained from the fact that four electric generators with a total generating power of 22,000 kilowatt and a steam engine of 18,000 horse-power, are in constant use. The belt that drives the main plant is said to be the largest in the world. It is 240 feet long and 72 inches wide, and over 750 hides were used in its manufacture.

* * * *

THE CYPRESS.

Along the shores of the myriad lakes and streams that are to be found all over the southern portions of Louisiana, Mississippi, Alabama and Georgia, and throughout Florida, there is to be seen, intermittently silhouetting itself upon the horizon, a great tree, a veritable monarch of the forest, that, heavily draped in its somber garb of Spanish moss, robed in the native majesty and glory that signals it out from its brothers of the forest, seems to stand sentinel at the water's edge as though to challenge and halt the approach of the iconoclast.

It is the cypress, "the tree eternal," the tree that has outlived the centuries, impervious to time and the elements; that has delighted the heart of nature lovers since the day LaSalle first explored the mighty reaches of the Mississippi; that has inspired the artist and the poet and compelled music from the lips of the songster.

But it is Louisiana more than any other state that this noble tree calls home. Here can be found huge forests of cypress—the famous red cypress of Louisiana—the cypress that attains a height, a diameter, and a texture that no other does—three million acres altogether, or more than twenty billion feet—twenty billion feet of solid cypress growth, unbroken save for an occasional tupelo gum or other marsh-loving tree.

Up to a very few years ago these noble forests were looked upon as interminable swamps, even their magnificent timber having little intrinsic value. True, there were many who recognized the lasting and other qualities of cypress, but the extraordinary lack of knowledge concerning it on the part of the nation as a whole, the immense cost of cypress lumbering operations, the lack of adequate lumbering machinery, and the difficulties of transportation, precluded any comprehensive development of the industry.

In the last few years, however, conditions have been revolutionized, not only on account of the great improvement in the transportation facilities of Louisiana, and the introduction of machinery adapted to the logging of cypress, but because of a wider appreciation on the part of the consuming public as to the superiority of cypress in all classes of building construction in which durability is a prime consideration, and also because the capitalist, recognizing the future of the industry, has invested millions of dollars in it.

Today the cypress industry, with nearly 150 mills in operation, with 15,000 men in active employment and with an annual value to those engaged in it of some fifteen million dollars, is second only in importance to the much older yellow pine branch of Louisiana's wonderful lumber industry.

Perhaps no wood in the world has better weathering qualities than cypress. In the alluvial deposits of Louisiana almost perfect cypress logs have been uncovered hundreds of feet below the present level of the Gulf of Mexico, that are said by scientists to be at least six to ten thousand years old. Some of the oldest houses in New England, constructed by the Pilgrim fathers in the pioneer days of this country, are also of cypress construction, as are practically all of the homes that, scattered throughout Virginia and other Southern states, survive their day and age, living monuments to the pristine greatness of the ante-bellum South.

Cypress, the most valuable of all Louisiana's commercial woods, is now regarded as one of the richest of Louisiana's many untold treasures, and even the despised swamp from which this valuable timber is cut—the swamp that for so many years was regarded as the breeding place of the mosquito, the home of the moccasin, and the harbinger of fever, pestilence and plague—is recognized as the future soil foundation of an agricultural industry that one day is destined to be a source of potent wealth to the state and to the nation.

FISHERIES.

Not the least of Louisiana's many untold treasures are her wonderful resources of the sea. More rivers and bayous enter the Gulf of Mexico from Louisiana, it is said, than from the balance of the territory that borders America's Mediterranean, carrying with it, in immense quantities, all manner of food for almost every form of fish life, with the result that Louisiana waters abound, in their season, with redfish, Pompano, mullet, trout, red snappers, sheepshead, Spanish mackerel—all the other commercial fish for which the Gulf of Mexico is famed, and inexhaustible quantities of oysters, shrimp, crabs and various other mollusks and crustaceans.

* * * *

OYSTERS.

If Louisiana had no other resources whatever, her wonderful oyster beds would entitle her to a ranking position among those states of the Union who depend on their sea-products for a large measure of their wealth.

With a larger acreage available for oyster culture than even the famed Chesapeake, with greater natural beds than any other state in the Union can boast of, and with better climatic conditions than practically all her sister states, Louisiana has the natural foundation for a greater oyster industry than is now known in the world.

Louisiana has a total water area of 4,720,502 acres, of which 409,220 acres are available for oyster culture under just as favorable conditions as the grounds of Narragansett Bay or Long Island Sound. Her natural reefs, confined, it is true, to three parishes, are 62,740 acres in extent, her famous Point-au-Fer reef, in Terrebonne Parish, being approximately 50,000 acres in extent, and having an annual production of a million barrels of oysters that up to the present time have been nearly all killed each year by the flood waters of the Atchafalaya because of the absence of a market large enough to permit of its harvesting in time to forestall destruction.

The advantages that Louisiana offers to the oyster grower are many and pronounced. All the natural conditions are peculiarly favorable to oyster growth. The water is warmer, the food supply greater, and the oyster enemies, like the star fish, the mussel and the ray, so common in the North, and so detrimental to the oysterman's welfare, are few and unimportant, the Louisiana oysterman not being compelled to dredge and clean his beds continually, knowing that unless he does so the destruction of his crop will be as complete as it is speedy.

Just as the Louisiana farmer can produce two crops a year, so the Louisiana oysterman can produce two crops of oysters while his Northern brother is making one, for an oyster reaches maturity in the warm waters of the Gulf of Mexico in less than half the time that the oyster grown in the colder waters of the North, a year and a half to two years being the average time in which a Louisiana oyster will mature, as against four to five years in any of the North Atlantic states.

No story of the Louisiana oyster industry would be complete without a mention of some of its famous oysters, such as the Cyprian Bay, the Bayou Cook, and the Fort Bayou, those oysters that have delighted every visitor to New Orleans, and have compelled recognized connoisseurs to place them on an equal footing with the famed Blue Point, Cotuit, and Lynnhaven, in the blue-blooded aristocracy of oysterdom. While it is hard to make comparisons, there are many who feel that the Louisiana oyster has a flavor and a consistency that is common to no other oyster in the country, and whether this be so or not, it is certain that the warm waters of the Mississippi River carry into solution certain salts that give these oysters a piquancy peculiar unto themselves.

Although more than five thousand men are engaged in the oyster industry of Louisiana, 1,700 of whom are employed in the packing houses and on the dredge boats, and while the state is now producing 900,000 barrels of oysters annually—valued at nearly a million and a half dollars—and is deriving approximately $50,000 a year in revenue from leases and other sources, the industry is yet in its infancy, for at the very lowest estimate Louisiana has an acreage sufficient to produce at least 100,000,000 bushels of oysters annually, or more than the present output of the entire country.

* * * *

SHRIMP.

The shrimp industry, too, is also becoming yearly more important to the State of Louisiana. This industry, which has had a slow but healthy growth since the War, is today valued at about $400,000 a year, and represents an investment of over a million dollars.

Owing to the close season enforced by the Game and Fish Commission of the state and to induce propagation and thus prevent the annihilation that without some measure of Government control would be inevitable, together with the fact that in the winter time the shrimp seek warmer waters. this industry is carried on only in the months of February, March, April, August, September and October, the 3,000 people employed finding other occupations the remainder of the year.

Shrimp are found chiefly in Louisiana in the waters of Grand Isle, the Timberley Islands, various sections of Barataria Bay, at the estuary of Bayou La Fourche, and in the lakes and bays of the Mississippi Sound, in the Parish of St. Bernard.

About 75 per cent of the annual shrimp production of Louisiana is canned at one or other of the oyster and shrimp canning factories that are to be found at intervals along the entire Gulf Coast of Eastern Louisiana and Western Mississippi and shipped chiefly to New England points, the Pacific Coast. Great Britain. Australasia. and South America, the balance being consumed in raw state in New Orleans and the larger commercial centers of the Mississippi Valley and the Middle West

* * * *

INDUSTRIAL DEVELOPMENT.

In industrial as well as in agricultural and mineral development, the State of Louisiana is also forging forward in the mighty current of progress that is sweeping the whole South. Not alone in New Orleans, Shreveport, Lake Charles, Alexandria and Baton Rouge, is there a decided trend to real industrialism, but in every town and hamlet in the Commonwealth there are springing up many new industries, incipient industries, it is true, but industries that appear to be founded upon the rock of stability that spells permanence.

The strategical position of Louisiana in relation to the great centers of population of the Mississippi Valley and the Middle West, her navigable waterways, her splendid railroad and other transportation facilities, her raw materials, cheap power, and the supply of labor that is bound to follow the peopling of her lands, all point to the day when she will be almost as great a manufacturing as an agricultural state.

* * * *

NEW ORLEANS.

The opening of the Panama Canal, too, is bound to divert an enormous amount of the commerce of the world to the Gulf of Mexico. Already the prow of the tramp steamer is turned toward what is destined to be the Mediterranean of the tomorrow, and New Orleans the Genoa of Italy, but a greater Genoa than the Latin Kingdom ever knew is even now beginning to feel the effects of a movement only three years away.

And this is as it should be. Situated at the mouth of the greatest system of inland waterways in the world, occupying a strategic position in relation to the great centers of commerce that no other city in the United States can boast of, enjoying a climate that is acknowledged by world travelers to be the counterpart of the Riviera, New Orelans, the Queen City of the Gulf, is passing through a period of evolution that should make her one day one of the mightiest cities of the world.

There have been many cities in the past decade that have grown up from the very plains themselves, magnificent tributes to our modern civilization, but few that have undergone such revolutionary changes as the romantic old City of New Orleans, the city that under five flags has played such a picturesque role in the history of the New World.

Already the third largest port in point of commerce in the United States, New Orleans is each year increasing her importance in this regard.

Speaking in this connection no less an authority than Herbert Knox Smith, the Commissioner of Corporations, said:

"New Orleans is one of the most important as well as one of the most interesting harbors in the country, particularly in its advanced terminal facilities, its organization, and its methods of public administration. It is a river harbor, about 100 miles from the Gulf, but easily accessible for ocean vessels.

"Both the commercial and industrial functions of the harbor are important. It has about six miles of publicly owned wharves, over twenty-five in number, and about fifteen large steel sheds and warehouses. There is a very considerable amount of modern transshipping machinery for grain, fruit and coal."

Another institution that is doing much to forward the interest of the Port of New Orleans is the Belt Railroad Commission, a municipal board that in the last few years has built and operated a belt railroad along the water front of the city. This is an 11-mile double tracked railroad, and has about forty industrial spurs.

It is intended ultimately to encircle the entire city with a double track railroad which will increase the length of the road to 22 miles. This road is publicly owned and publicly managed, and is giving universal satisfaction.

New Orleans has splendid dry-dock facilities, for besides its great government steel floating dock which can accommodate with ease ships of 18,000 tons, there are two other docks of 5,000 and 2,000 tons capacity, permitting the merchant ships of the world to undergo necessary repairs without having to proceed to some distant port.—National Magazine.

THE SOUTH

THE SOUTH has the grandest destiny the world ever saw. No people have such a future. Her soil, her climate, her products, her mineral resources, her manufacturing resources, her manufacturing facilities, present a combination of advantages such as are found in no other land. The high moral tone of her people, the strength of her Christian faith, the culture of her highest classes, place the South where no other people stand.

"The small buddings on the great oak prove that it has survived the winter, and spring is at hand. The survival of the misfortunes of the past is one of the grandest evidences of the strength of our civilization, and betokens the coming of a better day. Indeed, that day has already dawned. Go where you may, over the South, you will see evidences of improvement in every department of industry. The fact that Northern capital is taking possession of the railroads of the South shows that the North has faith in the future of the South. Never before were there so many great railroads being constructed in our region.

"The northern coast of the Gulf of Mexico is the natural center of trade for the Western Hemisphere. The configuration of the continent, the direction of the great rivers, the sweep of the ocean currents, and the prevailing winds all point to the mouth of the Mississippi as the natural center. There is land enough adapted to the growth of sugar, contiguous to New Orleans, to supply the wants of the continent, and to furnish vast amounts for exportation. It only needs the proper application of machinery and labor to effect this great result. As to cotton, the lowlands along the Mississippi River can produce ten million bales annually. New Orleans is to be the grandest emporium of trade for the continent. As ship communication is now made across the Isthmus, New Orleans must become the great center of trade for North America; and nothing can divert it but an imperial despotism holding huge investments of capital elsewhere.

"Take it all in all, the smiling sun never looked upon a better country, or a grander people, than we have here in the South."

WHY YOU SHOULD SETTLE IN LOUISIANA

Because it is the best country known to the man of moderate means.

Because you will find a country of rich soil awaiting the settler.

Because there are uplands, prairie lands, and alluvial river bottoms.

Because you can be certain of profitable returns from whatever you put into the soil.

Because the winter does not consume what the summer produces.

Because there are more and better opportunities for diversified farming than elsewhere.

Because the seasons are regular, and no fear of crop failure.

Because the country is never scourged by cyclones and devastating storms or blizzards.

Because no better fruit country is known—oranges, plums, pears, peaches, apples, grapes, strawberries, figs, pecans, and others fully maturing.

Because everything grown elsewhere can be produced here more abundantly.

Because truck farming is a success; products, being early on the market, obtain high prices.

Because there are more chances for profitable investment of capital than elsewhere in this country.

Because you have no long winter months to encounter, with no excessive dry heat in summer.

Because the climate is more uniform than elsewhere, no extremes of heat or cold.

Because you will find the most open-hearted people on the globe.

Because education is paramount; public schools and churches of every denomination are to be found in all communities.

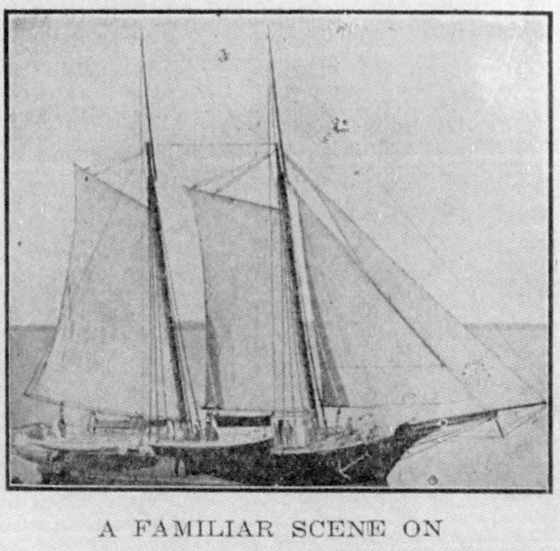

A FAMILIAR SCENE ON LOUISIANA COAST LINE

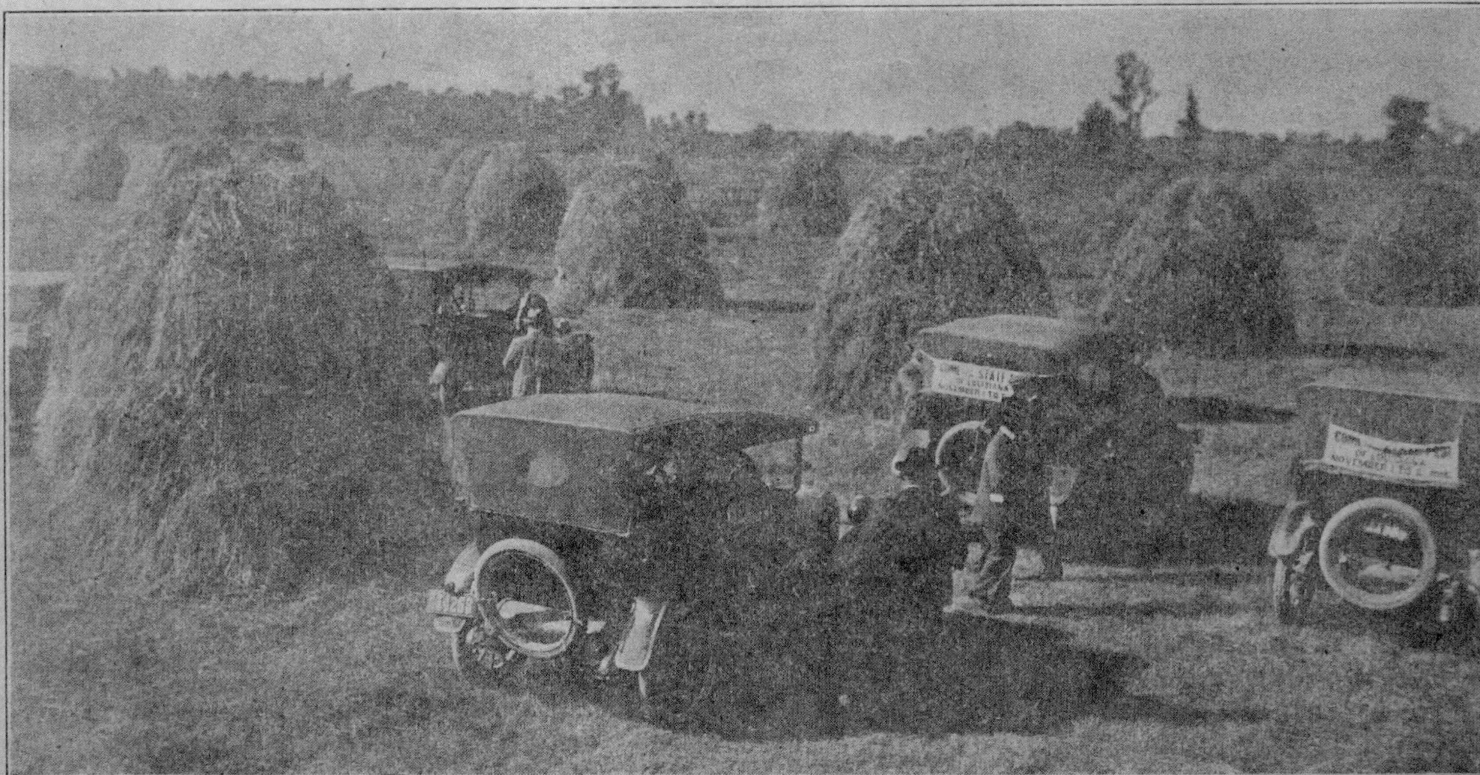

A LOUISIANA HAY FIELD